ALISTAIR MIRFIN

WALKING WITH LIONS:

NOTES ON A ROUND THE WORLD JOURNEY

14/10/2008-12/09/2009

Defiance Publications

Defiance Publications

Published by Defiance Publications

ISBN: 978-0-9566908-0-7

This is a work of non-fiction and the author has stated that the contents of this book are true.

These journals are dedicated to those underprivileged peoples of this world who never have their stories told: people who suffer at the hands of injustice and to those who have fought against all forms of apartheid and oppression by one group of people over another.

CONTENTS - WALKING WITH LIONS

ITINERARY – WALKING WITH LIONS

2008

UNITED KINGDOM

October 13	Manchester to London
October 14	London to Abu Dhabi, United Arab Emirates

UNITED ARAB EMIRATES

October 14	Abu Dhabi to Al Ain
October 15	Al Ain to Abu Dhabi
October 15	Abu Dhabi to Johannesburg, South Africa

SOUTH AFRICA

October 15-16	Johannesburg to Windhoek, Namibia

NAMIBIA

October 16	Windhoek
October 17	Gobabis
October 17-30	Harnas Wildlife Sanctuary
October 30	Windhoek
October 31	Windhoek to Johannesburg, South Africa

SOUTH AFRICA

October 31	Johannesburg to Abu Dhabi, UAE

UNITED ARAB EMIRATES

November 01	Abu Dhabi to Al Ain
November 01-05	Al Ain
November 05	Al Ain to Abu Dhabi
November 05	Abu Dhabi to London

UNITED KINGDOM

November 05 – 08	London

SINGAPORE

November 09	Singapore
November 10	Singapore to Sydney, Australia

AUSTRALIA

November 10 – 22	Sydney
November 22-24	Cairns
November 25	Great Barrier Reef
November 26-27	Cape Tribulation
November 27	Cairns
November 28 – 29	Townsville
November 30- December 01	Magnetic Island
December 02 – 03	Airlie Beach
December 04-06	Whitsunday Islands Inc Long Island
December 07-09	Agnes Water/1770
December 10 – 11	Rainbow Beach
December 12 – 14	Fraser Island
December 14	Rainbow Beach
December 15 – 18	Noosa
December 18 – 22	Brisbane
December 22-24	Byron Bay
December 24 -January 06	Sydney

2009

January 06 – 07	Canberra
January 07 – June 19	Melbourne
June 20 – 22	Great Ocean Road
June 22 -24	Melbourne
June 24	Melbourne to Sydney
June 24-27	Sydney
June 27	Depart Australia for Auckland

NEW ZEALAND

June 27	Auckland to Santiago de Chile

CHILE

June 27 – 30	Santiago
July 01	Valparaiso and Vina del Mar
July 02 - 04	Santiago
July 04	Santiago to Lima, Peru

PERU

July 04	Lima
July 05	Lima to Cusco
July 05 - 21	Cusco
July 22 -25	**Lares Trek**
July 22	Pisac
July 22	Ollantaytambo
July 25	Aguas Calientes

July 26	Machu Picchu
July 27 – 30	Cusco
July 31	Cusco to Lima
August 01	Lima
August 02	Lima to Caracas, Venezuela

VENEZUELA

August 02 – 04	Caracas
August 04	Caracas to Santa Elena de Uairen
August 05 – 29	Santa Elena de Uairen
August 29 -30	Caracas
August 30	Caracas to Trinidad & Tobago
August 30	Trinidad & Tobago to Miami

UNITED STATES OF AMERICA

August 30 – September 11	Miami
September 11- 12	Miami to Dusseldorf, Germany

GERMANY

September 12	Dusseldorf
September 12	Dusseldorf to Birmingham, United Kingdom

UNITED KINGDOM

September 12	Birmingham to Manchester

INTRODUCTION

If one wants to discover the origins of this trip, one must go back a few years to two quiet, sunny afternoons working for Bury Primary Care Trust. Each afternoon faded into mediocrity after completing University, as I could gradually see my life slipping away before my eyes, not living any dreams or fulfilling anything. The first afternoon of note came in the days preceding my graduation in 2006 where I was sat working for the Dental Bureau in a cramped little office at Carne House, Bury Primary Care Trust, overlooking the smoke and the red-bricked walls that make up the buildings of Bury. On an impulse during my lunch break, I decided to take a walk in the sunshine because, let's face it, there are not too many to waste in Great Britain. On walking past a well-known high street book retailer, I decided to call in and, as I wandered around, I found myself being drawn to a book within the biography section. Little did I know at the time but this book would change my life forever. I continued to walk around to see anything of more interest. However, I was still being drawn back to this book, with its bright red colour and the most iconic image of the century emblazoned on the cover. The book, Che Guevara: A Revolutionary Life by Jon Lee Anderson. For weeks afterwards, as I travelled to United Arab Emirates to visit my Uncle Ronnie and saw the sick excess to which Dubai and Abu Dhabi has to offer, I carried this book with me. I was like a sponge, soaking up information on this man who, agree or disagree, led a fascinating life. However, it was his experiences as a young 23 year old student travelling around Latin America with his friend Alberto Granado that caught my imagination. I was inspired by the bravery, the determination and, most of all; the humanity of this individual who I felt held similar sentiments to me. Many people use the words 'dreamer' and 'idealist' but the way I saw it was if only there were more dreamers or idealists in the world then maybe, just maybe, it could be a better place.

I had always wanted to set off on a voyage such as Che and Alberto's, but I had never had the reason to go. I had always had it easy in Manchester and, let us face it; I was lazy in pursuing my dreams. We all are – you as much as me. However, another sunny afternoon on Friday 18th May 2007 would change all that. The night before, we had a reunion in Preston for University and it turned into a late party. Needless to say, copious amounts of alcohol were consumed. At around 06:30am, I got up as normal to head off to my days work. I felt fine for much of the day until, shortly after 15:00; I had an epileptic seizure to which I recall nothing much from that moment until waking up in hospital after the 'twilight' period. It was perhaps more shocking for the people witnessing it than it was for myself as consciousness was lost completely. Apparently, in the ambulance, I thought it was Monday and, also, that my Mother was my boss. It was in the aftermath of this seizure that I decided to change things – I now had the reason to start living my life. I was bored with my life, bored with my job and generally bored pissing my life away. Upon being informed by the consultant that I was not allowed to drive for 12 months, I made immediate plans to sell my car and with the proceeds, organise a round the world trip that would allow me to work voluntarily in some of the poorest countries in this world, to work for the sake of working and not being a slave to money. From having the seizure to selling my car to organising my trip, it took about a month and a half. This was how determined I was. The only person I discussed it with was by best friend for about 22 years, Adam (Wes). If anyone was going to come with me, I would have wanted it to be him as we understand each other. However, this was something I had to do on my own and I found it hard to make other people understand the importance of voluntary work when people are so wrapped up in a career over living a productive life and, to them, anything that didn't make money was idealistic bullshit. All I needed to do now was to pay for the trip, in instalments, for the next year or so. I knew what I was doing was right.

The intended date of departure was 05th June 2008. This was intended so I could have my farewell party in Manchester on my 24th birthday and then call time on my trip on my 25th birthday. However, my parents made an announcement about a month or two after I announced my intentions to travel – they intended to get married in October 2008. Ultimately, this meant I had to delay my trip by a few months. At first, I was a little put out by this decision, maybe thinking (with justification) '22 years to get married and they choose now'. But, honestly, it worked out for the best and those extra few months gave me extra time to prepare mentally for the trip. The wedding, on 03rd October 2008, was also one of the best days of my life, prior to the trip. So, not wanting to waste any time, the trip was booked and I would leave on 13th October 2008. Many were worried about my intentions for leaving as they all (and I mean ALL) are too preoccupied with earning money to see the bigger picture of living life. The myth of 'the American Dream' never appealed much to me before I left. The idea of the perfect nuclear family, make as much money as you can and have the flashiest possessions is, for want of other words, bullshit. It is an illusion – a myth. I did not want to stay in a job I did not want to do for the sake of money and, being a dreamer, I always wanted to explore, to set off in search of the world.

> ***"Money is money. Life is life. Money is not life. And life is not money"***
> *Alistair Mirfin, 14-10-2008*

In many people's eyes, this was a grandiose trip and, by one such person, it was described as 'epic'. The scale of this had escaped me and the only thing that I had in my mind were the people I would meet, living my life to its fullest, without the restraints and the shackles that stop us from living life to your full potential. All I could see ahead were the roads, rivers, oceans, rainforests and deserts that had to be seen to be believed. Because when we die, we want people to say 'Yeah. They lived life to the full and achieved a lot. They saw what the world had to offer and made a real difference to it'. That is what matters to me.

> ***'The key to immortality is first living a life worth remembering'***
> Bruce Lee

It was time. Let the adventures begin

CHAPTER 1 – First Reflections

"These travels are not extraordinary feats achieved by one man. They are not an act of bravery, or courage. They are a journey of discovery. Into the unknown, in search of truth, in search of life, in search of me. Brave, courageous men fight illegal wars, with no concept of what is wrong or right. This journey seeks to do what, in my opinion, should be right. Not to fight an illegal war on the grounds of money. Not to subjugate people by social apartheid. Not to justify my actions in terms of a monetary reward. But to speak the truth of what I see, in and around of me". Alistair Mirfin, 15-10-2008

And so, with an embrace and a tear in my eye, my goodbyes were said to Mum and Dad upon embarking the train. All I can do is to speak the truth from the world as I see it, when I see it. The fleeting remarks and judgements may sound naive at first, even uncompromising, but these words are of a man writing on his impulses, how he judges the world at a particular moment in time. Maybe they are too contrite or narrow-minded. All I have to speak of is the truth –nothing more and nothing less. However, as Hemingway commented in the book *Death In The Afternoon*; whoever reads this can only truly make such a judgment when he, or she, has seen the things that are spoken of and knows truly what their reactions would be.

The first few days, everything seemed so surreal and to have finally broken free from the voices that tell you 'no' and seem to make you doubt your own judgement felt liberating. I can't try to put into words how that freedom felt, to be responsible for your own decisions – you and you alone are in charge of your own destiny. Then, gradually, life seemed to settle into this bohemian, travelling life I chose for myself and, you know what, nothing in the world compared to watching the sunset in Africa as you hear a lion roaring in the distance. Nothing can compare to seeing the harsh desert plains of Africa, the sparkling blueness of the Great Barrier Reef, the perfect white sands of the Whitsunday Islands, the engineering magnitude that is the Sydney Opera House and Harbour Bridge, the Urban Metropolis that is Melbourne, the night-time buzz of Santiago as you kiss a Latina with the Andes towering in the background. Nothing can compare to reaching Cusco, the heart of the Americas, touching the ruins of a civilisation you cannot begin to comprehend, ultimately leading to your dream in the clouds on a misty July morning in the Peruvian jungle – Machu Picchu. Nothing can compare to battling through the crime riddled streets of Caracas with one, busted knee after tackling a robbery, travelling a 25 hour bus journey to the south, seeing La Gran Sabana. Nothing can compare to sitting with South American children, teaching them to read and write, giving time to simply help others and care. Caring is important. Finally, nothing compares to being a man wandering the world meeting the people with no fixed intentions on the future or anything from which your furthest horizon is tomorrow. Nothing compares to this.

Eleven months of a man's life is a long time and he can think many things along that road – yet it is the people who speak here as well as me. As you read this, I ask you to bear in mind one thing: the fire that burned within me before undertaking this trip never waned. There were times living in Melbourne where I became frustrated at my lack of progress, where all I had to talk of were the football results, but that soon faded once I started meeting the people – true people. You may find those journal entries about the football a little dull, but you'd be missing the point. As you will find, I was happiest when I was either in Namibia or South America as I felt closer to the real people of this world. People who do not care about material possessions and who have little concept about a world they will never be able to know. These are the people whose furthest dream is always tomorrow. Listening to their stories inspired me and opened my eyes even more to the plight of the poor in this world, who are being forced to live beyond their means by a system that simply does not work. They were happy to have someone to listen, someone who cared, which is what I wanted my travels to be about. These are the people who walk 4 hours to work in mines, in the most dangerous conditions imaginable, struggling for water and whose only purpose in life is to find where the next meal will come from. Helping construct a waterhole for animals in Namibia showed me the true value of a hard day's work. I do not think I have sweated so much in my life, literally to the point where I was flat on my back. However, this taught me to appreciate one of the most important commodities we in the Western World take for granted – water. You accept whatever water you can get in the Namibian bush as it is scarce in its existence. Teaching in Venezuela made me realise that if we all make a concerted effort to make things better then the world can become a better place.

Re-writing these notes has brought back to my mind the full extent of where I have been. There were many fun times and, for me personally, there were many difficult times when seeing the plight of some people just pulls at your heart. Although, I should imagine this to be the case for anyone who actually cares. Sometimes, during these journals, I have questioned human nature. I questioned why so many people walk around with their heads buried in the sand, simply not caring about those in a distant land. However, as Gandhi said:

"You must not lose faith in humanity. Humanity is an ocean; if a few drops of the ocean are dirty, the ocean does not become dirty."

As you read, you will find that no-one is safe from criticism – not even me. The figures of the world like Nelson Mandela have come in for criticism as well as the corrupt Catholic Church and the Monarchy. The main crux of my frustrations lay at the door of UK and United States Imperialism whose rapacious economic system leaves most of the world beyond their reach and condemned to a lifetime of poverty and hunger. Institutions such as the International Monetary Fund (IMF), the World Bank and the World Trade Organisation are institutions governed by the US, which merely serve to reaffirm the debt of third world countries.

Many will judge the remarks I have made but that is fair enough. But, in reality, these would have been your own judgements <u>if</u> you would have gone. And what is stopping you? Life is too short to be doing things you do not want to do. It is time to start living. After all, the world is too great a place to waste it on 2 weeks holiday on a beach each year. So as you read, I say this – go, break the boundaries and explore the world. As the quote goes:

> ***"The world is a book. Those who do not travel read only a page."***
> St. Augustine

Monday 13th October 2008, Manchester to London

Everything is in its place and all is of its time
I think its so funny I left you so far behind
You might have another story but I can see your smile
Money it don't buy you love redemption, hope or style
Ian Brown; So High

I am not too sure why I cried when Mum and Dad dropped me off today at Piccadilly Station. I suppose that is just the way I am. Maybe I was grateful to them for all they have done for me and, the reality hit home, that they have not been as fortunate as me. It is an emotional day and this is the first day of the rest of my life. The train journey to Euston Station, London, was not too eventful apart from the businessmen with laptops trying to make money from anything they can, showing off that they have laptops. I am glad that, for now, the shackles are off and I am no longer a slave to the system. At last I've made my own little stand and I feel freer than at any other time in my life.

But, after the initial upset (which is not like me) I was fine and the sandwich bought by Mum at Piccadilly Station came in useful. I felt like a schoolboy being sent away on his first trip with a packed lunch, crisps and a drink. Who knows when I'll be back though?

I sat there and read John Pilger, Freedom: Next Time for about 30 pages (which is a book that really strikes a chord with me) and I felt somewhat exhausted. Steph met me at the top of the ramp at Euston Station and the weight of the rucksack felt immense – I had sweat on my back like a layer of frost. This is all I need now for a year - me, the rucksack and the road, away from home. So, we got the tube back to Archway and then walked the 5 minutes back to her gaff, where we saw Stuart, her boyfriend. We ate a meatball spaghetti dish and went to the pub in Archway (it's location is opposite The Sweeney pub, because I can't remember its name). It was typical London (or what I'd imagined London to be like). The Italian barman asked if I wanted a 'top' on my lager, to which I retorted 'No, I'm not a shandy pants Southerner' as we call them up North. The Fosters tap didn't work. Nor did the Becks. So Kronenbourg it was for Stu and I, and it was cheap apparently at £2.50. But, after 4, it was time to make the walk back, which was a bit better this time without the 25kg on my back. So, now, I'm nervous about the tube tomorrow and getting to the airport on time. I don't trust Steph's confidence on 06:45am departure though.

Tuesday 14th October 2009, London – Heathrow Airport

I awoke very early this morning at 04:30am because I could not sleep. A bit of nerves, excitement and a load of other feelings I cannot yet explain. I made a brew and sorted all my things out. Stu woke to find a huge wasp infestation on his balcony when he went out for a fag. A couple entered the flat but, after a couple of decent whacks with a paper, we conquered the beasts. Or so we thought as they totally disappeared.

Not fainthearted, we departed for the tube, forgetting to tell Steph about the infestation so no doubt she would have a shock when she woke up this morning! We got the tube at Archway to Kings Cross, where we said our goodbyes (por ahora). I got on the Hammersmith Circle Line to Paddington, which was conveniently waiting there. I went up to platform 6 + 7 to get my Heathrow Connect Train, which again was there, waiting. London transport seems good – or maybe I'm lucky! I got to Heathrow Airport Terminal 3, checked into block E and they had all my details i.e. that I am going to Windhoek, Namibia. So, now, as ever, I am playing the waiting game at the airport, waiting for my gate to open for Etihad EY012 to Abu Dhabi. I hate airports. But my fears about any problems this morning were unfounded. I am off now to get ripped off by buying some food here at the airport.

Heathrow Airport to Abu Dhabi

The plane journey seemed to drag on today but it was pleasant all the same. I was seated next to a guy from the United States of America, who took pleasure in informing me that he does work setting up networking for the troops in war situations.

What a great asset to human existence he is – setting up networks to take the lives of innocent people, although in the UK he would (wrongly) be called a 'hero'. A bit of a tosser. I'm not too sure if he glanced at this quote on the back of my John Pilger book, Freedom: Next Time, but he shut up really quickly. The quote reads:

'...men in decorous offices far away impose a ruthless political order with tariffs and embargos, bombs and bullets, distorting the very language of freedom, causing suffering they never know, spilling blood they never smell'.'

This guy was a smug Yankee who I have no time for and is part of a corrupt Western military I do not want to be associated with. On saying that, I am going to visit my Uncle Ronnie, whose whole life has been part of 'our military.' The other guy to the side of me as French, on his way to Bangkok, on his own. I wondered what for? Due to lack of interesting conversation, I spent the rest of the journey watching Rain Man alone in my thoughts.

Wednesday 15th October 2008 Abu Dhabi Airport – Al Ain

Uncle Ronnie met me at the airport and drove me back to luxury at his house. It is the most palatial place I will stay on my trip – mark my words. So, he made me a curry and we had a beer together. I sat in my room, which is bigger than some people's houses and my rucksack is a total nightmare. I have got to get up at 07:00am tomorrow morning to get a bus to the airport for my flight to Johannesburg so I went going to bed now to get some much needed sleep in this huge bed, knowing for a fact it is too big. My first days travel has gone well.

Al Ain – Abu Dhabi Airport

I awoke at 07:15 – Liam had to wake me up because I was exhausted. I did set the alarm on my phone for 07:00 but, me being me, I forgot to alter the time to UAE time. So, inevitably, when I was on the bus to the airport around 10:00am, my phone alarm went off. It is something I'll have to bear in mind in future time zones.

Uncle Ronnie dropped me off in Al Ain in time to collect the Etihad bus to the airport, which was a pleasant ride – only 5 people (including myself) were on it. They provided a gift bag including water, fresh mints and a face wipe for the journey. It was a nice touch I thought. Before leaving, Ronnie slipped me 100 UAE Dirham's. He is far too generous.

The journey took just over 90 minutes and I had a chance to film the desert in its majestic beauty. I checked in about 220 minutes ago and I'm enjoying a globalised Costa Coffee – I say enjoying but that is not strictly true. My bag is checked through to Windhoek so I have no need to collect it when I arrive in Johannesburg later. Looking around the departure lounge I found a few curious looking faces looking over at me writing. Again, I noticed a lot of people waiting until their time comes. It is now 11:00am and my flight is not until 13:50. A long day awaits me I suspect...

Abu Dhabi - Johannesburg

After Uncle Ronnie and I were waxing lyrically about the reliability of Etihad Airways, my flight was delayed my 20 minutes. Anyway, the flight seemed to take a lot longer than I thought it would but it did not matter to me because it meant less time waiting about once I got to Johannesburg. Typically, the plane landed shortly after 20:00 South African time. Immigration advised me not to go through with my passport as I had nowhere to stay. The lady on immigration could not believe it. She said it is far too dangerous to just walk the streets with my baggage like I was doing (or going to do). She had a point – Johannesburg is probably the most dangerous city in the world and me walking out with a huge rucksack made me a perfect target. So, I walked back up to international departures, passing the Etihad crew on the way who said 'it was nice to meet you.' So, I sat down in a chair in the international departure check-in. Almost immediately, I was approached by a big, huge-hearted Namibian gentleman, who is doing a similar thing to me – waiting for a plane. We had the talk about football (Manchester United) and then I headed to the South African Airways desk for information. They said I could go through to the departure lounge, which is what I did as I had about 10 hours to kill. They could not give me a boarding pass until check-in opened at 04:20am. I tried finding an internet cafe, which I would have to pay for, so I decided not to bother. Instead, I went to the bar to get a pint of Windhoek draught – it was Namibian (well, with a name like that I expected nothing less. It is like calling an English beer 'London'). On my way, I called into the bathroom and I was greeted by the attendant who shook my hand in the African way and ran the tap for me. I think he was put out when I left and didn't leave him any change but, for my part, I had no South African Rand. I feel slightly guilty now though. So, I got to the bar and chatted with the bartender (football again) and it turns out I can pay with British sterling for £2.50 a pint. My first impressions of Africa are great and I have not yet left the airport. The people seem very friendly who are not backward in coming forward.

Johannesburg Airport 22:50

I decided to come down to the other bar/restaurant in Johannesburg airport as there were 2 guys up in the other one I did not trust.

It is full of colourful characters. The first I spoke to was a German guy, Rainer, here on business. We chatted about Hamburg and the quality of German beer. Then, Thomas from the Isle of White, turned up and we got chatting. He thought that he was ripped off on buying a beer because he paid £10 and he got 90 SA Rand back. £1 = 15 SA Rand and it is 22 SA Rand for a beer. Anyway, he buggered off for a fag, came back and bought me a beer with the surplus because he is going home soon. So, that is me drinking it now. Apparently, he has lived in Kilmarnock and his parents are Scottish too. The first in a long line of people I intend to meet. Once Thomas left, I went outside with Rainer while he had a smoke and he told me how he had lived in Johannesburg but it was too dangerous for his wife and children. He then went to get his first class flight to Paris (on business) so I came back to he bar. I got chatting to another German called Patrick, who lived close to the border with Luxembourg. He told me he supported St. Pauli, which made my day as I have been to a St. Pauli match in Hamburg. I bought him half a beer and we were then chatting to a couple on their way to Rwanda for a wedding. The 3 of them left at the same time – Patrick was going to Nairobi.

I'm not too sure how they deal with money here in South Africa but I have seen people paying with pounds, dollars, euro's etc. I bought the last beer with a £20 and got £10 change, 50 SA rand and a load of coins, Christ knows where they are from. It has just turned 00:00 South African time and check-in for my flight to Namibia is in a little over 4 hours. What a night I have got in store. Everyone laughed when I told them my flight was at 06:20. The barman was called Thabo who supports his family on his meagre wage from working in the hotel bar. He has never had the opportunity to leave South Africa, instead working all his days to provide food for those who depend on him. Upon hearing this, I could not help but think about the disparities that exist between a person from the developing world and a person from the developed world.

But all I was doing was waiting to go to Namibia and I couldn't wait to get there.

E-Mail:

Dear All,

Just a quick message to say everything is going fine so far. I'm just in Abu Dhabi Airport waiting for my flight to Johannesburg at 13.50 UAE time. It is only 11.15 so I have a big wait ahead of me. That's what unites people from all over the world - the fact that we all have to sit around for hours in the departure lounge waiting for our flights. I managed to get the bus this morning from Al Ain to the airport with no problems and, even better, it was free. The flight from London went off without a problem and i managed to get to the airport hassle free - surprising because I had to surmount the rush hour London transport system.

The only problem so far occurred this morning when I set my alarm to wake me up at 7.00 but, me being me, I forgot to adjust the time to UAE time so 3 hours later on the bus my alarm went off. I was lucky i had someone there to wake me up. Also, Ronnie's air-con unit is on the blink so I woke up with a massive sweat going on during the night and a huge thirst. So, I'm off to look around the departure lounge here at Abu Dhabi and i'll have a long night ahead waiting at Johannesburg airport for my flight to Namibia at 6.00am tomorrow.

Chapter 2 – Search for the Desert

"We, the people of South Africa, declare that our country belongs to everyone and everyone shall share the wealth" *Freedom* Charter, African National Congress

Thursday 16th October 2009 Johannesburg – Windhoek

The journey to Namibia proved to be quite eventful, let me tell you. A very African journey I would describe it as. I was at the gate at 05:50am and we had to get on the bus to take us to the express plane. So, aboard we got and I looked forward to getting some much needed sleep. I happened to notice that it was taking a very long time moving when the pilot informed us that there was a problem with the steering column and we were awaiting a "spare part." Then, 15 minutes later, she came on to say that they could not fix it and we would have to board another plane, so another bus collected us to drive us to the other plane. I missed the eventual take-off as I was so exhausted. We eventually arrived in Namibia Hosea Kutako Airport around 09:30am and, after filling out an arrival form and sorting out my visas, I collected my luggage. However, the back support system was broke on my rucksack and I was severely pissed off. But I used my initiative and resources to quickly rectify this minor obstacle. I went out to the arrival lounge and the first guy I saw was Willem, who had a piece of paper with my name on it. He was a tall, lanky Namibian who spoke little English and wore blue, dirty overalls with an old, dirty red cap, which looked like his only clothes in the world. I had to hang around for 30 minutes or so as we were expecting 2 girls to turn up. They did and they were Beth and Vanessa from a borough in London. We proceeded to get our transport, which was a Hyundai Coupe, not a minibus or a 4x4 as we expected. I was then put on the phone to someone from the sanctuary where we would be working at, saying there was no accommodation booked for me for tonight – but I said I'd go with the 2 girls to their hostel in Windhoek – about 30 minutes away according to Willem. So, it turned out to be about 50 minutes away but on the way we saw baboons knocking about at the side of the road and I knew I was now in Africa.

We arrived at Base Unite Hostel shortly before 12:00 and we met 2 girls from Hull who were going to the Harnas project too so we hung around with them for the day. A mixture of people were spending time at Unite – people from Finland, Senegal, Macclesfield. We were told to be careful when heading down to the shops as cars pull up and rob people at knife point but, showing no fear, I took a wander and I was fine. The meal I got at the shop was an awful chicken and chips – the chicken contained some sort of a tumour and the greasiest chips ever. Listen to me complaining though – outside the shops were children begging for food, so skinny and fragile. I can hardly begin to think when their last meal was. All I could offer was a paltry scrap of what I had but it wasn't enough and how is that ever likely to be enough for a child, not knowing when or where his next meal will come from? This should not be the case when so much food in the world goes to waste. Monica Ali, in her 2003 book 50 Fact That Should Change The World said that every day, one in five of the world's population go hungry (some 800 million) yet every cow in the EU is subsidised by $2.50 per day – 75 % more than what African's have to live on.

The rest of my day was spent hanging around the hostel, drinking a few beers contemplating how lucky I am. I met a lad called Charles Mortimer, an 18 year old from Macclesfield, who was trying to somehow make his way to Cape Town. 'Good Luck mate' I said. So, about 11:30pm, I went to bed so I can be fresh for my trip to Harnas tomorrow.

Windhoek

"One Namibia, One nation" Namibian government motto

Historians differ on how Windhoek got its name. Some believe that Jonker Afrikaner named Windhoek after the Winterhoek Mountains near Tulbagh in South Africa, where Afrikaner's ancestors had lived. Back in the pre-colonial days, Windhoek was the point of contact between the warring southern Namas, led by Jonker Afrikaner, and the Hereros to the north. Afrikaner built a stone church that had the capacity for 500 people while at the same time also being used as a school. Two Rhenish missionaries, Hugo Hahn and Heinrich Kleinschmidt, started working there in the 1840s; they were later succeeded by two Wesleyan missionaries. Gardens were laid out, and for a while Windhoek prospered, but, as usual in this strange human civilization, wars destroyed everything and the victorious soldiers (dead or alive) probably returned home as heroes. In 1893, after a long absence, Hahn revisited Windhoek and was apparently left flummoxed that nothing remained of the once former prosperity. In June 1885, a Swiss botanist found only jackals and startled guinea-fowl amongst neglected fruit trees.

Today, however, Windhoek on the surface appears to represent a different prospect. The present Windhoek was founded on 18 October 1890 when Von Francois laid the foundation stone of the fort, which is known as the Alte Feste (Old Fortress). These days, you get a sense of revolution as you wander the streets, with Fidel Castro Street and Robert Mugabe Avenue, acting as symbols of those who fought and won against all forms of colonialism. Many may find this disconcerting, although if you speak to a few African's, Robert Mugabe is still held in quite high esteem in these parts, which is a different image from what you would find in the Western Media.

In central Namibia, live about 30% of the Namibians, mainly Herero and Damara and the majority of the white population, most of them in Windhoek and in the towns of Walvis Bay and Swakopmund. The least populated part is the dry south, where only 7% of the population live, mainly Nama and farmers of Afrikaans or German origin. Most of them live in the towns of Keetmanshoop and Luederitz.

Like South Africa and other African countries, Namibia has a high birth-rate and here the main problems are poverty, lack of education and HIV/Aids. Namibia is, besides South Africa and Botswana, one of the richest countries in Africa. Nevertheless, the per-capita income only amounts to a mere 120 Euro per month, whereby the majority of the population has to cope with an even lesser income. Approximately 40% of the population capable to work are unemployed, which, personally, I find shocking.

Friday 17th October 2008 Base Unite Hostel – Harnas Wildlife Sanctuary

Harnas translates into the archaic word for 'armour' – defensive arms for the body; clothing to cover or protect one's person in battle. The staff and volunteers at the foundation are the 'harnas' for the animals.

What a nightmare day it has been today. We were told that we were being picked up at 07:00am-09:00am to be taken to the foundation. So we all got up at 06:30, showered, ate breakfast and collected our things in preparation. At 08:00am, Vanessa had a call saying we would be collected at 12:00!! So, I went back to bed and the girls went into Windhoek. I awoke at 10:40 to be told that someone called while I was sleeping. But, at 12:00, our driver Rudolph showed up to take us to the airport to collect another girl (this time in a Vauxhall Zafira with a trailer). So, we got to the airport and it turned out 2 girls would be arriving. One, a German girl called Maika and a scouser called Hannah. However, there was not enough room in the car – not least because of the obese girl from Hull, who simply does not fit in, in Sub-Saharan Africa where poverty is apparent for all to see. It's not right that much weight on a young girl. Anyway, we waited at the airport for 2 hours while Rudolph went to get another car. So, we waited and waited and then, at 16:00, Rudolph turned up in a big van to take us all to Harnas. I hopped in the front as I was the only guy, and that was us all the way until Gobabis, where we stopped for a break at a Shell Petrol Station, where we could stock up on food while the children beg and starve outside.

Gobabis

Gobabis is the capital city of Namibia's Omaheke region bordering the Kalahari Desert located around 110km from the Botswana/Namibian border. The town is known affectionately as 'Little Texas' due to its high reputation for cattle farming. Indeed, Gobabis is so proud of this fact that a statue of a large bull with the inscription 'Welcome to Cattle Country' greets visitors to the town. The Gobabis district was proclaimed by the German authorities in February 1894 and in June the following year was occupied by a German garrison. While the military fort, built in 1896/7, has long since disappeared, one of the few buildings dating back to that era is the field hospital, or Lazarette, which has been declared a national monument.

Gobabis was a very humbling experience, for me in particular. I'm not too sure how the others felt but I was deeply moved by what I saw. For me, at 25, this was the first time I had witnessed extreme poverty. The hardest aspect I found, which is now burned into my memory forever, were the little children begging for food. Outrage would occur if this ever happened on the streets of Manchester but, to my people, to people who know me and I share a kinship with, this life in Namibia is meaningless. Not in close proximity so it does not exist. It should not be this way in this day and age. The money countries like the UK and USA have, yet poverty still exists. It is the only situation in my life where I have found it very difficult to watch. I will never forget that moment for as long as I live. There but for the grace of god (go I).

After another 60km driving up a cobbled, off road track, we arrived at Harnas, with my arse sore after the bobbly journey. We had to drive up an air-strip to get to it and we were immediately met on the farm by an ostrich and a few gazelles. We said our respective 'hello's' and then made our way down to the camp for tea. It was a fish with baked potato and spinach – with a bottle of Windhoek I bought. Our introductory talk was given by Frikkie, a tall, thin, white Namibian man with a moustache who calls a spade a spade. He told us to take in the sounds of the Namibian bush and how much we can learn from this experience. We sat there under the moonlight, in silence for a moment, listening to the bush and I glanced up at the night sky, the stars twinkling, and the realisation then hit me- this is it. I am actually doing this. I began to get flashbacks to moments in my life but none of them could ever match this.

So, now, it is 20:30 and I have found my hut where I am sleeping. I'm friends with a guy on Facebook called Steve, who is sharing my hut with me along with another guy, Stuart. My first impressions are optimistic of the next few weeks and I'm sure many of us are in the same boat. I have noticed mosquito nets can be good for not letting them in – but they do not let the things out too! I'll figure it out.

E-Mail:

Hi,
Arrived in Namibia yesterday morning, a little tired after a long night in Johannesburg Airport. I was quite fortunate that the guys on the check in desk let me go through to the departure lounge, where I found a 24 hour bar and proceeded to enjoy myself. I chatted away to a guy called Thabo who worked behind the bar and they seemed to accept any currency going. I paid for a pint of Castle Lager (a South African beer which is surprisingly good) and paid with 20 pounds. I got about 70 Rand change, a 10 pound note and a few other coins I'm not too sure what to do with.

Anyway, I met a few people waiting for their flights back to Europe, onwards in Africa and everyone seemed to be really friendly, apart from the Yankees. Trying to strike a conversation with them is like pulling teeth - very unlike the African or European people. The Africans are very friendly and offer a smile everywhere they go, but the Americans just distance themselves from everyone. Maybe they are a cut above the rest of us. At about 3:00 I decided I needed a sleep so Thabo said I could crash down on a couch in the bar, which I did. Then I headed back the other way through security as I needed my boarding pass and obtained it no problem. At about 6:00am on Thursday morning I boarded the South African Plane destined for Namibia. However, after 20 minutes of sitting there we were told by the pilot that there was a technical problem with the steering column on the plane and an engineer was coming to fix it. 20 minutes passed and she came on again to say it was irreparable and we'd have to get another plane. So we did. About 7:30 we took off and I missed it as I fell asleep.

We landed about 9:45 in Windhoek, Namibia and after getting my visa accepted (the worst looking visa in the world may I add, which consisted of a copy of someone else's visa and a load of names on the back - mine being one of them) I collected my bag. The back system was broke and I'm not too sure how but the heavy handed baggage handlers are my prime suspects. But after some ingenuity I fixed it and then I was met at the departure lounge by Willem, our driver. We had to wait around for about an hour for 2 girls to arrive from Gatwick. So they did and we proceeded for our accommodation in a backpacker's hostel in Windhoek. I received a telephone call from the Harnas rep saying no accommodation had been booked for me so I said I'd go to this backpacker's hostel with the other 2 girls. So that's where I ended up last night. I ended up spending last night having beers with a guy called Mika, from Finland who has to be the biggest bullshitter I've ever met and an 18 year old guy from Macclesfield called Charles who is somehow trying to make his way to Cape Town.

We were told we were being picked up at 07:00-09:00 this morning but, at 12:00 the driver showed up to collect us and take us to the wildlife sanctuary. We have just stopped off at the airport to collect someone else so i popped into this internet cafe in Windhoek Airport. It's going to be another 4-5 hour drive to where we are going. It is now 13:35 Namibia time.

Food has consisted of bread, cheese, ham and apples so far but I just ate a hot dog before with a coffee so I'm doing OK. I picked up some chicken and chips from the local shop close to the hostel yesterday but it was awful. The chicken had some sort of tumour on it. I was also accosted by people outside the shop, begging for food, which is not a nice thing to see. I haven't had the chance to take any photos yet but I'm sure I will. I've been briefed by a German girl in the hostel that there will be a lot of hard work and it will be extremely hot but that's what it's all about.

Forever,

Alistair

Day 1 - Saturday 18th October 2008

We awoke this morning at 06:30am for breakfast, which consisted of cereal and cold tea. Steve and I came back to find an ostrich sticking its head through our window, which is not the usual thing you see on a Saturday morning. The day was spent finding out about the animals and getting to know everything. This afternoon we were split into groups for our duration here and I am in group 4. Most people seem OK, apart from a miserable Swedish girl. It is headed by a cool guy called Roger from Norway – such a friendly guy, who wears aviators and has that laid back attitude that symbolises the Scandinavian race. We walked around with the group to find out what we needed to do and the baboons seemed to take to me a lot and I took to them. A sad incident occurred when we saw a little dog, Rambo, taking a bath, which from the look of his skeletal body and him shivering uncontrollably, it seems he has not much time left. I put my hand out to stroke him and he managed to summon enough energy to lick my hand. I do not feel as though he has much longer left and possibly it would be for the best to stop any more suffering. Then I had to go and assist in shepherding the ducks back to their pen – which is easier said than done when there are 30 of them to a flock and they do not want to go where you take them. Patience is a virtue.

Tonight, I spent the time making the barbecue, which consisted of kudu meat. This seemed to get me into the spirit of the group and I seemed to make a few friends. The idea was to stock everything up once it was cooked so that we all ate together. This seemed mightily stupid to me as some would get cold meat and some hot. So, famished and in charge of the barbecue, I snaffled a sausage (or 3) and I also made sure my mate Roger got in on the act. By the time all the meat was done, we were all pissed and no-one fancied any food.

I think I've got off on the wrong foot with a stupid Swedish girl, the 'non-smiler' who is really rude. So, me being me, I shot her down big-time but that never cheered her up. I can not put up with any form of rudeness and politeness costs nothing. Mosquito's tried to get into my net but I brush this aside!!!

Day 2 - Sunday 19th October 2008

When I awoke this morning, I was politely informed by Lasser, the German guy sharing my cabin, that there was a horrendous storm last night that shook the cabin violently. Being unbelievably fatigued after the past few days, a tornado ripping through the cabin would not have woken me. 'I didn't hear it' I said to him. Apparently, as it turns out, I am the only person in camp not to hear it as everyone over breakfast was talking about it. The morning has been spent watching food preparation, 'learning' what we need to do. Cutting up bits of meat and that is about it. It seems straightforward to me, especially when you have an obnoxious, immature 18 year old girl from the south coast showing you what to do. Anyway, the animals we get to look after are baby baboons, lost the leopard, ducks, a zebra, Goetters the cheetah, wild cheetahs and Gumbi the Hyena/Werewolf. It has been very boring so far... my impatience is growing rapidly and all I want to do is to work. Lunch consisted of Spaghetti Bolognese, which was cold, and I ate everything on my plate because I am still thinking of that poverty I saw on Friday. I do hope it does not ruin my trip.

So, this afternoon was spent lounging about at the lapper and then we did virtually the same thing as yesterday, apart from today it was our turn to count the sheep and goats. This consisted of counting 113 as we put them back into their pen for the night. Now, this is easier said than done as sheep and goats do not necessarily form an orderly queue for you to count them one by one. Plus, when you have all these sheep and goats running towards you, you do begin to feel that you are going to be crushed into the shit filling the ground, like that lion who was killed in the stampede in the Lion King.

However, I wanted to get the counting done ASAP as, at 17:30, there was a game of football taking place – bushmen v volunteers. It was a really fun game, but tiring for us as the Namibian bushmen can run forever – and I mean FOREVER!! I now understand why they always win the long distance running in the Olympics. It does bring you closer to a group of people who live a pure and simple life, free from materials or possessions. They didn't even have shoes to play football in. However, after a gritty, dogged performance at football, we stuck to our guns and ran out 4-2 winners. I scored one (deflected) goal, which I felt I deserved on my continuous running. After the match, Steve and I returned to our Cabin and I went for a cool shower, in the dark under the twinkling Namibian stars. It was the strangest shower I have ever taken. Tea tonight was chicken piri-piri, which I felt was exotic for this place. I am just sitting through a horrendous storm and it is going to be very tricky finding the toilets. They are about a 3 minute walk through the Namibian bush and I have been told to watch out for the Puff Adder and Black Mamba snakes.

Day 3 - Monday 20th October 2008

At last – I had something to do today albeit it was a bit of farm work. Morning started with breakfast – Rice Krispies and the worst cup of coffee I had ever tasted. Then, I was informed by our group coordinator, Roger, that I would be on farm work. So, those of us on farm work firstly had to let the baboons out of their jail (they were put there because of the storms last night). This proved to be a bit (a lot) of a ball breaker because they were so heavy. Not individually you understand, but because all 6 of them happened to sit in one corner of the cage holding hands, which, you guessed it, was my corner. The cage itself was no feather either. That nearly snapped my back in two.

Exhausted, we made our way to the garage where we had to load 10 bags of cement into the van, which proved to be even heavier. I had to load bags of cement into a van with an Irish girl, Sharon, who coped far better than I. By this time (which was not even past 09:00am) I was exhausted. However, we then had to make a 25 minute drive in the van with the cement, through the Namibian bush, to the waterhole we would be working on – ALL DAY. It turned out we would be building it for animals to drink out of (well what other reason could there be). The girls in the group got to clean it of any 'dirty sand' and us guys (Frikkie (65), Lasser (22) Jason (21) and I) had to drive 5 minutes to go to dig for fresh sand, and as we were in the bush, beware of any snakes that may be hanging around because there are not exactly hospitals or medical centres at the end of the street should a bite occur. The sun scorched my neck as the grill crisps bacon on a Saturday morning after one too many beers the night before. That thinking did me no good as I struggled to dig. It was so hot. Frikkie had no such problems. Indeed, he seemed to be mocking us young guys for being so exhausted. He is in his 60's and does everything with a cigarette to his mouth. He is a total freak of nature. We had to make two trips to and from the waterhole, loading and unloading the sand by hand (spade assisted).

During a break, Frikkie took us 3 guys and one other German girl for a swim in a water storage tank, which was about a 10 minute walk into the bush – but under the heat it felt like a lot longer. The tank was 30ft tall and the only way to enter it was by climbing a pipe that led to the summit. Once we climbed it, we found the filthy water full of wasps, dragonflies and stinging beetles, and other things that no man should want to know. But we had a swim all the same as it was so hot – it felt great and I'd call it the best swim ever apart from a skinny dip with Megan Fox but this will do for now. By the time we had walked back to the water hole, the lunch had arrived so we sat down under a tree and devoured what was brought to us. Disappointingly for me, it was a waldorf salad, bread and a hardboiled egg but I cannot complain at all. We had to pay a token for a sprite, which I thought was a little unfair after we were busting our balls making this water hole. However, I soon got over this attitude when I thought back to those starving children last Friday.

The afternoon was spent making cement for the waterhole and I have never perspired as much in all my life but, in a way, it felt good to push myself to my physical capabilities. I have never appreciated water as much as I do now – even the hot water we had today. I have never worked as hard as I did today. At 17:00, it was finished and we headed back to the farm. Stuart and I collected our laundry and then I headed for a much needed beer. During the first beer 6 'newbies' got called way to the wild cheetah's enclosure (which I thought was a little weird as I was one of them) and Frikkie led the way, while I carried a large, olive green tarpaulin. After a 5 minute venture into the unknown, for me, we found a cheetah, lying under a tree, dead. We gently lifted it into the tarpaulin and took it to the cooler where it will stay until tomorrow when it will go to Gobabis for an autopsy. It reminded me of being a young kid and lifting my old dog, Nell, into a blanket and putting her in the garage after she had died. A theory is that this cheetah had been bitten by a snake, which we only found out after we left the enclosure. This put a real downer on the day and everyone seemed a little deflated. I never expected to find a dead animal here but that is nature I guess. We all stayed at the lapper and had a few beers. I decided it was a good idea to chat to one of the Namibian staff at the lapper, who serves beer, as it seems none of the volunteers chat to him and some even take the piss out of him. His name is Jarni, he supports Manchester United and he was delighted when I said I was from Manchester – I have made a friend. We talked for a while about his work. He said he only works at Harnas for 3 months in a year and, when asked what he did for work the rest of the year, he could not answer. He said he tries farming but work is hard to come by. This job at Harnas is a blessing as it pays better than he could ever imagine. It is the same for the other guy, Petrus who does a similar job to Jarni. Jarni and I chatted away, while the other volunteers looked on, seemingly questioning why I was talking to this guy. For Jarni, it is a dream to visit Europe – a distant dream he knows he will never be able to reach. That is pretty much symbolic of the underprivileged of this world. All I can do is to listen and to empathise – a hollow empathy in itself as I cannot understand how these people feel as I have many more opportunities. How can I possibly comprehend something I do not understand?

I then made the 2km walk back through the bush to camp where we had tea, which was curry, with another beer to toast the late cheetah. Now, I find myself with 3 annoying girls in my cabin (about 18) with Steve. I feel so much older and wiser now and I am still unsure whether I am going to find what I am looking for in my trip with such people around me. I am fairly annoyed with them but I am going to stick it out and probably get laid - its nature.

Day 4 - Tuesday 21st October 2008

I awoke this morning to a terrible ache from all the work yesterday but, for some surreal reason which I cannot explain, it felt invigorating. Breakfast (again) was awful as the milk was off so that fucked up my cereal and tea. It's becoming a bit of a theme here. I was told by Roger that I would be on food preparation. This involves cutting up limbs off a donkey and feeding it to the cheetah's, leopards and hyena's. I took in Lost the Leopard's milk and meat, and she jumped up at me but when I showed no fear and carried on walking straight, she was fine. She was only testing me, and she only used her paws and no claws were shown. I seemed to click really well with the baboons and I am going to go on a baboon walk tomorrow, which I am looking forward to. I may also arrange to sleep out with them later on this week or next week, which no-one has had the balls to do yet but, why not?

I have been chatting to the bar staff again today as I get the feeling no-one talks to them When you ask a question, their eyes flash brighter than a shooting star, amazed by the fact that a volunteer guest would ever talk to them. I'm noticing here, in Namibia, that apartheid still exists – but it is social apartheid. The black people get to the work the shitty jobs for the white landowners, polishing rocks in the gardens but working as if their lives depended on it. All the best work goes to the whites. No black volunteers exist. It is us rich Europeans and Yankees who have a job to give up volunteering here. I look at a little, old black lady cleaning rocks in the gardens with such vigour and determination, head down and focused. Then I walk passed with my IPod and Camera. Why is there this gulf?

Day 5 - Wednesday 22nd October 2008

This morning was quite a success and a little bit sad too. I got to go on a cheetah walk with 2 cheetah's called Cleo and Pride. However, due to the unbearable heat, they did not walk too much and decided to lie down under a tree. The only bit of interest came when a wild lion was spotted in another, separate enclosure, to which the cheetahs were excited by this. I did manage to get a few nice photos and I was on the walk with Maja – a beautiful Danish girl. I asked myself a question – how lucky am I to be here right now? It is a moment I will treasure, just to be able to lie under a tree, resting my head on a cheetah and listening to the sounds of Africa, with a lion prowling close by. It was sad as we had to bury Rambo the dog who sadly died yesterday after his illness. After the ceremony, Jason and I filled in the grave and we stuck a cross in the ground to remember a much loved dog. It was another moment filled with sadness, naturally, but I have ability to judge death as being a part of life – even when it comes to people. Death to me can be quite matter of fact – it is something we all do sometime. We need to celebrate a life and be happy it existed.

At 12:30, we were picked up and headed back to camp for lunch – ratatouille, leftover Waldorf salad, coleslaw and a bread roll. It tasted OK. Michelle, over lunch, informed me that I would be doing a baboon walk this afternoon so, at about 14:30, I went to the lapper to spend some time with them before we did it. The baboon walk, when it eventually took place, went really well for me. They all love me because I am a guy and I seemed to have 2 baboons on my shoulders most of the time (3 at one point as one was clutching my waist). We sat down in the middle of the bush for a minute or two and one baboon even came up to me and gave me a big hug, ducking under my clutched hands, resting on my knees, to do so. All the ladies naturally thought it was sweet and, honestly, it was. The walk seemed to take it out of me, however, and I could not even eat dinner tonight, which was lasagne. I have come back to my cabin to go to bed. It is only 20:00.

Day 6 - Thursday 23rd October 2008

I feel remarkably well this morning, considering how I felt last night. I even volunteered to go on enclosure patrol as Roger was struggling for volunteers. He is such a great guy and I cannot speak highly enough of him. Enclosure patrol was walking around for 2 hours checking all the fences in a 10km area, looking for any holes or gaps in the fences and testing the electricity. The last job involved walking about 1km through the wild dog enclosure to get back to the foundation. However, the wild dogs started stalking the entrance before we even got in and were looking nasty bastards. Maja was scared but I was fine and determined to tackle them. I was the only guy out of the group of 4 and I picked up a big stick and said that if we all stuck together in a group, we'd be OK. It is only when you are alone that the dogs will tear you apart limb from limb. They prowled around us a bit but I was not worried at all. My sense of fear has totally gone.

We made it back for lunch in one piece, which was couscous – a completely boring meal. When I slag food off I think about those starving children but, today, I am making an exception because couscous is awful. It is nothing and a waste of energy making it. I don't know what those Moroccan's think when they eat it. This afternoon, I was given the opportunity of looking after the baby lion cubs. It had to be the greatest experience I could ever have.

They are so cute but, even at this early age, they are still dangerous. Their claws and teeth are razor sharp, as I found when Maddox (my favourite by the way) bit me in my chest. I managed to snatch as many photo's as I could so my Mum will be happy. There was a slight mix up at feeding time at 18:00, which led Frikkie to go mental but, once I explained the score to him, he patted me on the back saying 'it's not your fault.' It is now 22:15 and I am going to bed, the latest since I have been here.

Day 7 - Friday 24th October 2008 – LION WALK!

Some days you will remember for the rest of your life and some just slip into the void of misery surrounding us, along with each other day. I think I can definitely say that today is one I will remember for the rest of my life. This afternoon I got the opportunity to walk with an adult male lion, which is a once in a lifetime opportunity and I am still struggling to put into words how I feel I should not be doing things like this.

Frikkie took 5 of us on a lion walk with Zion, through the dusty Namibian bush, through the intense heat. We were allowed to stroke it, sit with it and generally be with one of the most powerful creatures in god's kingdom. It is only now that it is beginning to sink in. Harnas is only one of very few places where a lion walk is possible. I sat in the van transporting the lion, in the passenger seat and when it jumped in the back, I sat there in awe, in amazement pinching myself that this was real. Again, I am so privileged that I have the opportunity to walk with these beasts. I owe it all to Roger, our coordinator, as I was scheduled on food preparation all day but he, kindly, took me off that this afternoon so I could go on the walk. He even gave up his place as he has done one before, but the point I am trying to make is that he did not have to. He is a great guy and I have made a friend and his girlfriend, Siri, is here and she is great too. If ever two people were perfectly suited, it is those two. I'm lucky to have met two great people. But, we only get a handful of truly memorable moments in life and, without any hint of being obnoxious, walking with Zion was one of them and I am proud I have been able to grab life by the balls. It still has not properly sunk in yet. Maybe in the next days, weeks, months, years ahead, I will look back on today and feel extremely lucky to do what most people will never get the chance to do. Alistair Mirfin: Walking with Lions.

<u>E-Mail:</u>

Hey.

I just thought I'd take this time to send a quick e-mail.

Things are going great here in Namibia and I'm getting the chance to spend time with some amazing animals. The first days work on Monday was the hardest day's work I've ever done. A few of us were dragged into the African bush to help make a waterhole for some animals. Frikkie (the guy in charge of the volunteers) took me, and two other guys further to dig for fresh sand. Us young lads were knackered after 30 minutes but Frikkie is crazy. He is a 63 year old white Namibian, who does everything with a fag in his mouth and never stops. He put us young guys to shame. The 4 of us had to fill 2 trucks full of sand and take it back to the water hole and unload it. At lunch, Frikkie took us guys for a swim in a tank that was raised about 30 ft off the floor, and the only way to get in was via a pipe about 35ft from the ground. The water looked really poor and it was covered with wasps and other various insects but it felt really good to have a swim! Anyway, at about 18:00 we finished the waterhole and now some animals have a place to drink etc.

Tuesday was spent preparing the food for my groups animals, which consists of a Cheetah. Lost the Leopard, Gumbi the Hyena, some teenage baboons, ducks and some wild cheetahs. On Wednesday, I took a Cheetah walk into the bush with 2 Cheetah's called

Cleopatra and Pride. Then on Wednesday afternoon I went on a Baboon walk. The baboons really took to me and I had about 2 on my shoulders the whole time (3 at one point). One even ran up to me to give me a hug. We are planning to sleep out with these baboons next week, which should be fun. We can't take any photos of them unfortunately, as they steal EVERYTHING, so we have to wear only our clothes and take everything out of our pockets before going in with them.

Thursday afternoon was great as I was in charge of looking after the baby lion cubs. They are all a handful and one seemed to really like me - a little one called Maddox. I've taken some amazing photos, which I'll send when I get to Ronnie's.

I'm on food preparation again today, but my group coordinator (a quality Norwegian guy called Roger who is a big Man UTD fan) has said I can go on one of the big lion walks with Freaky. So this means getting the adult lions and taking them for a walk into the bush. I've heard it is an amazing experience.

We are also constantly getting snake warnings as one was spotted outside our cabin last night and a black cobra has been spotted near the showers. It's all fun but it makes it difficult walking in the dark to find the toilets at night!!

Hope everyone is OK. Good result for United the other day: 3-0 v Celtic and 4-0 v West Brom. This'll keep all the fans happy here.

Day 8 - Saturday 25th October 2008 – FEAR FACTOR!

Quote: *'Sometimes in life, things happen that are out of our control. Things, bad things, that no-one can predict... but we must not dwell on these and feel sorry for ourselves. We must find positive, constructive ways to move forward'* *Frikkie von Solms; 25/10/2008*

What an amazing day it has been today. It did not start off that way, however, due to what Frikkie called an unforeseen accident with one of his grandchildren, although in my opinion it was reasonably foreseeable. His grandson, who is 10 years old, fell off the tailgate of the van on the airstrip at about 40km per hour when Frikkie made a turn. He needed emergency surgery on the airstrip, then had to be airlifted to Windhoek. Needless to say the medical facilities were scarce. Naturally, Frikkie seemed devastated and, to make matters worse, he was driving at the time but, thankfully, his other two grandsons' were fine. It begs the question: what were they all doing on the back of the van in the first place? Health and Safety counts for nothing in Africa. All the commotion started when Karen and I were sat looking after the baby baboons and we had a guest sat with us from the USA. He was boring us with his belief that he had an 'epiphany' and needed to come to Africa and so on. I took it with a pinch of salt, trying not to judge the guy for being a clear tosser. Luckily, he was a neurosurgeon so, when the boy fell off the van, the Yankee was the first person everyone turned to and he performed a tracheotomy on him and he also ended up going to the hospital with the kid. It was all pretty dramatic yet unsettling.

But, undeterred and showing remarkable courage, Frikkie still planned this afternoon's activities, which was the Harnas Fear Factor, consisting of several challenges. Firstly, all of those that had not previously done the Fear Factor had to sit down at the tables at the lapper and we were each given stale bread with peanut butter on it (along with a few flies). We were told to eat it as it was the best thing we would get all day. So, I ate it. We then had to go outside and we were split into two groups, told we had to do various challenges to promote team bonding and the winning group would receive a cooked breakfast on Monday. The first challenge consisted of sitting in a circle within our groups.

We were then brought a plate of disgusting animal food. It was dog biscuits, zebra pellets, baboon food, insects and other shit they put in there too disgusting to mention. The group to clear the plate first would get a point. I was determined not to lose so I just whacked a huge load in my mouth but, on trying to swallow, I gagged. Nevertheless, we won that point. 1-0!

Secondly, Frikkie said we needed to wash it down with something. So, they brought out one huge jug (per team) of sour milk, which had been lying out in the African sun for 2 full days. As if this was not bad enough, they decided to add a few delicacies to this drink, which were worms, flies, beetles, onions, Tabasco sauce. As before, the first group to finish the drink, got a point. We had a good rhythm going and Steve, Jason and I drank a lot. It tasted a bit like yoghurt – although that is what I convinced myself as I was necking it. Anyway, we won. 2-0.

Thirdly, we had to do a physical and mental exercise. We had to solve riddles, run to find animals at the lapper, solve more clues to find a bottle of whisky in the stream and drink the whisky – in the shortest time. We just could not find our numbered tortoise and we lost by 4 minutes. I timed the other team who did it in around 18 minutes so when 18 minutes expired on my watch, which was it as far as I was concerned. Frikkie said bring back any tortoise and find the whisky. I asked what the point was - we have already lost the point. Frikkie said 'I do not like quitters'. I responded with 'I do not like losing but shit happens'. I was more pissed off as I put my name down for being our designated whisky drinker and we still had to find the whisky in the stream and, knackered from all the running, I had to drink a jam jar full of whisky, which nearly killed me. So, we lost that task. 2-1.

Fourthly, we had to go into the wild dog enclosure to retrieve a t-shirt from the top of a tree, which belonged to one of each team members. We had to be tied together by the ankles to someone in our group. I was with a sexy Danish girl Rikke and we led from the front staring down the wild dogs as we proceeded.

We found the tree where the t-shirts were but we were hampered for 2 reasons. Firstly, our t-shirt had been placed much higher up than the other team's making their task much simpler. Also, we had a fat girl from Hull who could not walk under all her weight and she also cried. Rikke and I were not happy with this needless show of emotion. We completed it in 11 minutes 47 seconds and the other team in 7 minutes 30 seconds. 2-2.

I could see my chances of a cooked breakfast slipping through my fingers. But I was not going to let this happen and I made sure I pushed my team all the way so I got a cooked breakfast. I undertook the role of the team captain, leading from the front as we headed stronger into each challenge. The Wild Dogs experience was tough but it ultimately did what it was designed to do – it forced us to face adversity and work as a team. That is what Harnas is really – it is about overcoming a lot of fears and working together as part of a team to reach the ultimate goal – a cooked breakfast!

Fifthly, as a team, we had to go into the wild baboon enclosure digging for a can of coke, which had been buried under the sand, then drinking it. This was particularly dangerous as if the baboons see you with anything, they will fight you for it and they are very wild. The idea was to distract them while others dug for it. We lost this task too so we were now 2-3 down.

The last task involved throwing about 30 keys into the swimming pool and only one opened a padlock. The team who found the key the quickest, won. We did it in 1 min 42 and the other team in 7 minutes 50 seconds. It was 3-3 and we were into a tie-break. It involved both teams getting back into the pool at the same time to find the key again. Hannah, the Scouse girl in our group, found it for us and it sparked rapturous celebrations. It was great fun and it really did pick everyone up after an upsetting morning. Now, on Monday, we get a cooked breakfast and I cannot wait.

The night has been spent having a few beers in Michelle's cabin where a load of us went to get away from the silly kids although I feel that a growing division is occurring in camp, which I do not feel should be happening as we should all be trying to enjoy this experience together. I had about 7 cans of Windhoek draught and started doing my best impression of Iggy Pop, Lust for Life. It has now just gone 00:30 and I'm going to bed.

Day 9 - Sunday 26th October 2009-09-28

The day today has been far less eventful than yesterday as, basically, we had a day off. This morning, I decided to take this opportunity to embrace myself in the Namibian culture so I had a walk down to the bushmen's church, which was a really rewarding experience. The bushmen, children, wives all go and everyone are so thankful for things they have, instead of not wanting what they do not have, like in the greedy Westernised world. Everyone sings and it is treated as a celebration. They are so happy and at the end of the service everyone shakes hands and it makes you feel good about life.

Sadly, this afternoon, the football game did not go ahead, which was disappointing as most of the volunteers were looking forward to it. Tonight over dinner, I chatted away with Rikke, the girl from Denmark who is really sweet. I like her a lot. But, now after much discussion, I am tired so I need to go to bed earlier tonight.

<u>E-Mail</u>

Hi,

Just to let you all know that I am still buzzing from the lion walk on Friday. It was such an amazing experience. Apparently, there is nowhere else in Africa you get the chance to walk alongside an adult male lion

Yesterday was amazing too. We had to do a fear factor to get us used to the Harnas experience and the winner would get a cooked breakfast on Monday. I just thought I'd do anything for a cooked breakfast. We thought we were in for a good lunch up at the farm, but reality soon kicked in when we sat down. We were given a stale piece of bread each with flies and peanut butter on. The flies were fine but peanut butter is awful. Then we went outside and were split into 2 groups. We had to sit in our groups in a circle and each group was presented with a big plate of dog biscuits, baboon food, zebra vitamin pellets, and a load of other crap too awful to imagine. It was a race between the groups to finish it. I just shoved everything in my mouth and we won that task. 1-0. The next task involved them bringing us a jug per team of milk that had been left out for 2 days in the Namibian heat. In it they added worms, tadpoles, flies, Tabasco sauce and all other rubbish. It was a race to finish that too. I necked a good percentage of it and we won again. 2-0. The third task involved solving riddles to find our animals, but we lost by 4 minutes as we couldn't find our number tortoise. But we still had to find our number bottle of whisky in the lake and I had to drink that too. I was pissed off at this point as I was timing our team and I knew we had lost the point as the other team went first. 2-1. The fourth task involved going into the wild dog enclosure to find a t-shirt for our team, which was up a tree. We had to do it tied to another team member. I was with a sexy Danish girl Rikke, but our team was hampered by the fattest girl from Hull who firstly cried and secondly she couldn't move under all the weight. Rikke and I were so annoyed. Anyway, it caused us to lose it. 2-2. Then each team had to go in with the wild baboons to dig up a can of coke each, buried 4ft under the sand. This was the most dangerous apparently, as the wild baboons are vicious. Anyway, it was fine but we lost. 2-3. By this time I was really pissed off because I could see my dream of a cooked breakfast slipping away. I've talked about bacon all week to my friend, Roger. So then, the last task involved trying to find a key at the bottom of the swimming pool amongst 40 others. We did ours in 1:42 and the other team did it in 7 minutes. 3-3. The tie-breaker then involved each team getting in the pool at the same time to do the same again. It was a lottery, but luckily a Scouse girl in our team found the key!! 4-3 to us. Game over. I loved Scousers for all of 10 minutes. So, tomorrow morning at 9:00am our team get a beautiful cooked breakfast. It will be like a dream come true!! It was a great day, but if I'd have lost I wouldn't have been happy after putting in so much effort!!

Day 10 - Monday 27th October 2008

The morning has gone tediously slow. The only task involved Stuart and I sitting in the anthill doing a game count at the waterhole we made last week. We started at 09:00 and by 14:00 we had counted nothing. All we were able to do was to read our books and I am getting stuck into *For Whom The Bell Tolls* and Stuart has completed his book, which he started this morning. The highlight of the day was lunch. We both put it off until 12:00, then devoured the cold toasted sandwich (with hardly any cheese), the cold sausage, the hardboiled egg and I quenched my thirst with the sprite I bought this morning, which had inevitably gone warm in the heat of the anthill. We quipped that we would save the apple as an afternoon treat. 14:30 was our target. The question was: Could we hold off? The answer was no and we scoffed the rest of our food. We were there until 18:00 and boredom began to set in about 14:00, which was probably the only reason for eating our food.

Now the day is done, I am getting ready to go for dinner and I can safely say that this is one of the most pointless days I have had. Not for the fact it didn't amount to anything and I achieved nothing. It is not really what I came to Africa for. I am just sat on my own, at 18:36, on my cabin step writing this and the thoughts often run home, thinking of what is happening in my absence. A lonely mind is often a dangerous mind I tell myself as I hear the lions roar in the distance. I say that the negative thoughts must not be allowed to seep through the positive thoughts. But, my time in Africa will soon be up and I'll soon need to establish what it has done for me. Maybe I'll need more time.

Day 11 - Tuesday 28th October 2008

I am a bit down today if truth be told, but the fact is, I should not be. The morning started fine and we even received our Lapper breakfast. It tasted delicious but I thought as I was eating it, that if I received it back in the UK, it would have been sent back. But I was extremely grateful for it all the same. So, we had that and the rest of the morning we had time off to relax and do with as we pleased.

After lunch, which consisted of soup, I embarked upon another cheetah walk with Cleo and Pride, not that they did much but they never do. The main problem is my Manchester United polo shirt has gone missing in the laundry – the only thing to ever go missing. I know what has happened – the laundry women have taken it for their husband or kids. I am more annoyed at the fact it was a gift from work before I left to travel. If I found out who did it, I will break their fingers because I hate stealing. I am so annoyed. Now, I am happy in the fact that some person from Namibia has something that they would never have the opportunity to get. It is just the way it has happened but I am going to teach myself to be selfless and to stop thinking about myself. Stealing doesn't do any good though.

But, after a few beers tonight, it was decided that I am going to do a sleep out with Goetters the cheetah, which is where I am now with him purring away next to me. I made the 2km walk through the Namibian bush in the darkness, with only the light of my torch for company. I entered Goetters narrow, L-shaped enclosure, locking the gate behind me. Undaunted by the glowing eyes of the purring cheetah walking towards me, I walked towards him and set my sleeping bag on the mattress where only seconds before, Goetters was in a deep slumber. Luckily for me, he did not seem too pissed off. He waited outside for about 5 minutes, while I lay there, inside my sleeping bag, unsure whether or not to go to sleep in case he came in for a little snack.

Then, in he came and slumped down with his head on my shoulder as we lay and listened to the sounds of Africa. The insects buzzing, an occasional lions roar and then these sounds were disturbed by a stray cat entering Lost the Leopard's enclosure next to ours and, needless to say, the cat is no more. It was still slightly unnerving trying to get some sleep next to a cheetah but it is another memorable experience I will take with me for the rest of my life. This trip just gets better and better.

Day 12 - Wednesday 29th October 2009

It is my last day today at Harnas and I can say that I have enjoyed it. It has been an experience I will never forget but I'm still disappointed about the football shirt incident, which has left a bad taste in my mouth, but I hope it has gone to making an African child happy. I have just settled my bar account from the past 2 weeks, which was N$765 – around £51. This morning, we got to lounge around and, all of the people who are due to leave are unsure what to do. I decided (as I will not get any more chances) to go to sit with Lost the Leopard for an hour this morning and she gave me a frosty reception as I sat with her in her enclosure. It was such a great night tonight. We had a party and a meal up at the lapper. The meal consisted of a kudu pie with a fruit salad and custard for dessert. I have met so many amazing people here but if I did not meet any of them apart from Roger and Siri, I would not care. I've met a great friend in Roger and he said to me that 'if any of the people he meets in Cape Town are half as good as me then he'll meet some great people'.

I said him and Siri have made my time at Harnas really special. The night after the meal was spent taking photos and I think I got some really good ones to take away with me. We drank lots of beer and then headed back down to camp for a bonfire, wine and cheese, which was shared amongst us in the 'sensible' group. Rikke and I had the responsibility of putting the dogs Uma and Bubbles to bed and there was a slight moment under the stars. I have had a great time at Harnas and I think I've found a new friend who I can say is one of the best.

Day 13 - Thursday 30th October 2008

So, my Harnas experience has ended and I'm quite sad to leave it behind. We were each presented with a certificate this morning and then we had to get our transport to our respective accommodation in Windhoek, which meant another 4-5 hour drive. I was happy when I was put in the same coach as Roger, Siri, Erin, Stina, Julie and a few others. We did not speak much of the way as we were all tired and most of the others slept. I decided this would be a good opportunity to take in the barren landscape for the last time. We crossed over bridges where underneath should be a free-flowing river but instead lay the bare river beds, which stretch for as far as the eye can see to the furthest horizons. Trees struggling for life as the people are. Lonely souls walk aimlessly, in the middle of nowhere. In search of what? The heat crisping their skin and no water to be found. Then we drive by in our van, stocked up on food and drink for the journey because we come from that part of the world, which gives us the chance to buy water. Life is not fair when you see people in need of the basic commodities we take for granted in the Western world. But those who read this may just ignore the situation (as always) as it is the easiest thing to do. It reminds me of the book I read at University – Stan Cohen: States of Denial, which focuses on "the unedifying ways which most people comply with authority." Cohen has a vision of a social utopia where it is imperative to assist others in times of danger. There are, in fact, many people in this world who are suffering, but because they are pre-modern, they usually go unnoticed by the global community. I, like Cohen, believe that this needs to change.

At Windhoek, I was dropped off at Hotel Safari Court, which is where I am now. I showered and made my way to dinner around 20:00. It tasted amazing. I went into the hotel restaurant and I was seated by an old waiter who looked like Patrick from Eastenders. I ordered Mushroom soup to start with and then a fillet steak for main course. It was just what the doctor ordered. However, I must be losing my appetite because I left a little bit of the steak and I watched it go away on the plate with a feeling of guilt. Undeterred by this, I proceeded to the Flamingo bar for another 2 beers. I was going to chat up 2 very attractive Namibian ladies at the bar, but I decided against it.

So, I have just come back to my room to get an early night. Sleep is an important commodity for any traveller. You do not know when you may get the chance to have a decent bed again so I am making the most of it. I think I left a little piece of me at Harnas and taken a greater part of the earth, that suddenly means so much to me. For a haven to learn and discover the realities about yourself, I would recommend it as a sanctuary, not only for animals, but for humans.

<u>Day 14</u> - Friday 31st October 2008

Happy Halloween. It has been a busy day today to be honest. I awoke at 08:00 and made my way down to the restaurant for breakfast. So, I still could not find my appetite and I do not know where it could be hiding. I sat at the pool reading until it was time to check out. However, I checked out at 11:30 slightly later than I should have but Nelson on reception did not mind as we are mates now! Then, all I had to do was to wait until 14:30 when my driver picked me up to take me to Hosea Kutako airport in Windhoek. As I queued for check in, I saw MJ, the American girl from Harnas, in the line and it turns out she was going to be on the same flight as me to Johannesburg. We sat in the airport bar and had a drink, chatting so much we nearly missed out flight. But, we made the plane and we landed in Johannesburg at 19:00. I rushed to gate A7 to get on Etihad 601 to Abu Dhabi. I was seated next to a friendly chap named Oswaldo from Angola. He is really struggling with English so I helped him with the menu etc. We struggled to understand each other but the global language of football and beer makes it easier. I also enjoyed looking at the attractive Air Stewardess who is bringing me drinks on a pretty regular basis.

Now, I am going to try to get some sleep. I have just watched The Matrix movie and ate some sort of beef dish (it is about 01:00am). I am a little tired.

›ve: With Maddox – my favourite Lion Cub)

(Above: Lion Walk with Zion)

›ve: Challenge 1 - Animal Food!)

(Above: In with the wild dogs)

ve: nose with a wild baboon)

(Above: sleepout with Goetters the Cheetah)

Al Ain – The Garden City

Al Ain can be literally translated as meaning 'The Spring' and is also referred to as the Garden City. The area is still famous for its traditional irrigation system, the Falaj, some parts of which date back as far as 1, 000 BC. The six-lane roads in the city are lined with a wide variety of trees and shrubs, both indigenous and foreign. Jebel Hafeet is itself a fascinating landmark of Al Ain. This limestone monolith rises 1350 feet, providing spectacular views across the border between the UAE and Oman. A modern three lane highway lit by yellow halogen streetlamps snakes up the mountain to the royal palace and picnic areas at the top. There are also hot spring spa pools at the base, and the entire mountain is honeycombed with passageways accessible to any seasoned pot-holer. Indeed, on my first trip to Al Ain, I made the trip up Jebel Hafeet, overlooking Al Ain, Oman and Desert for as far as the eye can see.

Al Ain's population is around 374,000 being located 160km east of Abu Dhabi, capital of United Arab Emirates, close to the border with Oman. Many British ex-pats currently have flocked on Al Ain and the United Arab Emirates in search of a tax-haven and luxury surroundings. However, I notice that those from Pakistan and Philippines are not offered the same luxuries, instead working jobs such as taxi drivers and maids in order to earn a living. A huge disparity encapsulates the rich and the poor in this country and you can clearly see the segregation between the haves and have not's. The rich live in luxury apartments and, like my Uncle Ronnie, 6 bedroom mansions whereas the poor are placed in shacks, out of the way where they can be no blight to the landscape. They are transported like camels in the back of a truck after what must be an excruciatingly difficult day's labour. In fact, if I may say so, it is probably one of the worst places in the world for it. However, those on tax free salaries may simply choose to ignore this situation.

Day 15 - Saturday 01st November 2008

I had a nightmare upon arriving in Abu Dhabi Airport this morning – my luggage had been inexplicably left behind in Johannesburg. So, me and this guy from Cape Town had to wait around for 30-45 minutes for it to be sorted out. I proceeded (with my hand luggage only) to get a taxi to Ronnie's house, which was driven by a guy called Saeed. I spoke to Wes, who yesterday had been sick on a piss up with Ronnie and his workmates on an annual trip to the desert. It is typical Wes. I arrived at Ronnie's just after 09:00 after being awake for 27 hours. Ronnie made a brew and some toast, which I scoffed down in no time, still with a thought of the starving kids I saw in Namibia. Wes got up with a huge hangover to join us but I could see he was not at his best. Around 11:00 we all went to our separate bedrooms for a sleep. At 13:00, we all got up and headed down to the Rugby Club for club sandwiches, a swim and I had a beer or two.

Tonight, we came back to Ronnie's for a Chinese and his mates Marcus and Dave came around for a few beers in Ronaldo's bar. Wes and I watched the Man United v Hull game, where we managed to scrape a 4-3 win. Then we headed downstairs to Ronaldo's bar where we emptied his fridge of beer. Wes managed only 3 as he was still rough and Dave slipped away early for the same reason. But, I wish I had made it yesterday – it sounded like a good day. It is now 02:45am and we are off to bed.

Day 16 - Sunday 02nd November 2008

The day has been spent lounging about at Ronnie's house. We were going to go down to the Hilton for a swim but we decided to go down tomorrow afternoon. Wes and I spent most of the day on Ronnie's roof, just sunbathing and reminiscing about our life, trying to work out how both of us managed to end up here for two completely different reasons. Fate is the answer I think. I was rough myself if truth be told as I think last night's beers, coupled with my last 2 days escapades took it out of me.

At 17:00, Ronnie nipped out to meet a guy (who did not speak English) to collect my bag, which took about 2 hours to meet up with him. Nevertheless, he got it and, luckily for me, it was the right one. He came back and dished us up a Spaghetti Bolognese – beautiful. Afterwards we watched Bolton beat Manchester City 2-0. Ronnie then had to fuck off out with Wes at 22:00 to meet a guy to drop off Wes' visa as he is going to India with work. That took another 2.5 hours. By the time Ronnie arrived back he was knackered. I am so lucky he is in my family. He is one of the best guys I know and I'm so proud to be his nephew.

Day 17 - Monday 03rd November 2008

You'll never guess what happened to Wes today? Well, Ronnie left for work this morning and I got up at around 10:30. Wes and I were talking about his proposed trip to India, just as Ronnie came home around 13:00. Wes then had a phone call from work saying he had to go to Houston, Texas in USA instead and that he may end up in Mexico by next week. Uncle Ronnie and I could not believe it and, to give Wes his credit, neither could he. Anyway, the 3 of us went down to the Hilton this afternoon for a chill out, a swim, some food and me and Wes had a beer or two to say farewell. We were going to head to Paco's tonight, but Ronnie made a great curry and we stayed in to watch Lee Evans as Wes has got to leave for Abu Dhabi tomorrow. It has been good spending a few days here with my mate. I'll miss him after tomorrow. I wish him well.

Day 18 - Tuesday 04th November 2008

The last day at Ronaldo's was spent sunbathing. This morning, I woke and saw Wes off in his taxi. I gave him a guy's hug. That is where both of you are uncomfortable to do it but it means more than a handshake does.

This afternoon, Ronnie and I went back to the Hilton where I aimed to get rid of my t-shirt tan once and for all and, in doing so, I think I overdid it as my chest is now like a cooked lobster. On the road back to Ronnie's we stopped off for a haircut and the Gulf Barbers. I tried explaining what I wanted to this Arabian fellow to no avail. He literally took a number 2 razor and shaved my head. Ronnie's eyes in the mirror showed what he thought, but his declarations that it was a 'good trim' sounded a little hollow. It is a haircut so I am not too bothered and it should last me a while. We came back to Ronnie's where he cooked us a steak. We watched Chubby Brown and, now, it is 21:00 and I am going to bed.

E-Mail:

I've just said goodbye to Wes this morning at my Uncle Ronnie's house. He is now off to Abu Dhabi and god knows where after that. I'll give him a call tonight to make sure everything is OK. I fly back at 08:15 to Heathrow Airport tomorrow and there is a chance Wes maybe on the same flight as me. Pretty coincidental how things work out. I'll be spending a few days at Steph's flat in London with her and Stuart, going out for a few drinks and chilling out before I get my flight on Sunday morning to Australia. I've already met some girls from Australia so I'll be looking them up when get there. I'll also look up my mate Mark who's somewhere in Australia. It can't be that big of a country so I'm sure I'll bump into him.

I did have an awesome time in Africa and I've experienced more than enough to take with me in the future. I'd definitely recommend doing something similar to everyone. However, it is not for the squeamish as some days (most days actually) involved cutting up a donkey leg (and other parts of a donkey) and feeding it to the animals. All the work was tough and in your face, but it was great. I enjoyed it a lot.

So, we've just got back from the Hilton and Ronnie will cook us a steak tonight. I'll be in bed early as I'll need to be up at 04:30. I can't believe I've got to come back to the cold of the UK for 5 days!! At least I can show off my tan. One more thing - Ronnie and I have just been to a "Gulf Barbers" where the guy gave me one of the severest trims of my life and a very close shave. So I've got a really short, but good, haircut for 10 Dirham's. I feel great and I'm having a great time!!

Day 19 Wednesday 05th November 2008

It has felt like a really long day today and, if I'm honest, it has been even though I am not tired. I woke up at Ronnie's at 04:30am for my flight at 08:15am UAE time. I was packed off in a taxi to the Airport and the flight was all on time. No problems.

The plane landed at 11:30 UK time and I proceeded to make my way to Archway to meet Steph, who I will stay with for the next 4 days. I arranged to meet her in a pub at 14:00. However, I arrived there earlier than expected at 13:15 and the original meeting pub was closed. So, I went to the one over the road (which Steph said was really rough). I had a couple of pints and then Steph turned up and, as I found out, it is actually a good pub. We proceeded to head back to Steph's, had a sandwich and watched some afternoon TV, while

I waffled on about my African experiences. At 16:30, we went down to meet Stuart in a bar in Angel to go for Tapas. After filling our bellies on delicious tapas, we came back to Archway to watch the United v Celtic game and we just managed to scrape a 1-1 draw. Here is an admission – London is better than I have given it credit for.

<u>Day 20</u> - Thursday 06th November 2008

The day today has been spent walking around London and I went to Hyde Park – by myself. Wandering around London, I arrived at the conclusion that it is not so bad, although it is big. We have a negative view of it up in the North, but my opinion has changed. I am man enough to admit it.

Stuart and I went to a gig this evening on Holloway Road to see his friends playing in a band called Ice Station Zebra. A few beers were sunk, while listening to eclectic bands playing.

<u>Day 21</u> – Friday 07th November 2008

I managed to venture to the Kings Road today and I nipped in for a pint in a pub called "The Chelsea" full of city workers who cannot take their beer. Money was the talk of the day as I 'eavesdropped' and these folk are a world away from the African Deserts I have just visited. Karl Marx always said that the working classes need enlightening but I believe that these city bankers with a capital 'W' also need to have their eyes opened. Money is not the be all and end all of life.

Tonight, Steph, Stu and I went to a bar in Angel for karaoke night. I, as it is one of my hang-ups, decided not to sing but we did see and speak to Maggot from Goldie Looking Chain. Many beers were consumed as I listened to Steph doing numerous renditions on the karaoke. She is probably not bad but, after about 20 beers, anyone sounds good. Happy days.

<u>Day 22</u> – Saturday 08th November 2008

This morning, Stuart made a quality fry-up to set us up for the day. After we devoured it (because it was delicious) we went to a pub in North London (around the corner from the Emirates Stadium) to watch Arsenal v Manchester United. It was full of Gunners fans (good humoured I have to say) and we lost 2-1. There was a frosty atmosphere though when I first walked in with my George Best Manchester United t-shirt on though. I'm gutted we lost but glad I went out to wind them up!!

Tonight, we all went out to meet Steph's mates in the social, near Oxford Circus. One of Steph's mates thought I was fit, but nothing was ever going to happen (unless I was going to get wrecked but I couldn't as I'm off to Australia tomorrow). I have just had a kebab and I am off to bed as it is 01:00am and I have a big flight to Australia tomorrow. I'm not even watching Joe Calzaghe fight Roy Jones Junior in the boxing.

Day 23 – Sunday 09th November 2008

London – Sydney

I awoke this morning around 07:00 and made my way to the airport. I made a slight mistake by getting off the Heathrow Connect train at terminal 1 instead of terminal 4, but I rectified this situation and we were away. The plane is OK(ish) and I noticed that there were more male cabin crew workers than female. But, for some inexplicable reason, I cannot seem to sleep on planes yet everyone else can – and they snore at the same time. But, apart from that, it has been uneventful. A word of warning to all those people wanting to travel to Australia from England – do not do it with a hangover. It is bad enough at the best of times but you are just asking for trouble. Next time, I will take my own advice.

Day 24 – Monday 10th November 2008

Singapore – Australia

I arrived at Singapore Airport at 08:00 and spent a brief period on the internet, reporting in and then got on a "short" 7 hour flight to Sydney. The flight was uneventful and I landed in Sydney shortly after 19:00 Sydney time. I checked into my hostel and I went next door to the Scu-bar, attached to the YHA where I am staying, to meet a few people. I met a guy called Jamie from Wales who seems OK, a guy from the Wirral (whose name I forget) and another lad, Scott, from Wales. It felt really weird, as I also met up with my friends from University and Hamburg – Mieke and Miriam, who are in Australia to do a sailing trip on the Whitsunday Islands. It was so nice to see Mieke and Miriam again and felt really weird that we were catching up in Australia

Chapter 3 – Half The World Away

Sydney – The Harbour City

Australia's largest city, Sydney has a metropolitan population of around 4.4 million people, representing one of the most multicultural cities in the world, acting as a beacon for immigrants into Australia. It was initially founded in 1788 when the first fleet arrived in Australia from England although many believe it was initially inhabited by Australian Aborigines.

Sydney continued its modern growth throughout the 20th Century and by 1954 its population was over 1.4 million. Sydney Harbour Bridge opened on 19 March 1932 being opened by Jack Lang (1875-1975) who was Premier of New South Wales in 1925-27 and 1930-1932 (although a man called Captain de Groot cut the tape before the Premier could). The new Bridge was 3,770 feet long. The span of the main bridge was 1,650 feet. Clearance for vessels passing underneath was 170 feet. A bridge climbing tour began in 1998 although I was unable to participate in this due to my epilepsy.

Sydney Opera House was opened in 1973 by Queen Elizabeth II. Sydney Tower was built in 1981. Furthermore the Chinese Garden of Friendship opened in 1988. The same year, 1988, Bicentennial Park opened. Also in 1988 Sydney Exhibition Centre opened. From 1988 the Darling Harbour district was redeveloped and is now known for its shops, restaurants and entertainment. Sydney Harbour Tunnel was then built in 1992. Although beautiful at Darling Harbour and Circular Quay, the CBD of Sydney proved suffocating due to the many tall skyscrapers that exist and the dense population.

Day 25 – Tuesday 11th November 2008

I got up at 08:00 for the orientation at 09:00, slightly worse for wear after the activities of last night. I had a breakfast in the cafe and went to the hotel reception to meet the others. I saw Stina from Denmark, who was at Harnas with me, which was a bit coincidental. She'd be worth a fuck if she didn't have a boyfriend, but that has not stopped me in the past I seem to remember. But she's a sweet girl and, me being a changed man, I didn't try anything. I wanted to help her though because she has managed to cut her head on a fan and made a right mess of her pretty face. We walked through the streets of Sydney together to our orientation and, Sydney is claustrophobic, with skyscraper after skyscraper engulfing you into a submissive surrender.

Orientation lasted 3 hours and, after I bid farewell to Stina who went off to Melbourne, me and the 3 lads from last night went for a pint to Scruffy Murphy's – an Irish bar in Sydney Central. I won a jug of beer off the lads as I correctly guessed the nationality of a sexy Brazilian barmaid but unsuccessfully managed to get her number. About 12 jugs of beer (each) and 2 meals (each) later, we were asked to leave because the scouser in our group fell asleep. So, we left and went to another Irish bar for a pint but then decided to go back to the hostel, change and head for a night out in Sydney (minus Jamie who could not keep up the pace despite his boasting about Rugby, Rugby, Rugby). We started at the Scu-Bar.

I had an argument with an Aussie guy over pool who was so rude but I shot him down to size – I lost but I shot him down to size. I spoke to a girl from orientation called Liz, from Norwich, who is a pain in the arse. She said after orientation, she went down to the harbour and the Opera House. She was shocked when I said we went to the pub for 7 hours. I am pretty pissed now, but I've got my face seen around Sydney!

Day 26 – Wednesday 12th November 2008

I met up with Mark Lowe today, which was awesome. We went down to Coogee Beach as me and the 3 lads had to look at a couple of flats. Anyway, Mark and I chilled on the beach and he convinced me to sack the idea of a flat and go with him next week to Cairns to travel down the East Coast. I don't know how to tell the other guys as they are expecting me to move in to split the rent but i'll probably just not tell them and bugger off. But the best flat we saw was $225 per week, which is a bit much. So, i've booked my flight to Cairns on 22/11/2009, which I did on an impulse in the reception of the YHA. No need for thinking – just do it.

Tonight, Mark and I went for food with a girl he knows from Melbourne called Meredith. Then she left the bar and we were joined by Mieke and Miriam. We all went to another pub then headed for a kebab, which was the best kebab in the world as me and Mark concurred. We seemed to stay on the streets for ages. Mark and I were really pissed, so much so that he missed his train and had to stay on the floor in my hostel much to the chagrin of the Frenchies in my room. I think the guys I'm sharing with are pissed off as i've not been to bed earlier than 03:30 yet. I did chat with one guy today from Milan called Antonio who seems OK. Typical Italiano – smooth, good looking. I hate the bastard (only joking) – he is a quality guy.

E-Mail:

Hey,

Arrived in Australia OK. The past few days have been spent knocking about getting to know the place. I went down to Coogee Beach today with my mate Mark from school and then went to check out 2 flats near the beach with 3 guys staying in my hostel. We are all discussing moving into a flat but, me being me, I think my circumstances have changed and I'm going to catch a flight to Cairns next week with Mark and spend the next month or so travelling around the East Coast. It also gives me chance to see the Whitsunday Islands, which should be great.

When I arrived on Monday night, we went straight to the pub next to the hostel where I met up with 2 German girls I went to Uni with. They are here on Holiday and then on Tuesday morning I bumped into a Danish girl I was staying with in Africa. It's a small world. We had the orientation meeting yesterday morning and, afterwards, me and the 3 lads went to an Irish bar where we stayed until 19:30. We would have stayed longer, but the Scouser in the group fell asleep and we were asked to leave. But don't worry, he is an Everton fan and hates Liverpool as much as the rest of us!!

Anyway, it is 20:30 here on Wednesday and marks on his way to the hostel then we're off out for food and to meet the German girls for a bit. Sydney is OK by the way. Full of high rise buildings and beautiful ladies on the beach today. I may get a chance to see more sights tomorrow and book my flight to Cairns! I'll also have to break the tragic news to these 3 lads that Alistair will not be coming to live with them for the time being.

Hope everything is OK in sunny Bury and is not falling apart without me!

Day 27 – Thursday 13th November 2008

Awoke this morning at 08:30 and Mark had buggerred off without packing my sleeping bag away, which leaves me a job later. I tried calling him but he's not answering – obviously hungover.

So, I headed down to breakfast and I'm now sitting overlooking one off the most famous views in the world – Sydney Opera House and Sydney Harbour Bridge. It is so beautiful. It is hard to describe when you see something so famous from TV, up close and personal. It does take away your senses. Lots of people taking pictures and it is just as it seems on TV. I still can't believe I am here and I cannot get it out of my head how lucky I am to be able to see sights such as this. Why me? Champagne Supernova is just on in the coffee place I'm sat in, overlooking the harbour. It cannot get any better than this as the sun crisps my skin. I just wish I had someone to share my experiences with. 'People believe they are gonna get away for the summer.' Why am I so lucky? I've just been stung $3.40 for a coffee on saying that.

I'm not happy about the situation occurring with Jamie. He gave me $3000 in traveller's cheques and cash the other day to keep in my bag because he did not want to carry them. But, I've not seen him since that first day and I've still got them. I don't like the responsibility as I can hardly look after my own things let alone his. 'He deserves you to rob him' in the words of Mark Lowe.

Tonight, a few of us from orientation got together for a piss-up. We were sat at the kebab shop next door to the YHA, peacefully enjoying a kebab when some Korean fella went crazy inside the shop. Danny Smith and I tried to calm him down and he disappeared down a back alleyway next to the kebab shop screaming. As Danny and I tried our best, this guy picked up a big plank of wood and proceeded towards our direction, seemingly intent on destruction. He wanted to batter the owner of the kebab shop, who was by no means small – he towered over me. Danny and I managed to wrestle the wood from this chap, and he broke down in tears as we explained that you should not do this. As the police arrived, this chap had disappeared into the night. After that, a girl we were with, Holly, wanted to head down to Kings Cross to see if she could audition as a lap dancer. So, her, Danny, Liz and I went to this seedy, grotty place in Kings Cross, which looked to be full of pimps. At the front a woman, mid-30's was working and her eyes looked demoralized. However, Holly still wanted to audition and she did for Danny and I a little pole dance, which, if I must say, was rubbish. Lap dancing bars are not my scene at all. We went over the road so she could do another audition and then, in the cab on the way home at 05:00am, I said I do not think she should be a pole dancer as it is full of seedy blokes and she deserves more. Holly did ask the question 'Why didn't you say that before the pole-dance Alistair?' What an eventful night though.

Day 28 – Friday 14th November 2008

"No man is an island, entire of itself; every man is a piece of the continent, a part of the main. If a clod be washed away by the sea, Europe is the less, as well as if a promontory were, as well as if a manor of thy friend's or of thine own were. Any man's death diminishes me, because I am involved in mankind; and therefore never send to know for whom the bell tolls; it tolls for thee..." *John Donne*

Now, normally, back home a Friday would be spent by working, treating myself to a McDonald's breakfast and wondering what to do with my pathetic, fucked up night. Instead, I have spent it down Coogee Beach with Mark, Meredith and Gareth, having a barbecue and a few beers. It was an amazing feeling.

We got down there at about 14:00, bought the essentials, and then headed to the beach. I nipped into the sports bar to find my camera (which was stolen the other night in Coogee) but it was gone. No sign. I'm fucking annoyed someone stole it the other night. Anyway, we had the barbecue, a few beers and had a kick about with a few guys from Saudi Arabia but I forget their names. 'Yeah, you can join us for a kick about' I said, not realising it was their ball we'd been using for about 30 minutes. I finished reading Ernest Hemingway; For Whom The Bell Tolls, which is one of the best books I have ever read. Meredith and I then took a swim but, Mark touching his toe in the water like a tart, found it all too cold and baulked at the prospect of a good swim. Give him credit though – it was freezing! On the bus home, having consumed too many beers, I thought the desperation for the toilet was going to knock me unconscious but, struggling to run the last few yards back to my hostel, I got there and spent the next 20 minutes, in pain, relieving myself.

Tonight, the 4 of us went for a meal in China Town where I had a massage. 'You very stressed' she said. I said 'Yes. I have been on the beach all day drinking beer. I am very stressed indeed.' I virtually fell asleep in the restaurant after this week's activities. Mark ate way too much and I'm sure he was doing it because he knew I wanted to go to bed! I've never seen anyone of his size eat that much Chinese food! At one point I did nod off in the restaurant at which I had to call it a night. It has been my best day so far in Australia.

Day 29 – Saturday 15th November 2008

Today, Mark, Gareth and I went down to Sydney Harbour where we took some good photos down there – on Mark's camera obviously. We had a coffee in Starbuck's and then Mark and I left to buy me some shoes for tonight's night out. After a few (and when I say a few I mean a lot) of shops, we found an expensive department store called David Jones where I bought nice pair of tanned shoes. Then I met Gareth back at the Star bar where we had a Chicken Schnitzel and chips – they like their Schnitzels in Australia!

Tonight, we met at Gareth's room at the Mercure Hotel and we were joined by Meredith. We drank a box of Goon between us (for all those unaccustomed to Goon, it is a 4 litre box of cheap wine, with some nasty ingredients but it gets you pissed). We then proceeded to meet Nat, Gareth's ex-girlfriend, which made it awkward, and went down to Darling Harbour to a quality bar called Cargo. Meredith was flirting with me big time and, due to the awkward situation, we ended up together for the night. It was the best night I've had since I have been in Sydney and I look forward to a few more.

Day 30 – Sunday 16th November 2008

I awoke this morning surprisingly refreshed as everyone said Goon gives you a really bad hangover. So, I texted Jamie, Scott and Chris and we headed to Manly on the ferry. Manly is so expensive but the beach compensates for that. We found a decent bar on the beach front where we spent the next few hours playing pool and watching rugby. Lowenbrau on tap is amazing! I annoyed a Kiwi fellow when I asked him where his New Zealand Choker was. He knew what I meant as New Zealand always choke at the big tournaments.

Pissed up, we decided (I decided) to get a box of Goon on the way back home, ultimately leading to a dentist's chair job on the streets of Manly, until the box had gone. We just managed to make the ferry home after a tiring run through Manly, which was eventful as Jamie and I because we (for some inexplicable reason) were singing all the way home to my IPod, which was funny for us, not the other passengers – especially when we broke into a rendition of Robbie Williams, Angels.

Later tonight, we went to Cheers bar where we watched the Everton v Middlesbrough game, which ended 1-1. A few Americans wound me up so I left, got a kebab and came back to the hostel, falling over my bag in the dark, lying on the floor of an 8 bed dorm, flummoxed like a turtle lying on its shell.

Day 31 – Monday 17th November 2008

Mark, Gareth and I went down to Bondi today where we knocked about for a bit and got a good meal by the beach. Bondi is not as good as everyone says it is but it is still a reasonable place. We were going to do the Bondi-Coogee Beach walk but Gareth has a really sore ankle so we opted against it. I do prefer Coogee Beach to Bondi if truth be told.

Bondi, although respectable, just seemed a bit overrated. Not in a bad way but I just did not seem to connect with the place. The bars and restaurants were nice enough but there were a lot of crazy people walking about like zombies, on another planet, forgotten by the world of travellers and socialites that seem to encompass this area. It is an interesting place if you sit back and look at it from that point of view – to get all these people from different walks of life, together walking side by side.

Tonight, Gareth and I went to Paddy McGuire's for a few drinks and watched as people passed along the streets of Sydney, to destinations unknown. Gareth is a nice lad, although I am unsure if I will keep in touch with him in the future. I will leave it at that.

Day 32 – Tuesday 18th November 2008

Today has been a bit of a disaster to be fair. We went down to Palm Beach as Mark was buzzing as that is where Home and Away is filmed. However, when we got there, it turned out to be so quiet and empty that there was nothing to do. No shops, no people. Just houses and a cold beach. The highlight was visiting a cafe where Mark and I had the best bacon and egg roll – ever. It has been decided. It was that good I had two. But, after failing to spot Alf Stewart outside the Surf Club when we went there to see filming, and as it started to rain at 17:00, we fucked off back to the city – disgruntled.

Tonight was Gareth's last night so we all went for a pizza in his hotel then headed out for a few beers. He is a good guy, if somewhat pretentious. I'm not too sure what to make of him. He strikes me as one of those ugly guys who tries to show off his money to attract women but then gets really annoyed when it does not work. He is pretentious and, although he thinks he doesn't, he does think he is above everyone else as he is a pilot. That's why he was pissed off when I hooked up with Meredith. I am now looking forward to Cairns at the weekend. I am glad Mark is here in Australia.

Day 33 – Wednesday 19th November 2008

It has not been a too uneventful day today but, for once, I am first back in my hostel – or so I thought! I came back and, due to the food, beer and other unhealthy dietary foods that has signified my time so far in Australia, I took off all my clothes, naked as the day I was born, and let off a huge, rip-roaring fart in the middle of my room, safe in the knowledge I was all alone. Then, looking across the room, I saw a body tucked under a duvet, and it turns out is the Argentine girl, hidden away like she has seen a ghost. Not my best moment.

This event came after going out with 4 new hostel roommates. 3 girls from Cornwall (Nicola, Sarah and Niamh) and one Dutch guy Arthur. I am in love with Niamh – she is such a beautiful girl and we got on so well. But, me being me, I came back early as I have to check out tomorrow.

Today at 16:30, I met Mark and he is trying to sort out me staying with his Auntie for a few days before Cairns. But I hope it gets sorted out by tomorrow because I have to check out at 10:00. But, Sydney is not as good as it is seen on TV. It is fading away into the void, which is now surrounding me day after day on living here. The storm outside expresses how I feel about the city. A new adventure looms, but don't look back in anger, I heard you say.

Day 34 - Thursday 20th November 2008

What an eventful day it has been today. I woke about 08:30 and bid farewell to the beautiful girls in my room and checked out of the hostel. I put my things into a locker at the YHA and then I went to meet Mark where we sorted out our accommodation for Cairns. We then came back to his Auntie's where we intend to spend the next two days. We met his cousin Anthony who also seems like a nice guy, who gave me a glass of Irn-Bru. Anthony is into his Scottish culture and we seemed to chat for ages amongst ourselves about the history and places we have visited. He is a sound lad.

We made our way into the city at 18:30 and ate a nice chicken schnitzel and chips at the Shark Hotel then proceeded to Scruffy Murphy's and then Paddy McGuire's for a jug off beer each. But, this was all a prelude to a Hawaiian party at the Scu-Bar, where the consumption of alcohol was at its peak since we arrived. There were a few people there I knew and we all had an amazing time. Mark and I managed to concoct a new drink of Sambuca/Red Bull, which got us pretty much on our way. The next few hours consisted of me getting up on stage having a dance off and Mark doing his usual pole dancing routine. We then went to a place called The Gaff where some guy wanted a fight with one of our mates, Danny Smith, so there was a big standoff at one point to which none of us backed down. On the way back into the city, one of us managed to steal a Mars Bar from someone, which led me, Danny and Mark to be sprawled out in the middle of a road in Kings Cross, tussling for the spoils. It was then decided that a Sydney kebab was needed, but after trying to find the best place, Mark and I settled on a location on George Street and Danny went home - ill. Mark and I decided we needed somewhere plush to eat our kebab and, somehow, we ended up in a boardroom of the Hilton Hotel. We made it to the 36th floor where we ate apples and then made it back down to the 4th floor, where we entered a function room, which had a load of boxes filled with Guaylain chocolates, Gucci perfumes, handbags and other accessories. Mark rifled through everything and we gorged ourselves silly on chocolates while Mark proceeded to break a lamp fitting. Writing this, I cannot believe we got away with it but it was the funniest thing we've done yet - although I don't want to think of the consequences if we were caught.

At around 04:00am we got the train back to St. Leonard's but fell asleep and ended up about 4 stops further on. It was lucky Mark woke up as I was out for the count and the train would have travelled for about an hour further on.

Day 35 – Friday 21st November 2008

I am just lying here on the floor mattress in the basement of Mark's Auntie's house. It is a really nice house to be honest yet I am not too sure how I feel to be leaving Sydney. Another frontier has come and gone and, like the others, I have nothing to show for it. I am just wondering what the point is at the minute. I am a little down today and it is not that I miss home, which is probably for the reason that I do not know where home is. I'm not too sure if I have one or where I belong. Maybe I'll keep travelling until I find out what the point is – all I know is that there has got to be one.

I awoke this morning and thought I'd broke my new camera as the lense would not work. After a brief panic by Mark and I, I clicked it into place and we are back in business. Panic at the disco over. But we actually did not get up until 14:30 and at 17:00 we walked 2 miles to Crows Nest where we found a restaurant where we ordered 3 curries for $10.50, which we both ate until our bellies were stuffed. I'm still bloated now but it was a good curry.

Tonight, we watched the film Green Street and then Men Behaving Badly. I am totally shattered now and I am ready to do some good sleeping. Cairns tomorrow and I have no idea what to expect.

E-Mail:

Hey,

Just to let you all know that today is my last day in Sydney for a while. Tomorrow, we are off to Cairns where we will travel down the East Coast, hoping to end up in Sydney by Christmas/New Year. I'm actually looking forward to getting out of Sydney as it doesn't appeal to me as much as I thought it would. I went out for a drink the other night with some girls sharing my room who say Cairns is much cheaper and that it should be amazing.

I'm just staying at Mark's Aunties gaff for a couple of days until we go tomorrow, which is a really nice place. Last night, we went on a Hawaiian night with some friends I made in my first hostel and it was quite an eventful night. Mark developed a concoction of Sambuca Red Bull, which was an experience!! I've included a few photos it was a fun night and I know a few people around Sydney for when I get back here next month.

Amway, when we get to Cairns and make our way down, we are going to go to the Whitsunday Islands, Fraser Island, Brisbane etc. I have some idea that I want to do the shark diving at some point but I may have to get to Adelaide to do that. It does sound like an awesome experience - not a lion walk, but it could be good. We're off now to get our last meal in Sydney for a bit.

Chapter 4 – Heading North

Day 36 – Saturday 22nd November 2008

We woke up this morning at Mark's Aunties at 07:30am and made our way to the airport via a taxi for $40. We arrived there, checked in through one of the longest queues in history and decided to eat breakfast, being completely ripped off but, after eating it, we discovered a McDonald's and, our injustice still seething through our little minds, we decided upon a second breakfast. Little sense was made of a second breakfast but it filled us up for the day. Mark got on his flight at 11:00am to Cairns and I then had a 3.5 hour wait to get mine and, needless to say, it was not too good.

On arrival in Cairns, I noticed it is very different to what I anticipated. It is mountainous, tropical, and very humid but I like it. I imagine it to be very similar to what Venezuela will be like. I like the mountainous backdrop to the city and you get a sense of living in the clouds. So, tired, hot and sticky, I made my way to Cairns City Backpackers to check in. Mark was there and we were sharing a room with Sam, Claire, Danni and Kay.

Tonight, Mark and I headed to Gilligan's with Clare and Sam for a meal and a few much needed beers. We watched the Rugby League World Cup Final between New Zealand and Australia, with the Aussies is super confident mood ahead of it. Due to this, I plucked for the Kiwi's and they thumped the Aussies in surprising fashion. We then headed to the casino where we watched the football – Villa v United. Mark won a decent amount of cash on roulette but then lost it all as he got drunker and drunker on vodka red bulls. I lost my temper with a bunch of Irish fellas who were basically dick heads and, as the argument became heated, we were thrown out at 05:00. This sense of injustice united both groups and a laugh was had by all.

Cairns

Captain James Cook sailed up the North Queensland coast on his first Voyage of Discovery in June 1770, aboard his ship the HM Bark Endeavour. Captain Cook was the first known European to visit the site where today's City of Cairns is located. Many, however, would debate this and say that the existence of Cairns dates back to 170 years prior to Captain Cook's adventure when Dutch explorers arrived on Cape York. Whilst it is accepted that they reached the western side of Cape York there is no evidence that they made it down the east coast to arrive in Cairns.

There are many stories documenting the conflicts between the white settlers and the indigenous Aboriginals throughout North Queensland. There were many deaths on both sides and it easy to understand the fear and lack of trust that was prevalent. The local Aboriginals had lived in this harsh area, having come to terms with the natural hazards over thousands of years. Within a few short decades they were being told what to do, where they could and could not go and how they could live. Some early explorers were violent, setting an example for other Aboriginals who may have considered retaliating against these strong arm tactics. As is often the case in history though there were many brutalities on both sides and even today, the rift, whilst much smaller, still exists in modern Australia. We had to be careful travelling through Aboriginal territory in Cairns.

Personally, I cannot picture life in the early Cairns compared with that of this modern city. Early Cairns offered a rugged terrain, proving difficult to explore. However, modern Cairns is just like any old town, although it remains hugely tropical, susceptible to Cyclones. Awareness of the Great Barrier Reef sparked this tourism growth and in 1984 an international airport opened and a major tourism boom began which converted Cairns from a sleepy regional town to the thriving city of today.

<u>Day 37</u> - Sunday 23rd November 2008

What an eventful day it has been today. We awoke (gingerly) at 12:30 due to the late night activities last night and made our way to Coles Supermarket to get a drink as we had mouths like Ghandi's Flip Flops. In Coles, Mark commented that we needed to find a place to bet on the Ricky Hatton fight. I had a flashback and remembered seeing that it started at 13:00EDT. We rushed to the casino, placed a bet just in time for the fight to start. I had Ricky to win in either round 9 or 11 and Mark had rounds 6 or 10. So, Ricky won in round 11 and I won $130, which completely made my day. We then proceeded to book on a Great Barrier Reef Dive on Tuesday, which will be awesome and, on Wednesday, we have booked on a stopover tour to Cape Tribulation, where we will live in the Rainforest. This is going to be amazing and the trip just gets better.

Tonight, Mark and I were joined at the Woolshed by Danni and Kay for a meal. Mark and I paid $10 and got Chicken Parmigianina, a pint and dessert which we thought was excellent value. So, we still have a free meal ticket left over too. For anyone visiting Cairns as a traveller, you need to visit the Woolshed. Cheap food, excellent beer and a good party spirit. Now though, we are so full, but we still managed an ice-cream on the walk home, which melted all over my hand and chin in the humid atmosphere.

<u>Day 38</u> - Monday 24th November 2008

We achieved quite a lot today. We got up early (for Mark) at 10:30, had our respective showers and breakfasts, then made our way to town to book a few trips down the East Coast. We headed into a place called PeterPans's and a pretty girl named Larissa with a tight fitting 'I love Paris' t-shirt dealt with our queries and we were provided with an itinerary for a trip. Mark and I wanted to mull it over for a while, so we headed to McDonalds for lunch and then headed for a swim in the lagoon for a few hours, soaking up the humid atmosphere, overlooking the brown, muddy coloured sea.

Around 17:00, we went back to see Larissa and, after the initial wait, Larissa sorted it out for us at a cost of $900 each, but we have booked a lot of things. I couldn't concentrate on what I was doing as I am a sucker for a pretty face and my mind was on doing other attractive things!

When we booked our trip, we went across the road to the Woolshed for our free meal before picking up our underwater camera for tomorrow and we went back out to the Rhino Bar for a few beers, which I did not take to.

<u>E-Mail:</u>

Hey,

*Just to let everyone know that I arrived in Cairns OK on Saturday. It is so humid and the temperature is about 38*C every day. We went yesterday and booked a trip for Tuesday to the Great Barrier Reef, which includes a free Scuba Dive so I'm excited about this. We also booked for Wednesday a trip to Cape Tribulation further north, which will let us see the rainforest. It is meant to be amazing up there. So, we will stay up there for one night and, maybe on Thursday or Friday, we will get on the Greyhound bus and make our way further south.*

Today, we are looking into sorting out a trip to the Whitsunday Islands and Fraser Island about the 8th December, which will let us do some sailing and 4x4 driving on the beach. The Whit Sundays are supposed to be amazing.

Cairns is very different from what I first imagined. It is surrounded by mountains and is very tropical in nature. I imagine it to be like Caracas in Venezuela, which I will see next year. It is about 100 times better than Sydney, which didn't have much going for it if I'm honest. Cairns is what you'd imagine Australia to be like if you'd never visited it. Also, me and mark went to watch the Ricky Hatton fight in a hotel casino here in Cairns so we had a $5 bet on which round he would win in. I bet round 11 and I got $130 back, which paid for one of my trips.

<u>Day 39</u> – Tuesday 25th November 2008

An amazing day has been had today by Mark and me. We got on the Ocean Spirit 3 Boat Shortly after 08:00am. It set sail for the Great Barrier Reef at 08:30 and we met 3 brothers from Leeds and then, funnily enough, a couple from Bury called Vanessa and Dan, who knew similar people to us back home. Anyway, we were put in the same group for the scuba dive. We were the first group to go down with the instructor and I have to say it was so amazing.

It was something completely different I have never done before and I still can't believe I have done it. The colours of the fish and the corals are perfect – indescribable. Once I mastered the breathing underwater, I was away and I wanted the shackles to be let off more, yet the instructor insisted we stayed by his side. It was still perfect to be able to share this experience with 2 other people from Bury who I am sure I will see more of, if I return back to the UK.

Dinner on the boat was amazing with langoustines, prawns, and so many delicious fresh fruit. The day just got better and better. After we were bloated from the food at lunch, we went out to a Kay to start our snorkelling, which was simply out of this world with an abundance of fish and marine life. Stingrays were spotted but, unfortunately for me and Mark, we did not see a Sea Turtle. But the day has been amazing and I do class myself as extremely privileged to have done a scuba dive on one of the Seven Wonders of the World.

Tonight, Mark and I went to the Woolshed with 2 Scottish people in our room and then met up with Daniel and Vanessa for a drink again before they set off south, down the East Coast.

Cape Tribulation

So called when Captain Cook's ship ran aground, Cape Tribulation found its name. Cook recorded that "the north point [was named] Cape Tribulation because here began all our troubles..." Cape Tribulation nowadays can still see what the world looked like more than a hundred million years ago. Although most of the dinosaurs are gone, the cassowary has survived until today (when you see them walking you will notice the likeness to the creatures in Jurassic Park) and the crocodiles are still around (they have been around for that long they have seen the rise and fall of the dinosaurs).

In 1985, the Jungle Lodge, the first backpacker's hostel, was built in Cape Tribulation. The huts where it used to cost $5 a night to sleep are now part of Ferntree resort on Camelot Close and now you pay around $180 in the same huts, though they have been upgraded a bit. Cape Tribulation, in particular PK's where we spent our time, developed a reputation as a major backpacker party place amongst the crowds that shag and drink their way around Australia. Highlights included drinking games, limbo competitions, dryer riding, and beach bonfires, all washed down with copious amounts of sex and alcohol.

Day 40 - Wednesday 26th November 2008

We were picked up outside our hostel by our driver, Andy, at 07:00 this morning and then we had to collect 14 other people from their hostels for our trip up to Cape Tribulation. Second (after us) to be collected were the 3 Hewitt brothers from Leeds – Ryan, Ollie and Johnny. They were, similar to us, all hungover but they had managed to acquire a bottle of vodka for the trip.

The journey up there was amazing with some breathtaking sites as we wound up the mountains, deep into the heart of the rainforest in North East Australia and into the clouds above. The weather proved to be the most tropical since we arrived yet it was utterly gorgeous. Mark and I checked into our room (number 7) at PK's hostel in Cape Tribulation and we were joined by a drop dead gorgeous Canadian girl, Emily (19), who seems pretty sound. This afternoon we went to the swimming pool where we met 2 more people from our hostel in Cairns so we spent a decent amount of time with them.

For tea, we cooked a weird concoction of Spaghetti, mince with a sweet & sour sauce. It sounded awful, it looked awful but, remarkably, it was bloody good. We cooked it on a shitty stove in a wood but it sorted out our appetites. We spent the evening with the Hewitt brothers and a Swiss girl, Anna who we were trying to teach how to speak like a Northerner but she didn't get it. Ryan and I seemed to have the same appreciation for what we were doing and couldn't believe that we were away from our respective cities of Manchester and Leeds. He is a decent guy and we may meet up again in the future.

Day 41 - Thursday 27th November 2008

You know when you see such perfect beauty; it hits you in the face as soon as you look at it? Like when you see the most beautiful of women. I am talking about visiting the centre of two world heritage sites at Cape Tribulation. On one side is the Daintree Rainforest and to the other is the Great Barrier Reef. Stood in between is me – I've never felt so humbled or insignificant in all my life. Mark and I wandered down to the beach where we found the Reef on one side and the Rainforest on the other. I must admit I had another moment to myself, just sitting in the sand, thinking to myself why a scummy guy from Bury gets a chance to see such magnificence. It has to be the greatest sight I have ever seen. I am not joking. I keep asking – why am I so lucky? I would describe Cape Tribulation as a sanctuary where you can maybe forget about things. Things that are bad that you once knew that do not exist here. Nothing exists here except tranquillity and the breeze from the reef as you stand in awe. For a moment I felt isolated from the rest of the world, even though Mark and Ryan were nearby. There was a moment where we all just sat about 50 meters apart, just thinking to ourselves. I cannot speak for the other guys but I thought about my life and what I have achieved. In all 24 years, there is nothing that compares to what I am doing at the moment. To sit here and feel freer than any man on this earth is, for me anyway, one of the defining moments of my life. It is hard to put into words.

The bus collected us at 14:00 and, after a brief detour to an ice-cream parlour (which did a gorgeous blueberry flavour) and a worthless visit to upper class Port Douglas, we got back to Cairns at 18:30. We are now ready to leave Cairns, after a drink with Anna who we met in Cape Tribulation. I love Cairns and I would definitely recommend it to anyone. I would return anytime.

Chapter 5 – Journey South

Day 42 – Friday 28th November 2008

The morning started quite badly and, to be fair, it has got worse ever since as it has not stopped pissing it down. We had to get up ridiculously early at our hostel (05:45) and had to make the 15 minute walk to the bus terminal with the weight of the rucksack breaking my back in the tropical heat. The bastard bus driver would not let me on the bus with my McDonald's breakfast so I had to eat it all virtually in one bite, which I thought was hugely unfair. I whacked it down my throat, nearly choking myself in the process. Once on the bus, it started to rain but the bus is so shit it leaked in and, the place with the worst leak, happened to be right over our heads. It is bollocks. We stopped for 20 minutes and the weather got worse. To cap it all, we had to endure a 4 hour traffic jam because some fucking truck driver decided it would be a good idea to collide with a passenger train yesterday. Unfortunately, the gentleman in question did not make it, which is a shame.

So, we arrived in Townsville at 15:00 and checked into shitty hostel called Globetrotters. It will do I suppose. Mark and I cooked dinner of chicken satay with rice. The rice was a bit gluey but it was fine and edible. Then we sat up drinking goon until midnight.

Townsville

Townsville is adjacent to the Central Section of the Great Barrier Reef and is Australia's largest city north of the sunshine coast and is considered, by many, to be the unofficial capital of North Queensland. As you climb Castle Hill and look down over the city, you see that it is rapidly expanding to the West, North and South. The problem for Townsville, as in most of North Queensland, is the threat from Cyclones. Shortly after I left this area, Cyclone Ellie hit land causing widespread flooding and forcing people to flee their homes. These cyclones occur during the cyclone season, between November to May, right at the time I arrived in Townsville.

Day 43 – Saturday 29th November 2008

I had a strange sense of achievement today. We woke early, had our free breakfast then, with the other guys in our room, walked up the mountain in Townsville. It wasn't too high, but I was breathing heavily near the summit. I had to laugh at Mark as he managed it up the rocky steps in only his flip-flops but that made the decent precarious. At least I had some decent footwear on. I had a feeling I had done something worthwhile – it'll set me in good stead for my hike to Machu Picchu. We came back for a walk in Townsville, around the botanical gardens and then purchased some items for the barbecue tonight. Mark and I also got our Australian SIM numbers, which is great because we get cheaper calls. But the exhaustive activities this morning were spoiled by the activities tonight. We ate the barbecue, which was quite unhealthy and we consumed a lot of alcohol. We went out with the guys in our room and were joined by 2 German girls. I don't know where Mark is now (possibly off fucking one of them) but I decided that the other one was not for me so I sacked them off at a bar in Townsville, which was funny – rude but funny ending up in a bar on my own with a group of locals!!

Magnetic Island

Magnetic Island is located just offshore of Townsville on the North East Coast of Australia, accessible through Nelly Bay. It has long been established as a holiday resort as I found out upon arrival on the island, but many visitors take walks around the many local forts from World War II. Apparently, the name derived from its 'magnetic' effect it had on Captain James Cook as he passed the island when sailing up the East Coast of Australia in 1770 – and I can see why.

Personally, I enjoyed the island for the vast array of wildlife to be found there – with Koala Bears being the main attraction. For fish lovers, such as myself, it is ideal although the travellers diet was not conducive to eating much of the fine fish Magnetic Island had to offer. In 1971, Cyclone Althea crossed directly over Magnetic Island, causing 90% of damage to the houses, lifting many from their foundations. Much has been rebuilt these days and the draw of Magnetic Island still attracts the travellers.

Day 44 – Sunday 30th November 2008

This has to be one of the best days I have had since arriving in Australia. I awoke early to wake Mark up and we said our goodbyes to Townsville at 11:00 (with slight hangovers) and got on a ferry to Magnetic Island. Once there, we had to get a bus to base camp and we happened to get chatting to two girls from Norwich called Rachel and Nikki. Nikki has such an unfortunate face and, one (or Mark) could say, ugly as sin. Rachel maybe worth one but Nikki is a 100%, definite troll – but nice enough all the same.

Once settled, all I wanted to do was to find a place to watch the Manchester United v Manchester City derby clash today. There are 2 bars on the island and I was told that everything closed at 23:00 (if I was lucky), which didn't help as the match kicked off at 00:00 – I was a bit gutted but I never gave up hope.

Mark and I ventured out for a walk and, after 5 miles of trekking in the intense sun of Magnetic Island we found a supermarket that did the best ice lollies (Splice's) and I devoured 3 in no time. Then we hired a Mini-Moke for $81, which is a vehicle used to get around the island. So, immediately, we headed to Arcadia and found a sports bar at Arcadia Hotel, which would be closing at 23:00 (or so the barmaid said). By this time I was giving up hope of seeing the game. Demoralised, we came back to the hostel for a lie down, which is beautiful as it is right on the beach and has the best atmosphere. At 20:00, we headed to the kitchen to cook ourselves a carbonara, which I am so proud of – especially as we had to eat it in the dark. It was fantastic.

Still trying to watch the match, we gave a last try up at picnic bay, which we got to in our moke but, upon arrival shortly after 21:00 the bar was closing, plus they wanted I.D off Mark. We then walked up the pier at Picnic Bay and had a lie down, looking up at the stars and it was so quiet and peaceful. For the first time, I reflected upon what I was missing at home, feeling nostalgic. My head was not in the right frame so we headed back to the hostel where I needed a jug of beer while we played pool. On arrival, I noticed a bald headed United fan wearing a 'Road to Moscow' t-shirt. 'Fuck it' I thought so I had a word. He said he was going back to Arcadia where he was staying to watch the match as the manager would be reopening it for him and they have Fox Sports. For a free lift back in our moke, I asked if we could join him to which he said yes. I was ecstatic.

Pissed up with a jug each, Mark drove us down to Arcadia. However, upon arrival at the bar, no-one was to be seen and I felt like my heart had been ripped out like seeing your girlfriend in bed with your best mate. Murray tried the door (more in hope than expectation) and, to our delight, it opened and we had a free bar to ourselves. It was like we had won the Champions League there and then if you'd have seen the celebrations. We scrambled to find the TV Box to turn on Fox Sports, which took 5 minutes. Then the game came on and the 3 of us sat there watching it with a free bar to ourselves. Beer was poured, Mark ate himself silly on crisps and it was amazing. Rooney scored nearly straight after I'd whipped the froth off my first beer and we won 1-0. Around 60 minutes, the manager and his mate came back banging on the window, really pissed off. Mark and I were ready to make a swift exit but instead managed to wise him up and he let us watch the rest of the game. He was more worried as he had left the bar open, unattended. It was quality and whenever United play City at Eastlands, I will always remember the time on Magnetic Island.

<u>Day 45</u> – **Monday 01st December 2008**

We spent the day walking around the forts of Magnetic Island with the two girls from Norwich. The heat was sweltering as we wandered around the mountains but I enjoyed it. We saw a couple of Koala Bears, which were sleeping in the middle of a tree – such cute animals. The mini-moke we got yesterday has proved hugely useful. However, at 17:30, Mark and I had to bid a fond farewell to it, saying our respective goodbyes to a friend that I wish we could keep.

Tonight, we cooked Spaghetti Bolognese with sausage meat, which worked surprisingly well. After the meal, in the darkness, sat by the beach we had a drink with the two girls from Norwich and the troll Nikki is such a dull girl, so I left her chatting to Mark. I say chatting as, I looked over at one point to find her talking to him, while Mark was lay on a ledge, eyes closed and looking fall intents and purposes, asleep. I spent the time with Rachel who I got on well with. We were getting a little close sat under the stars but nothing materialised.

Day 46 – Tuesday 02nd December 2008

We woke this morning to the three dick head Canadians in our room making so much noise and it was really hot as some prick had switched off the Air-Conditioning during the night. Mark was totally pissed off and I wasn't too far behind him. In a bad mood, I took a shower and then joined the 2 Norwich girls for breakfast, which was bacon and eggs, and it was FREE!!! That cheered me up although I did have to sit and look at the troll during it, which was a little off-putting. I am not trying to be mean to her as she is a nice girl but god – she is ugly!! They left early and we got on our bus to the ferry terminal at 10:40, got the ferry back to Townsville and from there we managed to get on the Greyhound Bus journey for 5 hours to Airlie Beach.

I slept most of the way on the bus, which is unlike me as normally I can't sleep on public transport. We were collected by a sexy girl at the bus terminal although everyone seems attractive at the moment (apart from one person. God she was ugly). I was really pissed off tonight, however. We ended up going out for a few beers on our free vouchers and we ended up in Mama Africa's. Anyway, we were sat there enjoying a beer, Mark was chatting to a Dutch guy and these 2 dicks came onto the dancefloor in front of where I was sat, blowing kisses at me, turned their arses in my face in a suggestive manner and generally fucked about. I ignored this with the restraint of a saint (twice). Then they thought it'd be funny to come over, prodding me, talking to us etc. I told them to jog on as they were winding me up but they persisted in talking. So, at one point, I confronted this 6'5 guy but he backed away saying something like 'you're not hard mate.' I may have retorted with 'Ok. Let's find out how fucking hard I am. Let's go.' I was ready to go there and then. But, what annoyed me more, was Mark took their side. Nothing like going into battle with your mates at your side. It showed me up, which I do not like. It ruined my night; I'm upset and totally pissed off. I should really tell Mark but I'll leave it.

(Below: With Gareth, Mark & Meredith at the Mercure in Sydney

(Below: At Bondi Beach)

(Below: Bury - with Daniel, Vanessa and Mark)

(Below: Cassowary at Cape Tribulation)

(Below: Period of contemplation at Cape Tribulation)

(Below: Top of Castle Hill at Townsville)

Airlie Beach

Airlie Beach is a town located in the Whitsunday region of Australia and offers the best access to the Whitsunday Islands. It is almost certain that the town was named for the parish of Airlie, in Scotland, as the name was suggested by the chairman of the former Proserpine Shire Council, who was born in nearby Montrose, Scotland. The official name was Airlie from 1936 until 1987, when it became Airlie Beach.

Day 47 – Wednesday 03rd December 2008

I've come to a point of self realisation today, involving my travel towel. I have not washed it since I started my travels and, if I'm honest, it is really starting to stink. Mark thought his was bad but mine is awful. I mean – it actually sickens me but I have to use it. It has travelled from Africa to UAE to London to Australia. Maybe time has come to wash it! Mark is using my travel towel as a Canary down the coal mine for signs of when he should wash his.

Today, we managed to sort out some internet things, after a huge queue in Peterpans. Then I went down to the lagoon for a sunbath with two white South African's who are sharing our room. We had a decent discussion regarding the Apartheid debate and they basically reconfirmed what I have been saying for a few years – racial apartheid has merely been replaced by social apartheid, which is not as frowned upon as much. 'Heroes' such as Mandela have cashed in upon this but, call me cynical, does 26 years in jail for advocating guerrilla attacks on government properties justify this? OK Mandela's actions are to be applauded and he is an amazing man. But, much work now needs to be focused on economic apartheid existing, not just in South Africa, but around the world.

Mandela has been lauded with approval yet he and de Clerk negotiated his release from prison with the assistance of big business. As John Pilger wrote "much of the new cronyism came from Mandela himself... he enjoyed the company of Captains of industry such as Harry Openheimer with his immediate aim to get money for the ANC". And for those who believe Mandela brought an end to Racial Apartheid, I feel you are a little naive. In fact, Washington, as always, signified the end as it as it was bad for big businesses. Mandela merely acted as a symbol for this. Che Guevara was a guerrilla warrior too yet he has been lambasted by Western governments as a ''Communist Murderer" for wanting to bridge the gap between rich and poor. Soldiers who fight illegal wars with no reason in US and UK are defined as Heroes. Repatriation ceremonies treat them as such yet who asks the questions: how many children died as a result of your misplaced bomb? How many people have converted to 'terrorist groups' as a result of your actions in the Middle East? How many people have you killed? Who makes the weapons in the Westernized world, which kills our soldiers?

Are these heroic acts? In my definition, a hero is meant to save lives, not end them. If armed forces fighting illegal wars are labelled 'heroes' for following orders from a democratically elected government - isn't that all the German soldiers were doing during WWI and WWII? OK – that is taking the point a little far, I will admit, but you know what I mean.

It's funny how UK and America defines greatness. I define greatness as someone who stands up against Imperialist Domination and wants to do something worthwhile for humanity. Like the South African's said today:

'There is still a divide in South Africa but based on money now. As long as the rich get richer and keep people in their stupid state people will continue to starve to death'
South African Citizens

The fact that this current situation is sponsored by US and UK imperialists, makes me feel embarrassed to be a UK Citizen and hold a UK Passport. As long as the likes of the Thatcher's hold residencies in elite suburbs of Cape Town, nothing will change. It's no wonder much of the world hates UK and US – I can understand why.

"In 'new' South Africa, as in the old one, the symbolic relationship with Britain has a special place. In the 19th Century, British Capital opened up South Africa and laid the foundation for racial division and white supremacy, legally enforcing apartheid in 1950s and 1960s, crushing black resistance. Between 1956 and 1970, British investment doubled." (Geoff Berridge: *Economic Power in Anglo-South Africa*, 1981).

I caught up with Mark about 14:30. We took our luggage to Peterpans to store it for our trip to the Whitsundays. Then we walked 8km to Coles Supermarket for some food for our tea. We decided upon a cooked chicken, chippy chips from over the road and a tin of mushy peas. Shit is the best word to describe it.

Whitsunday Islands

Originally, these islands should have been called the "Whit-Monday" islands as this was the day Captain Cook sailed through this passage in 1770. However, due to an error in time-keeping, Captain Cook thought that it was on Whit-Sunday when he passed, which is what subsequently led to the islands being called the Whit-Sunday Islands. The Whitsunday Islands were originally formed by volcanic action.

However, after the last glacial period (30 to 50 000 years ago) the sea level rose, leaving the higher coastal peaks as islands. During the mid 1800s the Whitsunday Group were the first to attract the attention of the pioneers of the mainland coast. In the 1880s, grazing leases were granted for the islands. It was not until the 1920s that 'dreamers' built galvanised iron huts for guests. Cruise ship passengers rowed ashore for tropical fruits, tea and scones. The first day trippers from the mainland were the Proserpine residents. They arrived on the island aboard the weekly mail boat. In 1962, the islands became more accessible when the road from Airlie Beach to Shute Harbour and the jetty were completed.

Day 48 – Thursday 04th December 2008

Some things are just too perfect to put into words. I am currently sat here on a beach (Hazelwood Island, Chalky Beach) at the Whitsunday Islands. It is too perfect. The snowy like sand beneath my feet as it crunches between my toes. The sea breeze and the noise of the calm waves, 10ft in front of me make it hard to find anything other than peace. The way the sun, romantically in its eyes, is about to set behind a far away island. The occasional noise of a motor dinghy passes by to spoil the silence but I do not care. I am at peace here. For once I am lost for words. Wars and famine escape your mind here. If only I had that special young lady with me, I'd be complete.

We managed to do a bit of snorkelling before we came to the beach and I loved it. There is so much diverse marine life and the fish do not move for you. It is as if they are used to humans swimming amongst them that they trust us. The Whitsundays are amazing – untouched. I urge anyone, looking for paradise, to come here. Mark and I also tried our hand at sailing, which was a tricky experience but at least we can say we put up the sails etc. It's thirsty work.

However, it all came so close to never happening. We nearly missed the whole thing this morning as Louis, our South African roommate, had to wake us up at 08:00 as our bus was collecting us at 08:30 so we had to rush to the bus station and we were close to missing it. Too many beers last night were the cause. Mark left it to me to get us up and, naturally, I left it to Mark with no-one telling the other.

Tonight has been fairly pleasant. We sat on deck underneath the stars, drinking and getting to know one another and the others all seem really nice. I now know we have chosen the right boat. We went for a quiet, 13 people boat instead of the big 60 people party boats. It is more personal and we can chat with everyone. I still can't believe I am here writing this, on a boat, under the moon and stars, in the Whitsundays. I do not deserve it. Why me is the question I ask day after day. People like me do not deserve to be here. But, needless to say, I am making the most of it.

Day 49 – Friday 5th December 2008

I awoke this morning to a mutiny aboard the ship. Everyone (apart from me) was complaining about the bed bug infestation that has swept the boat. I knew it wasn't great but assumed it was only affecting me and Mark. Before we went to sleep, Mark literally said 'Fuck this' as bed bugs were falling on him from the bed above so he slept on deck.

I thought, fuck that, even though it happened to me. Once asleep, nothing woke me. It turns out, everyone had the same idea as Mark. Mark, our skipper, was really cool about it (even though most people were complaining and giving him a hard time). He dropped us off at Whitehaven Beach while he went to deal with the problem, but he told me he was pissed off with the people who complained. Whitehaven Beach is so amazing. Although a beach, it is one of the most beautiful sights I've seen so far. The sand is so pure and untouched until Mark and I had a big game of football. The skipper returned to say we would be spending the night at Long Island Beach Resort but we could still do everything else as normal, which I felt was great but some people still complained, which I felt was out of order. Bad things happen in life but we need to move on.

After lunch, we headed to Tongue Bay Lookout Point, where we could see over the Whitsunday Islands. Everyone concurred that this had to be one of the best sights they've ever seen. It is a privilege to witness it. The sand was so white, sea so blue and the sky – perfect. I just sat there, finding peace and contentment, amazed by what was in front of me. I can't describe what went through my mind at the time but all I could seem to do was shake my head and think of where I've come from to where I am standing. Unbelievable.

Later, we proceeded to Long Island and checked into our rooms, which are quality. Some annoying Swedish girl pissed me off saying its 'unacceptable' as some fucking table in her room was broke or there is a problem with the fan. I just said 'what do you expect – 5* luxury?'

She just complained about everything and I could not be arsed dealing with her. We all had our respective showers, and then headed to the bar for a few beers. Mark bought me and him a 'Long Island' Ice Tea, which was nice to have actually sitting on Long Island. A perfect way to finish the day.

Day 50 – Saturday 06th December 2008

Saturdays were not meant for waking up so early!

We had to get up this morning at 06:00 to meet our Skipper, Mark, on the beach to set sail so we could get some snorkelling done on our way back to Airlie Beach. I think he is still pissed off about yesterday and, to be fair, the way some people acted and moaned he had every right to be. He told me it would be his last trip and actually phoned his boss to tell him as such. I understood where he was coming from and I think he appreciated the fact.

We got to do some snorkelling and, as the other day, I was last to leave the water. I loved it. Although, a lady in another group nearly decapitated me with the motor from her dinghy, which temporarily ruined my period of tranquillity. I came within 0.5 of a meter of literally sleeping with the fishes and it is the nearest I have ever come to meeting my maker. The rotor blades came within a midge's dick of touching me and cutting me to shreds.

After lunch on the boat, we decided to make our way back to Airlie Beach. About 14:30, the skipper pulled up and let us all have a swim so we dived off the boat and it was fun. No-one cared about box jellyfish but maybe we should have!

Upon arrival at Airlie Beach, we had to go and do some laundry, which took us about 45 minutes and this was paid for by the travel company due to the infestation. It feels great now knowing everything is clean. It is also the first time I've washed my travel towel since travelling! 50 days man without a wash! Mark could not believe it, but it is now clean. We went for a cheap meal to Domino's where I found I've burned all my lips. I found it when I bit into the boiling hot tomato paste and I let out a cry of something to the effect of 'fucking fuck.' Too much sun. We then headed back to Beaches hostel at 20:30 where we had a bit of a party with our group. We were first there followed by Mark and Skye (then 30 minutes later the others arrived and the skipper was pissed off at that). Mark Lowe had to drag me away from the bar as I was settling in too much and we had to get the greyhound bus at midnight. However, on arriving at the bus terminal Mark said our names were not on the list. No wonder – our bus is meant to be for tomorrow. I was desperate to get on the bus as I'd offended some local drunk who, put it this way, wanted to kick the shit out of me. The bus driver took mercy on us and let us on and we are now heading to Agnes Water – unharmed!

<u>E-Mail:</u>

Hey,

We've just got back from spending 3 days on a boat in the Whitsunday Islands. It was a great experience, which everyone must see if they get the chance. The beaches are so untouched with the purest sand in the world and it is so, so white. I'm going to add some photo's on Facebook when I can get around to it. The sea is so blue and some of things we did were amazing. I also got the chance to try my hand at sailing, which was great - tiring, but great.

We had a slight problem on the first night as the boat was infested with bed bugs and everyone complained. Mark was the first up out of bed and he went to sleep on the deck. Apparently, he was followed by everyone else. I, on the other hand, decided to sleep it out and woke up in the morning to the controversy. The skipper (another guy called Mark) said it is not acceptable and we could not sleep on the boat on Friday. So, he dropped us off at the best beach in the world, Whitehaven Beach, where we had a game of football etc. A few hours later, the skipper returned to say we would be spending the night at Long Island Resort, which was a bonus for me and it meant we could still do everything but get a good nights sleep! I also took the opportunity to get a few beers in!!

But, we also got the chance to snorkel some of the best reefs in the world, seeing the most amazing coral and colourful fish. It was amazing and the waters were so calm and still. I had to get dragged out at one point as I could've stayed in all day .I have really caught the sun and I have never been so brown in all my life. It feels great!!! We are now knocking about at Airlie Beach as we have to get a Greyhound bus to a town called 17 70 at 00:00 tonight. It takes about 10 hours to get there so we'll do some good sleeping on the bus. We have not got any accommodation booked in this town as everywhere is full, so I think we may take the opportunity to sleep on a beach or something to that effect. It shouldn't be too bad. But, in 17 70 we have a 4 hour surfing lesson booked followed by a scoot around the town. Got to go now and do laundry because of the bed bugs.

Agnes Water

James Cook, on Wednesday 24 May 1770, went ashore near Round Hill Head with a party of men in order to examine the country, accompanied by Joseph Banks and Dr Solander. Cook's ship, the Endeavour, anchored about 2 miles off shore. The ship was 106 feet in length, 29 feet 3 inches wide and weighed 368 ton and had a 14 foot draught. Some of the provisions were 80 ton of water, 21228 pounds of bread in bags, 1200 gallons of beer in puncheons, 4000 pieces of beef and 2500 pounds of raisins.

This was Cook's second landing in Australia and his first in Queensland, hence the Town of 1770 being referred to as the birthplace of Queensland. Cook and his party landed within the south point of the bay where they found a channel leading into a large lagoon. "In this place there is a room for a few ships to lie in great security, and a small stream of fresh water'' Cook wrote. Many large birds were seen, namely pelicans. Upon the shore they saw a species of bustard, one of which was shot. It was like a large turkey and weighed seventeen and a half pounds. It was the best bird they had eaten since leaving England, and in honour of it they called the inlet Bustard Bay.

Cook's party did not see any natives during their shore visit, but they did find campsites, fires and artefacts. From the ship, however, members of the Endeavour's crew observed about 20 members of the Meerooni tribe on the beach. At 4.30am on Thursday 25 May 1770, Cook made sail out of the bay. There is some conjecture about the origin of the name Agnes Water. Some believe the area was named after the schooner ''Agnes'' which disappeared from nearby Pancake Creek in 1873. Others believe that the area was named after Agnes Clowes, the daughter of the first European settlers, Daniel and Rachel Clowes, who built large stockyards and ran cattle on the miles of unoccupied coastal country in 1878.

Day 51 – Sunday 7th December 2008

We arrived at Agnes Water this morning after an overnight Greyhound Bus journey. On arriving, we had nowhere to stay. The place we wanted to go to was full as was the second (and last option). At first, it looked like we would be spending 3 days on a beach as this looks like a Ghost Town. However, we were lucky to find a hostel that is not yet opened and the guy there, Lex, let us have a room for $25 a night. The people at this hostel are awesome and nothing is too much bother.

Lex (the guy who works here) let us have 2 bikes this afternoon so we could ride about the town and we took the opportunity to go shopping to get some things for our tea. We settled for a frozen lasagne with tinned peas and carrots. Naturally, our 'IPod time' came first. This is taking an afternoon nap whilst listening to the IPod.

Tonight, we had planned to ride our bikes 15 minutes to the local tavern at 19:30 to watch the football highlights. However, at 18:45 a huge storm erupted over the town of 1770 – I've never seen rain, thunder or lightening like this. Undeterred, we hopped on our bikes and went anyway, getting completely piss wet through. I've been drier taking a swim in the sea. We arrived, to the amusement of the locals, like a couple of drowned rats and, to top it all, the football wasn't even on. We had a beer and a game or two of pool all the same. The storm continued and we got wet on the way home. It was quite dangerous, with no lights on the road or our bikes, lightening shockingly bad. My camouflaged clothes did not help!!

Day 52 – Monday 08th December 2008

We went surfing this morning. I didn't think I'd enjoy it as much as I did but once I caught the first wave, I loved it. We met at the surf shop at 10:15 and had our introductory briefing from the owner, who was an Axel Rose wannabe. Then we headed down to the beach to meet our instructor - a former world surf champion. However, on seeing him, you wouldn't have guessed it. A 50 year old overweight guy with a camouflaged, tight fitting sun outfit, with a sun hat with flap to protect his neck. A thoroughly nice guy all the same though.

So, he gave us his 45 minute chat on what to do and at 12:00 we were away. The waves were shit but I managed to catch a few decent ones. Just as we were finishing at 14:00, it started to rain so we headed for food with a guy from Kentish Town, London called Rich and back to the hostel. Dinner was noodles but we had to chill out due to the rain, which led us to egg and chips for tea.

Tonight, we went back to the tavern again to meet Rich for a few beers and we got chatting to an interesting Australian chap called Wayne, who is in his late 50's. He is working nearby in construction for a period and had so many words of wisdom – I wish I'd wrote some down. Again, it's been a great day and I feel like I've achieved something.

Day 53 – Tuesday 09th December 2008

We had a good lie in this morning until about 10:30 when I decided to get up and have a shower. We made 'brunch' of noodles and eggs and then we decided to head out on our bikes to use the internet. I managed to upload some photos and backed everything up.

This afternoon was brilliant. We went on 'Scooteroo', which is getting on a choppa/scooter and riding around the town of Agnes Water at speeds of up to 70km/h and I have to say it was really fun. We even got the chance to look at a few Kangeroo's and then we all went down to watch the sun set, whilst eating wedges. Agnes Water is only one of 3 places on Australia's East Coast where you can watch the sun set and, again I found a peaceful spot to think.

Whilst the sun was setting, I thought of people, back home, those I've met on my trip and, generally, thought of people passing me by. I made a vow to never let people who I care about pass me by. I really enjoyed today and my time in Agnes Water/1770 has been quality.

Rainbow Beach

According to the 2006 Census, Rainbow Beach had a population of only 999. The town's name derives from the rainbow-coloured sand dunes surrounding the settlement; according to the legends of the Kabi people, the dunes were coloured when Yiningie, a spirit represented by a rainbow, plunged into the cliffs after doing battle with an evil tribesman. Rainbow Beach is a pleasant, quiet holiday spot which also serves as a gateway to Fraser Island and Cooloola National Park. Originally known as Back Beach, Rainbow Beach was renamed after the coloured sands located near the town which lies to the south of Fraser Island. It was gazetted as late as 1969 when it was established to service the local sand mining industry. Until that time there was no road to Rainbow Beach, with the only access being via boat from Tin Can Bay. Sand mining ceased in 1976 and it has since become a rather quiet and idyllic holiday, fishing and retirement getaway which promotes itself not only as the 'Gateway to Fraser Island', but as an 'eco-tourism' destination. This is not the place to be if you are after cosmopolitan-style pleasures but it does cater well to beach-orientated holiday-makers with hotels, motels and caravan parks. Although it has a permanent population of only around 900 about 70,000 visitors blow through town each year.

Day 54 – Wednesday 10th December 2008

Today, we were up at 05:30 to catch our bus from Agnes Water to Rainbow Beach. It seemed like a long journey but it only took us until 12:30 to arrive at our destination. Rainbow Beach is a tiny little place, with only a few shops. Mark and I went for some IPod time on a patch of grass near the beach, but our usual slumber was rudely interrupted by some sprinklers going off, soaking us and waking us at the same time, amusing a handful of old locals in the process. So, disturbed and thoroughly put out, we headed down to the sand to get some sleep there.

On check in at the hostel, Dingo's, Mark and I went to our room where I had a read for a bit. My feet are causing a huge commotion in the room with the smell. I feel 6 months in quarantine is no good for them as they are that bad. I have scrubbed and scrubbed them but a foul smell persists. My sandals are just as bad. Mark acknowledged it first but I had to admit what it was and it is bad when you can smell how bad your own feet are. The others in the room, including one sexy girl, are not impressed!!

I am slightly pissed off today if I'm being honest – yet I don't know why. Maybe it's homesickness. I was sat in our bar in Dingo's hostel when we arrived, watching Oasis in a gig in Wembley from only a few months ago and I felt all nostalgic. My mind wandered back to that eventful, Rock 'n' Roll filled, pissed up, monged out day of 2005 when me and Wes headed to Eastlands in Manchester to watch them. Like the song goes though, live your life like a Rock and Roll Star, Stay Young and Live Forever.

Or maybe it is because I am not finding anything interesting in the travellers here. They all seem to do the same things. Same places on the East Coast of Australia. Same trip from Thailand, Cambodia, Laos, Vietnam, Australia, New Zealand, Fiji, USA. I am not learning anything from these people and, more importantly, I am not learning anything about myself. All I can do is to do what I did at home – piss it away. But I do not want that.

Day 55 – Thursday 11th December 2008

A fairly uneventful day has been had if i'm honest. We had a bacon and egg sandwich for brunch and then we had to find out information about our Fraser Island trip by attending a meeting. We were put in our groups consisting of 11 people and I am a little worried about doing the driving with Mark as there are only 2 other guys (Alejandro from Galicia, Spain and Ben from Israel) and the rest are girls who are too young or don't want to drive. Alex and Ben don't want to drive either. So, Mark and I are designated drivers, but if we have an accident, the cost gets split between all 11 people. I insulted a girl, Liz, from Liverpool who is the girlfriend of the Spaniard, Alex. I told a couple of Scouse jokes within about 30 seconds and she told me to stop 'otherwise we won't get on this weekend'. I took this on board and she seems fine.

I have the top bunk in hostels (as what usually happens) with Mark on the bottom bunk. I prefer this for 2 reasons. Firstly, when I wake up suddenly with an alarm, I forget there is a bunk above me and have a tendency to whack my head when I am on bottom. Secondly, when you come back late or get up in the night, you disturb them and not them you. But, new people have checked in and are complaining about my feet. To be fair, they do stink. I can still smell them, which is bad.

Fraser Island

Fraser Island's colorful history continues over the years since its discovery by Captain Cook in May 1770. Captain Matthew Flinders explored Fraser Island in 1799 and the island was named after Eliza Fraser the Scottish woman who was shipwrecked on the Island.

Prior to European occupation the island was home to several thousand Aborigines. Over the years it has become the site for a number of shipwrecks, and in the early days the home to the timber industry and mineral sands exports. The mining of mineral sands was stopped during the mid 70's by the Commonwealth Government when they would not issue export licences.

Much of the island is now protected as the Great Sandy National Park; in 1992 the park was inscribed on the World Heritage List.

Now with the end to sand mining and logging, Fraser Island has become a valuable tourist attraction for fishermen and 4WD enthusiasts. Wild brumbies were once an attraction on Fraser Island, but were taken off the island in the 90's.

Day 56 - Friday 12th December 2008 - FRASER ISLAND

"Fraser Island will certainly put a smile on your dial. Have a good trip, get on with the group, look after the motor and make sure there's no hassle in the castle. And remember one thing on the Island: Don't destroy what you've come to enjoy" Merv, Dingoes Hostel, 12/12/2008

Today, we set off to Fraser Island. We had to wake up early for a shitty breakfast of free pancakes and I wish I hadn't bothered. We had to have our induction with a guy called Merv – what a quality guy he turned out to be. Full of quality phrases and the most Australian geezer I've met since I've been here.

Anyhow, we set off in our 4x4 around 09:30 and got on the ferry to Fraser Island. Mark drove us there and we drove to Eli Creek for a swim, which is also where we had lunch of beef and cheese sandwich. We swam in the creek and let the current carry us back down to where our 4x4 was. We then drove to Indian Head where we saw the Ocean in all its glory and we also spotted a tiger shark. It was quite beautiful. I decided to drive us back to camp, but it was full of back seat drivers who wound me up big time. I have no diplomacy with these people, unlike Mark who dealt with the situation remarkably well.

We set up camp around 17:00 and Liz, the Scouser, cooked us an amazing steak. Her and her boyfriend are sound as a pound. While the girls prepared dinner, us guys had a mess about with the football, a beer and a Frisbee. The other groups met up with us and set up camp alongside us and, tonight, we all got pissed and did what you do. On tidying up later on, Liz asked me for a word. It turns out that Mark, who got completely hammered, made a move on her and she wanted me to have a word. Typical Mark! She said she never wanted it to ruin the weekend but, on trying to speak to Mark, he was virtually unconscious. So, I made it my business to try it on with a sweet French girl but she didn't like my 'Scotland 1-0 France: Parc des Princes 2007' t-shirt. So that was that but rich pickings were had! I also spent a while speaking with Alex in Spanish, and he seemed to understand a bit of what I was saying. I'll need that confidence for South America next year. But, when it came to finding a place to sleep, Mark passed out in the van and then I had to search through 4 tents to find a place to get some shut eye. Pissed up, I dived in with 2 German girls and, in the middle of the night, I got a dig in the ribs when I had my arm around one of them, literally trying to spoon her. She was not impressed and, dare I say, a little scared.

Day 57 – Saturday 13th December 2008

Today, we took a trip to Lake McKenzie, which is a beautiful place to see and we saw a few Dingo's – not as many as last night as one group had their chicken stolen. But dingoes are a strange creature as they look so skinny and hungry yet you cannot feed them – that is their natural shape. Lake McKenzie is beautiful and, dare I say it, the sand was whiter than the sand at Whitehaven beach at the Whitsunday Islands.

We made camp about 17:00 and the 4 young German girls in our group cooked a really nice chicken stir-fry. All of the girls went to bed early and then a storm came in so it left me, Ben and Alex in the back of our 4x4 putting the world to rights with a few goons. Mark fell asleep in the front. I learned that Ben, the Israeli, is so pro what his country are doing in Palestine and takes it as an insult that I should question it. I said that if your countries regime forces Palestinian people to live in another form of apartheid and sub human bondage, then who can be surprised if they fight back.

Mark and I slept in the van as Alex busted our tent whilst setting them up today. It worked out well if I'm honest as I could fully stretch out on the back seats and Mark was up front. I lay there for a while, looking up at the stars above Fraser Island and the full moon overhead, thinking about what I'm doing and, still, I have to pinch myself to tell me it is real.

Day 58 – Sunday 14th December 2008

Today, we got up at 07:30 to the scorching heat burning through our van. We ate cereal for breakfast and, after we packed the van, we headed to peaceful Lake Wobby. We had to park up and then walk to it for 30 minutes as it is in a really secluded part of the island but, on first sights, it is a beautiful spot, isolated in the heart of the island. We had a swim and could run down a steep sandbank at the side of it, straight into the lake. We managed 104 keep ups at volleyball and also managed to make a human pyramid.

After, we had to rush back to meet the ferry to get us back to Rainbow Beach. We managed to squeeze in a cheese and tomato sandwich then we said our goodbyes to Fraser Island. I saw it fading into the distance from the ferry, I was already missing it.

Once back in Rainbow Beach, we went up to a vantage point to watch the sunset, which I thought would have been romantic if I had that special someone there. Liz and Alex seemed happy enough together and it made me feel I should have that so I've decided, when/if I get home, I'll make a dedicated effort to find her.

Tonight, we spent the time quenching our thirsts and we said a fond farewell to all in our group as most of us are heading our separate ways.

Day 59 – Monday 15th December 2008

We had to wake up very early today to get our Greyhound Bus. It wasn't as early as previous occasions but it still felt early all the same and, for some reason, more of a ballache getting up as I was sleeping so well. During the wait for the bus outside our hostel, Mark and I decided it would be a good idea to bring back the game Kirby but we found it difficult as all the streets and avenues are so wide in Australia. However, we were joined by a guy called Danny from Skegness who seemed more excited about it than us and we recounted the various rules to pass the time. The other folk from Germany and Christ knows where in Europe, looked on at the 3 of us like we were from another planet but Kirby rules!!!!

The journey on the bus to Noosa took round 4 hours and we arrived at Noosa Heads about 13:30. Our transit van to take us up to the camp wasn't due until 16:20 so Mark and I made the 3km walk to Peterpan's, which seemed OK even though it was all uphill and the rucksack nearly broke my back. The bus turned up at the designated time and, after a brief detour to Woolworths to get supplies to last us until Thursday, we proceeded to camp. The camp is situated in the middle of Noosa National Park Forest, right at the side of a river. Tents are erected all over the show, the kitchen is very basic and the dorm we slept in was covered in mosquitoes, spiders and other beasties I am not even going to ask about. Mark and I made (packet) carbonara for tea and we had a meeting to discuss the plans for the next few days. After that, I headed to put up my mosquito net because I want to use it at some point. It took me about 90 minutes to put it up and when I got in bed it fell down. At least, somehow, it managed to cover my head.

<u>E-Mail:</u>

I've just returned from Fraser Island off the East Coast off Australia, which was amazing. Apparently, it is the largest sand island in the world. We had a 4x4 self drive for a group of 13 of us but some people couldn't drive or didn't want to so it was left to me and Mark to do most of the driving. At night, we had to set up camp next to the beach, which was an amazing experience. Especially when we had to chase dingo's away who were trying to steal our food. On Saturday, we headed to Lake McKenzie for a swim, which is a beautiful place. We also had really great people in our group and we all mixed together as a team to cook, clean, drive, set up camp etc. We had no showers for 3 days so, when we returned yesterday that was the first thing everyone did.

Today, we got our Greyhound Bus from Rainbow beach and have arrived at Noosa, where we are off camping again. Tonight, we stay at a bush camp and then first thing in the morning we head off kayaking down the Noosa Everglades for 3 days/2 nights, so that should be really fun.

We've also just booked our Greyhound Bus to Sydney from Byron Bay, so we will arrive in Sydney at Christmas Eve about 12:30pm. After Noosa, we are off to Brisbane for 2 days, then Byron Bay. It doesn't feel like Christmas as the sun is so hot!

Alistair

Noosa

The Noosa River and lakes were flooded by sea during the glacial period 130,000 years ago making Noosa Heads into an island. The mountains in the area were formed by volcanic lava thrust upward that have withstood erosion over millions of years whilst the softer land around washed away and created the Great Sandy Park with its high dunes. The name Noosa came from the Aboriginal word meaning "shade" or "shadows", probably a reference to the respite from the sun offered by the tall forests in the area. The Aboriginal Kabi tribe had been visiting Noosa for 40,000 years before Europeans first arrived in the 1800s. The Kabi tribe lived in the region bordered by Redcliffe near Brisbane in the south, the mouth of the Noosa River to the north and Cooroy & Nambour to the west. Even then, the region was a special retreat enjoyed by the Aborigines for celebrations such as the annual Bunya nut festival held in the nearby Blackall Ranges.

Day 60 - Thursday 16th December 2008

I cannot believe it has been 3 months since I started travelling and I still love every minute. Most of the people we meet are of the highest quality. We had to get up at 08:00 this morning for breakfast and to get into our kayaks. We were all in a 3 man kayak as our group had 9 people. All are really sound and we headed downriver for 3.5km where we dumped our kayak and headed for a 4km walk to a beach, which was empty and we had the sea to ourselves.

Once a spot of swimming and football was done, we headed to a resort where we made the use of the swimming pools. However, we were quickly thrown out of the pool as it was 'private land' so we headed to another pool and the same occurrence happened. This time we were threatened with police action so we hastily fled the scene, through a pack of kangaroo's and back to our kayak. In the process, I dropped my paddle in the water and jumped out to rescue it, getting my feet stuck in the sand in the process, which nearly swallowed my sandal for lunch. Luckily, Mark helped by filming the whole thing and laughing at the ridiculous state I was in. The stingrays lurking beneath the surface did not help.

But, we headed back up the river (tide against us as was this morning) to camp where Mark and I have just enjoyed a nice relaxing game of chess, which I won. I thought he had when my queen went early on, but I used my wit and won through. Mark is trying to pick the bones out of where his game fell apart. We now have to camp in a tent tonight, which we set up before we had our tea.

Day 61 - Wednesday 17th December 2008

Today has been very eventful. We awoke in our tent about 07:30 and had the same breakfast as yesterday – a ham toastie. After picking up our 2 man kayak, we headed up the river to find a campsite where we'd be spending tonight. However, when we arrived at the lake we were supposed to paddle through, the wind changed direction blowing us in circles and not let us paddle to where we wanted. Hilariously, mark and I had a blazing row about techniques in the middle of the lake, much to the amusement of other groups nearby. At one point in our vigorous efforts to get the right way, we nearly capsized , so in order to prevent this, Mark was forced to abandon his paddle so I had to make a leap to grab it, letting go of mine in the process and I had to make a last ditch fling to grab mine. It was a $20 loss of deposit for losing a paddle but, more importantly, we could not get anywhere.

As the weather was too tough and the lake was shallow, we walked our kayaks along the coast, braving the stingrays on Lake Weyba. Lake Weyba can officially be translated as meaning "place of the stingrays". Even though crocodiles are said not to be found here, I still thought the water looked like it could provide sanctuary for these beasts so I was a little wary. We found camp and quenched our thirsts and filled our ravenous appetites with a barbecue where one kind gentleman gave me my first taste of kangaroo.

Tonight, after IPod time, Mark and I went to the local pub with an Irish couple – Niall and Anne-Marie. We managed to blag a carry out from the pub and headed to their tent to play cards. The ranger came over at one point asking us to cool it down as we were being overly noisy – but it was just because we were hammered. Pissed up, I went to bed and passed out.

Day 62 – Thursday 18th December 2008

The morning did not start how I had planned. Niall and Anne-Marie had to wake us up at 06:30 to pack away our tents and ten we had to make the 7km trip back to the bush camp. Well – it went exactly as planned but I did not fancy doing it as I had one too many beers last night so 7km was 7km too far. Anyway, we got to bushcamp and stayed there until 12:00 when we were driven back into Noosa to wait another 3 hours for our Greyhound Bus to Brisbane. During the wait, Mark and I filled our faces on pies and slushees from 7/11. Anyway, we got on our bus at 15:25 and it was uneventful all the way to Brisbane. We did pass by Australia Zoo in Beerwah – home of the late Steve Irwin. From discussions with folk who have visited that place, you do get a sense of his presence there, which is a good thing.

We rolled into Brisbane at 18:00 and checked into Cloud 9 hostel, which is a total dive. We went out to try to watch the Manchester United match in the World Club Championships but we were out of luck. Coincidentally, we bumped into 2 lads I know from Sydney. One of them, Danny, is now living in Brisbane. On first reflections of the place, I like it. It is similar to both Manchester and Glasgow in its layout and the people are all so friendly.

Above: Mark and I in our Moke)

(Above: With Louis from South Africa)

Above: With Mark on Whitehaven Beach)

(Above: Long Island Ice-tea on Long Island)

ve: 4x4 driving for Fraser Island)

(Above: kayaking at Noosa Everglades)

Brisbane

The city of Brisbane is named after Sir Thomas Brisbane, born in Ayrshire in Scotland. The city grew steadily until World War II when it become the main allied headquarters in the South Pacific and an influx of Australian and American servicemen stretched the population to three quarters of a million. Industry flourished and continued to boom post war and Brisbane firmly staked its claim as the third largest city in the country.

The 1982 Commonwealth Games were hosted in Brisbane and the city received a massive infrastructure and sporting facilities boost as a result. In 1988 the world expo was hosted at Southbank (across the river from the CBD), and the event also helped put Brisbane 'on the map' so to speak. Brisbane has always struggled behind Sydney and Melbourne in the cultural stakes, but the city now has a thriving arts scene and is responsible for some of the best live music and bands in the country. However, we didn't get the chance to witness this as it was merely a flying visit.

Day 63 - Friday 19th December 2008

Today, we just spent time knocking about the city. I managed to buy a new set of headphones for my iPod as I was desperate for them. Lunch consisted of fast food and we did not achieve much. It's sad all our activities are done. I have achieved so much over the past 3 months that lounging about here in my hostel seems a waste. But, I am looking forward to being in Melbourne in the New Year and getting work, which is one thing I miss about home really. Walking in Brisbane today, it does not feel like Christmas at all even though I saw the big Christmas tree in the centre. Tonight, we went to the cinema to watch the newest James Bond film, Quantum of Solace.

Day 64 – Saturday 20th December 2008

Again, the day today has been spent walking around Brisbane. It still amazes me how, in a country the size of Australia, one which you can fit the whole continent of Europe in, you can bump into so many people you know. We've met about 6 or 7 so far. Today, unfortunately I have to say, we met Sam and Clare from our hostel in Cairns, who have pretty much followed us from there. They were at Noosa on one night with us but they are insignificant to me so I didn't mention them. But I want to see the back of them. I was never keen on them and, now, my first impressions have not changed. Mark likes them but I just feel that reflects badly on him rather than me as I've said that you are judged by the standard of friends you keep.

Anyway, I had to put up with them as we all went down to the market, where Mark and I had a spot of Chilli tasting. Naturally, we accepted a bet to eat this mega hot chilli. Mark immediately recognised how hot and spicy this was. However, I tried my best to fight it but, inevitably, I lost this battle and ended up with a burned mouth for about 2 hours – and I did complain a little bit. It was a funny sight when the realisation kicked in that this was the hottest thing I've ever tasted. Sheer panic and terror and sweats filled my face.

Tonight, me and Mark went to Coorporoo to my mate Danny's house, which is nice – although it ought to be for $200 a week. We played a few drinking games, which I find boring these days and a load of us went to a few bars in Brisbane. We all split up and I wandered off with a local girl. On our walk back home, I noticed some Australian police brutality on a black guy, which I found pretty shocking. They had him pressed against a wall, while 3 police officers poked and prodded him aggressively. The guy did not seem to be doing anything wrong so I got my camera out and started to make a video. However, the girl I was with took offence to this and stopped me taking the video. We had a slight argument about this issue, as I thought it was wrong what was happening, and she took the hump and fucked off.

Day 65 – Sunday 21st December 2008

Another uneventful day in Brisbane. I can't figure out if I like it or not. I awoke really early and headed into the city to refresh my thirst and to use the internet, while Mark slept. A few hours later, we met in Tribal Travel, where Mark's memory card for his camera was corrupted and he's lost most of his photos. I'm gutted for him but, remarkably, he's taking it on the chin even though I know he's pissed. If this was me, I'd be absolutely raging and, once again, Mark shows he's a cut above when it comes to handling negative situations.

This afternoon, we headed back for IPod time and awoke in time to get our free barbecue at the hostel, which consisted of one roll and one sausage. It wasn't worth staying up for so we went back to bed and awoke at 20:30. We headed to the Pig and Whistle in the centre of Brisbane to watch the World Club Championship between LDU Quito and Manchester United. We arrived there at 21:00 with only 5 minutes gone and ended up chatting with a group of Manchester United fans. It felt great to watch the match and we won 1-0. Afterwards, we headed to Hungry Jacks and then went to bed. Some guy in our hostel had been sick downstairs and, apparently, pissed in a bin. I hate these fools who can't take their drink. But there was a lot of commotion.

Day 66 - Monday 22nd December 2008

That guy must have been fucked last night because we awoke this morning to find police outside his room. Anyway, that was bad enough, plus the 06:00am wake up, then we had to get the Greyhound Bus for 4 hours to Byron Bay. Upon arriving at Byron Bay, I find that it is completely overrated. I am not enjoying it at all and I can take comfort in the fact that we will only be spending one night here. What is awkward is that Mark loves it. I've come to the realisation that we do, essentially, have different interests. I need to learn things and help people when I travel – sort of like Leo Tolstoy did on his journey in the end. Mark just wants to see things and give nothing back to the places he goes to.

We went for 2 hours to the beach, which was shit if I must say so. After, we walked to the most easterly point of the Australian Mainland, which I thought was cool but Mark had done it before so it ruined it for me. That was it – officially the furthest point I've ever been away from Manchester and it kicked in.

Tonight, we went over the road to Cheeky Monkey's, which Mark had gone on and on about. It is the most overrated bar ever. Full of pissed up fools, dancing on tables, who have no concept of reality. It is these folk who give travellers a bad name and I have no desire to be associated with them. Mark loved it – I hated it. I could not stand one more second so I left at 23:50 but Mark wanted to go back. I told him to but I'd rather not bother.

I do not know what is going on. Tonight, I also managed to break the last zip on my rucksack, snap the lace on my shorts and, honestly, I do miss home and I've never felt this way. Sometimes you need to be around people who know you and think like you. Today, more than ever, I have never been so far away from home and that is a fact. It is also the time of year you need people around you most. I don't have it and I think I need it. But I'll carry on regardless even though I do not learn a thing from them.

Day 67 – Tuesday 23rd Decembers 2008

We just sat around Byron Bay today, killing time and I cannot wait to leave if I'm honest. I'm not into Byron Bay and my opinion has not changed today from yesterday. But, all we look forward to is a 14 hour bus trip from Byron Bay to Sydney. We went to watch the Everton v Chelsea repeat from yesterday, which was 0-0. After a spot of chess, which again I won, which takes the total to 6-1 to me, we had to go back to Cheeky Monkey's for tea. I ate fish and chips and then we got the Greyhound Bus. Some bastard had stolen all my food out of the fridge at the hostel and that just sent me into a rage that nearly tipped me over the edge. Mark had gone back into Cheeky Monkeys as we forgot our rucksacks with passports and other essential documents. All I thought about was my stolen food and I snatched the bag angrily off Mark and stormed off to get the bus. Mark had a firm chat with me and it made me see the error of my ways. An apology was needed and I offered my sincere apologies to Mark for being out of order. That was it – water under the bridge. All I wanted to do was get on the Greyhound Bus and leave Byron Bay. 14 hours to Sydney.

Chapter 6 - Fits and Festivals

Day 68 – Wednesday 24th December 2008 – Christmas Eve

Christmas Eve did not start in the usual manner if I'm honest but nothing does these days. I awoke about 04:00am on the bus with a deaf Canadian girl using my shoulder as a pillow, although this was sanctioned by me. She had me over a barrel. Last night, we all got on the bus and Mark and I planned to do a good sleep with our pillows but all we needed was a window seat. We both got aisle seats. During a coffee break at a petrol station, Mark said he's going back onto the bus to steal the window seat from the guy he was sat next to. I thought 'you can't do that' but he did and I was stuck on the aisle. About 20 minutes into the journey following the stop, the Canadian girl asked me if I wanted to have the window so I could use my pillow. How generous I thought. So, I accepted and began to nestle in to slumberland. However, she then asked, 'can I lean on you?' What could I say after she'd just given up her seat? So I had this thing on my shoulder for the rest of the trip to Sydney.

We rolled into Sydney about 09:30 not feeling too tired, being dropped off at the station next to the YHA. We headed to get some food at McDonald's even though we didn't want it and, after it being so shit, we vowed never to set foot back in the place. After we stuffed our faces we headed to Mark's Aunties to drop our bags off and get a much needed shower after the adventures of the past month. It was one of the best showers I've ever had. We then headed back to the city, suitably refreshed, where we bumped into an old mate, Dave Smith, who we went to school with. Naturally, it was whilst buying a few beers in a bottle shop.

Christmas Eve in Sydney was a total nightmare as it is full of people doing last minute shopping, for things they do not really need. I thought a lot about the Namibian Bush where I lived in October and the complete contrast to where I am now. Money is not all that important. I'd actually prefer to be at home on Christmas Eve with my friends. I'm so tired now. Mark and I just watched Catch Me If You Can and I passed out, alone on Christmas Eve.

Day 69 -Thursday 25th December 2008 – Christmas Day

I awoke this morning at 10:30 to see Mark's Auntie Gina walking down the stairs to see me lying there. I said 'Merry Christmas' and she replied bluntly 'Where's Mark?' I immediately felt unwelcome on Christmas Day. However, that feeling soon subsided once I went upstairs and met Mark's other family members who were all great, especially his Auntie Judy and Uncle Paul whose house we are staying in. It turns out that his Auntie Gina and Uncle Billy are not a full shilling so I let them off. I think I ruined everything they dreamed of as they informed me that their dream is to visit Mark's Mum Cheryl in Bury. They asked me how much a flight would be and, when I gave them a figure, it seemed like something they could never afford. They looked gutted. Anyway, when the presents were handed out, I was given a box of chocolates, which was nice. It's always nice to have something to open on Christmas Day.

The next thing involved sitting down at 13:00 for Christmas Lunch. Paul cooked 2 joints beautifully on the barbecue, which was a different way than I am used to. Judy made the best Cauliflower Cheese I have ever had and, if I say, it was the highlight of the meal it was that good. The rest of the day we sat around drinking and enjoying ourselves. Even though I am on the other side of the world, it felt nice to spend Christmas with a family.

But, speaking of family, I received a phone call tonight from Mum and Dad who are spending Christmas with Auntie Janet, Clare and Gran in Kilmarnock. I do wish I was there for one day. I never really appreciated family when I was at home but, now I am away, I'd give anything to see them for one day.

Day 70 - Friday 26th December 2008

We managed to have a good lie in this morning, sleeping off the exploits of yesterday. It feels great to be in the comfort of a house after travelling down the coast for the last month. Even though we are on mattresses on the floor with our sleeping bags, it is great to have a nice place to stay.

We ventured into the city today and it was packed full of capitalist shoppers trying to acquire more than they actually need. We did not achieve anything and, about 16:30, we came back to Mark's Auntie's house for rest.

Tonight, we came back to the city to the Shark hotel to watch Stoke v Man United. We won 1-0 and it felt great to sit in a bar, watch a full game of football and sink a few cold beers.

Day 71 – Saturday 27th December 2008

The evening tonight was spent at Scruffy Murphy's Irish Pub watching the Celtic v Rangers game at Ibrox. It was absolutely packed, as I knew it would be (mostly with Celtic fans). It was pretty good and Celtic won 1-0. However, what disgusts me is the sectarian singing that still occurs. The Celtic fans singing for the IRA are a disgrace and, personally, I feel there is no need for it in football. The Rangers fans are just as bad, as I found out in Manchester in May for the UEFA Cup Final.

The day, apart from that, has been spent shopping and I managed to pick up a pair of jeans and a smart Ted Baker Polo Shirt from David Jones. It was bought with the money Mum and Dad gave me for Christmas.

Day 72 – Sunday 28th December 2008

Today we visited Chatswood to attend a shopping centre because Mark said he needed some t-shirts with the money he received from the refunded gift his Auntie bought him because, for some reason unbeknown to me, they were not good enough – even though she paid $140 for them. Naturally, he wanted to keep the money or not get his hand in his pocket to buy anything so I was the only one who spent anything on a pink Ralph Lauren polo shirt and another pale blue Politik shirt for Hogmanay. Lunch was spent at Subway.

Tonight, we went to The Shark Hotel in Sydney for a cheap Sunday lunch. Mine was a little tough but still edible all the same. I'd recommend it as a place to go for the discerning traveller – cheap food, cheap beer and free pool. The Asian community have cottoned on to this and you will find hundreds of Japanese all making the most of what is on offer. We watched a few games of football on the big screen and I'm gutted that the Scousers beat Newcastle 5-1. However, we've got back to Mark's Aunties and saw Chelsea draw 2-2 at Fulham. I'm always on edge here though because I have to be quiet all the time, which I understand but I already know that without Mark telling me every time I want to draw breath. I mean, for fuck sake, calm down and relax a little.

Day 73 – Monday 29th December 2008

I managed to change my Qantas flights today to fly to Santiago, Chile on June 27th 2009 instead of February 17th 2009. It is something that needed doing so I am happy about that. We also managed to go for a haircut today, which was really needed. Mine was not too bad but Mark's hair had got ridiculously long and, I reckon he should have left it until he found a job. We both had a laugh about how long it had gone.

Tonight, we headed to the Crow's Nest for a $10 curry meal and spent the rest of the night chilling out and watching shit movies and, while Mark is still trying to sort out his lost photos, I watched a programme on the history of the mafia but Mark, remarkably calm, has yet to lose his temper about the loss of his photo's and, with it, unbelievable memories. He is an amazing fellow – I would've flown off the handle as soon as it happened.

Day 74 – Tuesday 30th December 2008

Well – nearly another year over. Have I achieved much? Probably more than last year but not as much as I would have wanted. It's funny how philosophical you get around this time of year. I mean, in my heart I am still in the same place, even though I am on the other side of the world. I am still that lost guy who wandered around Manchester, although now I'm doing it in Sydney. I don't know if this will change or I can't put an answer to it anyway. I say this, because I find this everywhere I go. I texted 7 people tonight to see what they are doing tomorrow. Guess how many responses I got (bearing in mind one is my cousin who is over in Sydney). Guess? 0. None. Nothing out of 7 people – including my cousin. Mark manages to get a few replies. It was the same at home, in Glasgow, in London and it is the same here. No-one seems to really give a shit and, if I'm brutally honest, they never have and maybe never will. So, Happy New Year when it comes. It may be the same as all the rest (for me and everyone else) – pointless.

<u>Day 75</u> – Wednesday 31st December 2008

What a day it has been today. It needed to be good to get me out of my depressive mood I was in yesterday although that is a clear sign of a Gemini – one day elated the next day down. It has probably been the best New Years Eve I have had.

We awoke this morning at 10:00 and headed into town to get a good vantage point for the New Years Eve Fireworks from the Harbour Bridge and Sydney Opera House. Unfortunately, we were joined by Sam and Clare from the hostel in Cairns who, although I can put up with them, I'd rather not. You should not have to at New Year. Plus, there are people we met down the coast I'd much rather have spent time with. Even Rachel and Nikki the Troll we met on Magnetic Island would have been preferable – although me and Rachel did have an ulterior motive for meeting up, unbeknown to Mark.

Anyway, we got in the Botanical Gardens at 14:30 and spent the next 10 hours sitting around and meeting people. We met a group of sisters from Dublin who were all Doctors and then our group just got bigger and bigger until we seemed to take over a big area. At 21:00 the first firework display went off to whet our appetites for the main show. The big one at 00:00 was by far the best way to bring in the New Year and, for me, it was an unbelievable experience. After we did that, we all piled out in Sydney Central and I decided it would be a great idea to call home to speak with Mum and Dad. Mum said she loved me, which was the first time I'd heard it. Maybe I heard it before, but I did not appreciate it as much. I also phoned my best mate Wes, who was with Andy Bollesty at the time. My two 'supposedly' best mates together. I missed it. I say supposedly because I've lost a lot of respect over the years for Andy, mainly due to the company he keeps these days. Deep down, I knew what I was doing tonight was the best way to spend New Year's Eve. That is all that matters.

<u>Day 76</u> – Thursday 01st January 2009

Happy New Year. Or so you would think. It has happened again. We were sat in our room at Mark's Auntie's house at 17:30 and I had another seizure. It is my first one since May 2007 (18 months). The funny thing this time is that I knew it was going to happen (or might happen) as I moved a glass and a few other objects out of the way. 10 minutes later, I went. I kind of remember being in the ambulance, but it was the same as last time. I severely bit my tongue, which is now a mess full of ulcers and it is so painful. I am embarrassed because I am unsure whether or not I lost control of my bodily functions although it could have been coke as I was drinking at the time. Mark later told me this didn't happen. Anyway, I owe a lot to Mark who dealt with things by ringing the ambulance and preventing me from choking. We had to wait in the hospital for 5 hours while I had a load of tests, but everything came back OK. The Doctors, Nurses and Paramedics were all really nice and sorted everything out.

The standard of medical care in Australia is pretty much as you'd expect from any developed nation. Lucky as I am, I cannot complain at all and the reciprocal agreement between the UK and Australia concerning healthcare saved me any trouble. I just wish all were as fortunate. All I was wearing when it happened were a pair of cargo shorts so, when I left the hospital, I had to return to the house in just the shorts – no shoes, socks, t-shirt. I don't know how to break the news to my Mum – she will be really worried. But, now, I've got to register with a GP in Melbourne, which is something else to add to the list.

After I was discharged from A&E, I needed food so we got the taxi driver to stop at a kebab shop where I treated me and Mark to a kebab (I paid, he had to go in to order). My tongue is so sore right now because I nearly bit it off when my jaws contracted. I have to go to bed now. I am so tired. What a way to bring in 2009.

<u>Day 77</u> – Friday 02nd January 2008

I've been feeling much better today. I went to bed early last night, which is a good thing. I didn't wake up today until about 11:30 but it was still earlier than Mark who was up until 03:30am downloading a software package on his laptop to rectify his lost photo's. We decided to head out around 13:50 but we had to stop to discuss things with his Auntie who, naturally, was worried. I had to explain what had happened and discuss my history of seizures. Anyway, we got into Sydney via the 14:33 bus and I had to get my prescription for phenytoin from the pharmacy. It cost me $41. Then we went to get me a Medicare card but I couldn't get it today as I did not have a copy of my visa with me.

Tonight, I had to face the task of calling Mum to let her know what had happened and, understandably, she was upset. Then I reassured her everything was OK. Later, I got the call from Dad checking up on me. What did touch me was when Wes texted me to see if I was OK. That's one thing I'd say for Wes. I mean, he may not say much but, when the chips are down, he does come through and show he is the best god damn friends in the world. That is all that matters, to me anyway. It means a lot. Plus Marks actions yesterday meant a lot.

<u>Day 78</u> – Saturday 03rd January 2008

I met up with my cousin, Karen, in Sydney tonight, which brought back memories of home. She said everyone was missing me and tried to make me understand the situation with Stewart. Maybe I have mellowed a bit and have forgiven him but, like I said, I am now based on the other side of the world. Karen was with her boyfriend Steve. Mark and I took them to Scruffy Murphy's and Steve did not seem to be enjoying it so we left. We got a kebab and a chauffeur driven Mercedes pulled up to give us a lift home, which is not the usual backpacker lift home. I am off the beer at the moment, even though I did share a drink with Karen as we are both 2 cousins in Sydney.

Day 79 – Sunday 04th January 2009

Today has been a non-event to be fair, watching a lot of shit television in our room at Mark's Auntie's. We managed to watch a lot of Top gear and, although I love the show, I am against Jeremy Clarkson's view on Left Wing Politics. He is too much of a conservative, Thatcherite bastard and, for me, anyone who is of a Thatcherite persuasion, are middle class, Daily Mail reading tossers and, to generalize, I have no time for. But that is by the by and Top Gear is good entertainment.

This afternoon we ventured into the city for a Sunday lunch. I felt my meat, as last week, was a bit tough but Mark had a decent cut. Mark enjoyed a beer with his meal, whereas I stuck to the soft drinks. I may leave the beer for good.

Mark is now asleep but I am staying up, streaming thee football on his computer. He is flat out but I plan on staying up for Gillingham v Aston Villa then Southampton v Man United in the FA Cup and that is followed by the PDC Darts Final – Taylor v Barney.

Day 80 – Monday 05th January 2009

Today is my last day in Sydney for a while as, tomorrow, Mark and I depart for Canberra for a day before heading down to Melbourne where we will search for work – sooner rather than later I hope. We went our separate ways as Mark had to go to Chatswood to sort out a recurring eye problem that is causing him a bit of stick since we've been travelling. I had to go into the city to go to Westpac Branch at 275 George Street to see if my bank card was in yet, but it was not, so I'll have to get them to send it down to me in Melbourne. Then, I went to get my medicare card sorted out but it was so busy near the town hall branch I decided to leave it and go for a coffee.

Tonight, we joined Mark's Uncle Paul and Auntie Judy for a delicious barbecue, where I stuffed my face on meat. His Auntie Judy wanted to give us a good feed before we left and I took delight in taking her up on the offer. Everyone else, apart from me, was on wine, beer, bourbon etc but I stuck to soft drinks. It is looking promising that I am off alcohol for good. I think that could be a contributing factor to me having my seizures. It is a shame but seizures are something I may have to live with and I may have to live without alcohol. Such is life. No time for feeling sorry for yourself when you realise how much worse other people have it.

Canberra

Canberra is Australia's Capital City and is actually Australia's largest inland city. It's location as capital is strategic in between rivals Sydney and Melbourne, so Canberra was developed as a compromise. It is recognised by a few as a Ghost Town but it is pleasant all the same and, as you may be able to tell, I do not have that much to say about the place.

Day 81 – Tuesday 06th January 2009

We arrived in Canberra today from Sydney at around 15:30 on the Greyhound Bus. Originally, we left Mark's Auntie's about 10:30, to nice goodbye's and his Auntie Judy says I am always welcome back at any time, which was nice of her to say so. She also told me to take care of my health, which I will do when I continue my travels. As long as I have a guy like Mark in event of another seizure, I'll be fine.

Canberra is totally not like the capital I imagined it would be. On first reflections, I notice that it is unbelievably hot and dry. But, I normally expect a capital city to be buzzing with people and activity, like you see in London. However, Canberra is pretty lifeless and very quiet – but I like this. I did not take to the huge skyscrapers of Sydney. A lot of folk say that this is a ghost town but I think I could spend a bit of time working here.

Tonight, all we did was to go and watch a film at the cinema called Slumdog Millionaire, which we did not know anything about before going in (not even the full title as we thought it was called Slumdog Mill, then it said Slumdog Milliona on our ticket) but it was an amazing film. It was directed by Danny Boyle and was slightly Bollywood-esque. I'd definitely recommend it. I am now desperate for some sleep above a pub we checked into, which is filthy but still it's a roof and a bed so who's complaining?

Day 82 – Wednesday 07th January 2009

Canberra is proving to be one of the hottest cities I have ever been to but I do like it. I think I would like to work here in the Public Sector as I feel a lot of government workers are based here. I like the people here and everyone seems really friendly. I also like how laid back it is for a capital city – none of the hustle and bustle that encapsulates you in London.

Today, we visited the war memorial in Canberra, which took my breath away. Firstly, I never realised Australian soldiers participated in so many of the wars. But, it also made me realise what a terrible thing war is and, also, what a needless thing it is. It pisses me off. In Western countries we treat warmongerers as heroes but they clearly are not. Anyone who illegally invades another country taking innocent lives is, in all intents and purposes, a murderer. I'm sick of all the bullshit sentimentality that goes on for fallen soldiers in the two modern wars – Iraq and Afghanistan. Defending Britain? No: Britain did not need defending thank you very much and what you are doing is illegal. Pure and simple. Iraq has been proven as an illegal war with absolutely no justification and Afghanistan was the Yankees war for 9/11. Let them fight it themselves. But we sided with them and in

November 2001, we go into Afghanistan. 7/7 occurs by British youths, disaffected with our countries actions in the Middle East. They were trained in Pakistan. Are we invading Pakistan? No. It might seem like these statements are unfair but I just dedicate my thinking to the innocent children and families who went to bed one night, happy and safe, until a misplaced bomb from a B-52 bomber falls through the roof of their house in Kabul or Baghdad. Then the guy who dropped the bomb returns home to a hero's welcome (dead or alive – to me it doesn't matter). Bullshit folks. It's bullshit.

I can't stand nonsense sometimes. We are now just killing a bit of time until we get our bus to Melbourne at 23:55 which will take about 10 hours. I have such a thirst on me, which I've been trying to kill all day as the heat is so intense. We are now stuck for somewhere to stay in Melbourne until Saturday but I may get in touch with Meredith to see if she can put us up. Maybe that is being a little cheeky but the way I have been taught is if you do not ask then you do not get. I doubt Meredith will want to put up with 2 travelling slobs for long. I say 2 travelling slobs when, in reality, I only mean 1. That is me – I do not mind admitting it. As we have travelled down the coast, I was always the untidy one whose belongings lay strewn across each hostel we visited. Mark's belongings were always neatly packed away in his case and locked safely away. We were, in essence, like chalk and cheese but it worked out well. You could usually tell where I was sleeping compared to where Mark was sleeping. I would put this down to me not really placing too much emphasis on material belongings and having a trust in my fellow travellers not to steal my things. So far, it has worked out excellently. Maybe I will change once I find a place to live in Melbourne. Melbourne – that city they call the sporting capital of the world. I can't wait to see it.

Chapter 7 – Melbourne: The Sports City

Melbourne

Melbourne is the capital of Victoria, and home to close to 4 million people. Many of the citizens of Melbourne live in the suburbs that are situated east and south of the Yarra River, sprawled around Port Phillip Bay and extending as far east as Mount Dandenong.

Melbourne was founded on the Yarra River in 1835 after an abortive bid in 1803 to establish a settlement inside the Port Phillip Bay heads. The Port Phillip District gained independence from New South Wales in 1850. Melbourne boomed in the 1850's as a result of the gold rush in the region to the north. Melbourne has a reputation as being more refined than its northerly neighbour Sydney, boasting the country's finest restaurants and is acknowledged as the country's most important financial centre. The International Exhibition of 1880 put Melbourne on the world map as a major city. Its Exhibition Buildings stand monument to an era that earned it the title of Marvellous Melbourne. The city developed into a major trade centre with wool, wheat and other agricultural products adding to its wealth. Though most Victorians will grudgingly admit the mantle has shifted to Sydney, Melbourne was the financial capital of Australia until about the 1970s and the headquarters of many of the country's largest companies.

Today Melbourne is home to about 3.2 million people. For reasons now forgotten, it had a major attraction for Greeks and Italians as far back as the turn of the 20th Century, luckily for me as I met one of my best mates, Constantine, there. In people terms, it is the third largest Greek city in the world and the largest Italian city outside Italy. In common with Sydney, it has a large Chinese community dating from the 1850s gold rush. Melbourne has long been a bastion of the Jewish community in Australia. Though the mix is somewhat different to Sydney, authorities say the city's residents come from 110 to 140 different ethnic backgrounds and I was proud to represent Scotland.

Day 83 – Thursday 08th January 2009

We arrived into Melbourne at 08:00 after the overnight Greyhound Bus journey. We were slightly tired but I think I managed to get more sleep on the bus as, firstly, I had a window seat and, secondly, I managed to liberate a pillow from the hostel in Canberra. Liberate/steal – call it what you will. I did some great sleeping!

So, we are here slightly tired. The first job was to find internet access so we could find somewhere to stay as, at present, we are homeless tramps. We headed to the state library and signed up for a library card and the library is one of the most impressive I have seen. We also looked for work etc. So, we found somewhere, which is a bit of a dump called Melbourne International Backpackers. We are only here until Saturday, however, when we move to the slightly plusher, Urban Central. I also managed to get my Medicare card sorted out so I will need to register with a doctor tomorrow to get this seizure thing sorted out. I've also just managed to sort out my flights within South America in February so they have been changed to coincide with my plans.

Tomorrow is a day when I can look for work in more detail. I need to get it sorted ASAP and begin to work so things with my finances do not get too far out of control.

E-Mail:

Hey,

It's been a while since I e-mailed everyone so I thought I better start off this year with an update. Today, I arrived in Melbourne after an overnight Greyhound journey from Canberra. I have just registered at the state library where I am looking for accommodation until Saturday as, after that, I have somewhere to stay. Canberra was a little unusual for a capital city. It is so quiet and virtually empty. It is a purpose built capital but, contrary to reports before I got there, I enjoyed my time there and I could see myself working there. It is more for the governmental workers I think.

Anyway, Melbourne is where I hope to find work. As some of you know, I also need to sign up to see a GP following my second seizure on New Year's Day, which led me to be rushed into hospital. It was a bit of a scare for all those around me but everything is OK. It is something I could do without if I'm being honest as I've got to have some follow up appointments and I've also been put on a course of tablets, which means I am now off alcohol. But I see this as a positive for now as i'll be able to save money. Anyway, the last few months of 2008 were by far the best months of my life so far. I did the most amazing things but I'd have to say that walking with lions in Namibia tops anything I've ever done or will do and having a sleep out with a Cheetah is close too. I'm definitely going back to Africa one day. The Whitsunday Islands off Australia's East Coast are also just about the most beautiful place I've ever visited (followed closely by Cape Tribulation in North East Australia). The only problem I now have is how to beat what I've already done, but at least i'll give it a good try. I'm really looking forward to South America this year, especially visiting Machu Picchu in Peru providing I get a job and my money lasts!!

Day 84 – Friday 09th January 2009

I've been applying for jobs today so hopefully something will come of that. All it is is just sending my CV off to prospective employers to see what they will make of it. The only problem now is that I have just looked for my USB stick with all my information on it and I cannot find it anywhere. I will be really, really gutted if somehow I have managed to lose it. I need this USB stick so much.

I also went to visit the doctor today at 16:00 (who charged me $68) and he has referred me on to a Neurologist at St. Vincent's Hospital in Melbourne. That means more and more tests to see if I have epilepsy. I don't want it.

Tonight, Mark and I (more is the pity) are off to meet Sam and Clare. I'll be glad to see the back of those fools! I am sick of seeing the pair of them. The day they go home will not be a day too soon.

Day 85 – Saturday 10th January 2010

We've moved across town today to our new hostel called Urban Central on 334 City Road, Southbank, Melbourne. It is a lot nicer than the other one we were in, particularly because it is clean. Most of the day today has been spent in the library looking for a flat. I received a nice e-mail from my Auntie Leslie, which perked my spirits up a bit. I am still annoyed about what I saw at the Crown Casino last night in the poker room. A young lad (about 20) was lent with his chin on a pillow, playing poker and he had a masseuse massaging his neck and shoulders while he played. It was awful and the reason I do not like casino's. Too much money wasted when something else could be done with it – something better.

Saying that though, we still had a bet on a high card game tonight and managed to win $40, which was pretty nice. We also watched Aston Villa beat West Brom 2-1 in the midlands derby. It is nice to watch the football. I am really looking forward to Manchester United v Chelsea tomorrow. Come on the reds. Football is going to be the reason from here until South America.

Day 86 – Sunday 11th January 2009

Considering we got up at 12:30 today after missing our free breakfast, then having the shittest noodles ever and, if that was not enough, losing around $40 each at the casino, today has been quite productive. This afternoon, we headed to the library to look for a flat on the internet and we saw one advertised for Clarendon Towers, which is right next door to Urban Central and right across the road from the Crown Casino. So, Mark called the guy up (a Chinese guy called Hu) and 30 minutes later we were meeting him having a viewing and we agreed to move in on Wednesday. It is a really smart apartment, with a gym and a swimming pool downstairs. I am really happy. It is only $140 a week but now I really need to get a job.

But, now, we have got time to kill until Wednesday when we can move into our flat. The sooner the better in my opinion because I am a little fed up with the hostel thing now. Don't get me wrong, I've loved every minute (well nearly every minute) but I am just sick of the small talk that goes on sometimes. Same conversation after same fucking conversation – stupid one's at that. I am not learning a thing, which pisses me off too. That's why I'm reading The Dalai Lama: The Art of Happiness, Don Quixote and John Pilger: Freedom, Next Time. Just to learn more about what goes on. Mark enjoys the small talk with the others in our room – I can't be arsed sometimes and I miss the chats with my friends, although to be honest the chat with them could be irrelevant to important issues. Anyway, it is now 22:10 and I am off to get a bit of sleep before Manchester United v Chelsea – 03:00 am here.

Day 87 – Monday 12th January 2009

I got up at 02:00am this morning to go to the casino to watch the United v Chelsea game (Mark did not want to go as he was too tired). It was a game worth getting up for too as we ran out easy 3-0 winners. It was full of Irish. I also spoke to Wes just before the game, which was nice and he seems to be doing OK although I expected nothing more from him. Then, after the football I came back to the hostel to have a few hours' kip.

So, I got up at 10:00 and the job search started. Mark initially seemed to have more luck as he has a meeting arranged at Hayes. However, it turned out to be just registration. I received a phone call from Hallis asking me to go down tomorrow. It is a shit job advising people on share options but it pays $20p/h and it has the chance of overtime so hopefully something will turn up.

Tonight, we headed down to the trivia night in our hostel bar. I was looking forward to it until we got there and all I could do was get pissed. Yes – I've started drinking again (what did you expect. Really?). I do hope a job comes to fruition in the next few weeks. If it does not I will be totally fucked. At the quiz, I met a girl from Burnley called Sophie who did CPE Law the same as me, which was a coincidence and we really hit it off. If she stays in Melbourne, we are going to go for a drink. Our team did not do too well in the quiz but, my team name 'Stephen Hawkings Football Boots' was cheated out of best name by the quizmaster. There was nearly a mutiny when '9pm Sharp' won it and ours was announced in second place. Everyone agreed we should have won it. Stephen Hawking himself would even see the funny side of it.

Day 88 – Tuesday 13th January 2009

Today has been quite a success, even though I still have not been offered a job. I got up at 08:15 and headed for breakfast to set me up for the meeting at Hallis. It basically consisted of filling out a load of details regarding my visa and I had to do a role play. Very embarrassing but it had to be done.

After that, I went to meet Mark and I managed to collect my Westpac Card, which I've needed to do since my first day in Australia. I've also received an e-mail with my tax number, which I also needed to do within my first week of arriving in the country. 2 months late isn't too bad.

Tonight, we met Meredith and went to watch a film at Central Cinema called Yes Man. Mark and Meredith loved it. I, on the other hand did not, and I think I may have caused an atmosphere – it just was not funny. Typical Jim Carrey nonsense and I need more from a film. It was a poor effort. Well, I just need more than stupid faces and silly jokes to amuse me. Afterwards, we all had a nice coffee to finish the night.

Day 89 – Wednesday 14th January 2009

We got up this morning at 08:00, had our breakfasts and then proceeded to move into our flat on 80 Clarendon Street, which is really nice although I think we are living with 6 guys from India – I am not too sure as tonight there are a lot of them. It does smell like an Indian Takeaway though, but good for some reason. I'm sure that could get on my nerves though. Mark and I cheffed up lamb chops, carrots, potatoes and peas. Mark was asking if us eating lamb chops offended the Indians and said we would stop if they did. Luckily, they said they did not mind but that is not the point. Mark should not be volunteering me to stop doing something. Now I respect all faiths and cultures, but this is my flat too. The lads seem sound though.

Before dinner, we headed down to use the gym and the swimming pool, which feels really great. It is so nice to be able to get healthy again and, today, it has been one of the healthiest for a while. I am going to sleep now at 00:20 as I have to get up to watch the United v Wigan game at 07:00. Mark does not want to come.

Day 90 – Thursday 15th January 2009

We still have not heard anything on the job front but I continue to send off applications. It annoys me so much because I think that, probably, I am more qualified than the people turning me down and I pray that something turns up. The capitalist system is unfair (we all know that). But Mark and I managed to achieve a bit, which proved more important for me than Mark. We got a Library card from the city library, which means I can rent books. I say it is more important for me than Mark because, essentially, I read and he doesn't. "Rest, nature, books and music" are Leo Tolstoy's idea of happiness. Sounds perfect to me. I decided to rent a book by Chomsky; Necessary Illusions, which is the only one of his I have not yet read, so I indulged myself in that for the day.

I am also happy to report that today has been a healthy day and we are getting our diet and fitness regime on track. Breakfast consisted of cereal with banana and, for tea, we feasted on pasta. Following tea, we had an hour or so in the gym and a half hour in the swimming pool, being joined by two flatmates of ours from India. They seem to have this idea that UK is a great place and, for want of other words, paradise. I did not have the heart to tell them otherwise. They detailed us with stories of how, in India, a person does not have the same opportunities that we have in the UK. It makes me feel so lucky in a way. I take things for granted so much and maybe it is something I have always done. I am now, each day, trying to change my mind and attitude to class myself as lucky. I don't want to fall into the trap that so many people in my country have done by complaining bitterly about things that, honestly, do not really matter. All you can do is to listen and learn from people who have seen and experienced adversity and look at how they find positive ways out of their situation.

Day 91 – Friday 16th January 2009

It's Friday night and all I (or we) have done is to go to the gym and have a swim for 2 hours. Hu (our landlord) turned up at 00:30 to collect the rent, with his wife and children, which I felt inappropriate as I was lying around half naked (top half not bottom). Luckily, I was in as Mark had gone out to make a call from a public payphone (although that is what he said). Hu was pissed off and thought it Mark's fault for not being here, even though he turns up on a Friday night when, in reality, Mark and I should be out frequenting the various bars Melbourne has on offer.

Anyway, this morning I got up and went to the gym for an hour, having a swim also. After that, we headed into the city as we needed some speakers for our room, which we managed to get for $65 from the Reject Shop. I enjoy walking around the cosmopolitan city of Melbourne, meeting an array of different folk along the grid shaped streets.

I happened to read upon a chapter in the Dalai Lama: Art of Happiness book today. It says that people are usually unhappy and angry as a result of bottling things up from the past. That is what has happened to me – I am sure. Mark says I am irritable, which I think is his euphemism for me being an angry bastard. He also said that, due to my education, I think I am better than some people, which I thought was hugely unfair. I see it as I expect more as a result of it. Maybe Mark feels inferior as result of his lack of education but, if I felt I was better than anyone, I wouldn't have done a trip clearly designed to be of benefit to others. That remark pissed me off but, to be honest, that conversation is assigned to history.

Day 92 – Saturday 17th January 2009

We went to the casino tonight to watch the Lancashire Derby of Preston v Burnley. I won a bet as I predicted a 2-1 win to Preston. I am glad Preston won as I class it as my second (English) city having lived there at University and kind of wish I was at home watching it. I've never taken to Burnley. Then we watched Chelsea v Stoke and Chelsea managed to scrape a 2-1 win with the last kick of the game. Unfortunately, like the bad pennies they are, we were joined in the second half by Sam and Clare – those annoying fools from Brighton who followed us down the coast from Cairns. I do not like them, but thanks to the Dalai Lama's teachings, I am managing to be more patient but they do irritate me so much. The day, apart from that, has been a non-event. I like the fact that we can go to the gym and for a swim when we want and I already feel a lot healthier. A healthy body leads to a healthy mind.

Day 93 – Sunday 18th January 2009

We went to the Victoria market in Melbourne today, which I enjoyed as it gave me a chance to purchase some fine foods while haggling with the various market traders for a good price. I love markets basically for the array of people you seem to find there. They are down to earth, ordinary folk who are just trying to earn a bit of money to get by. That is why I do not mind spending my money there – it is full of interesting characters. I can't wait to get amongst the markets in South America. The Victoria Market is located to the North of Elizabeth Street and is the essential place to go for cheeses and meats. I could spend a whole chunk of my money here yet Mark is content on buying cheap tins of soup, which, when we got home, we found had expired in 2005.

Apart from that, the day has fizzled out into mediocrity and the gym was paid another visit. We did manage to cook a nice pasta dish for tea, which we concurred was one of the best since we've been in Australia. We also placed a few coupon bets, so when we wake up tomorrow, we could have won a bit of money. Let's hope as I am running low!!

Day 94 – Monday 19th January 2009

Still nothing. No work has come in. No phone calls. Not a thing. Mark got up early today to go to the beach with one of his friends he seems to know here in Melbourne. That's nice. At least he has friends here. I don't. I don't know anyone but I just find it easy because Mark is here. I need to be getting to know Melbourne but I can't at the moment as I am constantly looking over my shoulder, worrying about the financial situation. But it is not just that – I actually miss work. Having a reason to get up in the morning. The not looking forward to getting up for work, now, seems so appealing. I just need something to occupy my days. For the first time I am wondering, maybe, if it was better if Mark was not here then I would be forced out to meeting people. Each time a suggestion is made on going out to a few bars, Mark never seems up for it. It might be time to go our separate ways.

Day 95 – Tuesday 20th January 2009

The highlight of the day today has been going over the road to watch a movie at the Crown Casino Complex. We watched The Curious Case of Benjamin Button. It was quite a melancholy film, but I really seemed to enjoy it. A lot better than that waste of time 'Yes Man' last week.

Again, no news of any jobs. All we could do was sit around and watch the tennis on TV. There is a constant fight for the TV as all the Indian guys want to do is to watch Bollywood DVD's – all day long that is what they seem to do but I need to learn to accept their culture.

Tea consisted of a dodgy chicken schnitzel, tinned spaghetti and hash browns. A real unhealthy effort. Now, where we come from, it is called tea. That is that. Nothing can stop me from calling it tea as, I've done that for 24 years and I am not going to stop. However, Mark has started to call it dinner – seemingly forgetting where he has come from.

Day 96 – Wednesday 21st January 2009

We went to Ticketek today and bought a ground pass ticket for tomorrow at the Australian Open Tennis Tournament. I am looking forward to it. Mark and I have just been to Coles

Supermarket to buy some provisions to keep us going throughout the day tomorrow (Mark still owes me money for the ticket).

Apart from that the highlight of the day was Barack Obama being sworn in as USA President, which can only be a positive thing for the world. I said a few years ago that he should be next president as, let's face it, George W. Bush is as bad as the devil himself (although I am agreeing slightly with Socialist President of Venezuela, Hugo Chavez Frias). I remember Dad saying when the race was going on for Democrat Leader that Hilary Clinton should win it. With respect: bollocks. She agreed with the war in Iraq and the last thing the White House needs at the moment is another fucking dynasty. Now, I am being critical here, but I wish everyone would lay off the whole race issue. Let's face it; anyone is better than George W. Bush (a.k.a that arsehole who needs to stand trial in The Hague). It is not a black or white issue. It is about the best guy for the job, about good v bad. But, all the Yankees are way too affected and all the tears are a bit too much for me to stomach. Why oh why do the cameras point to people like Denzel Washington and Aretha Franklin in the crowd? The media are turning it into a black issue, which is wrong for USA and it is wrong for the world. We are all the same at the end of the day, which is what the great Martin Luther King lived and died for. Hopefully a change will come to the world, which has become so troubled, particularly over the past 10 years due in large part to fucking Yankee Imperialism. Let's hope a new government in the White House can try to erase the illegality of the past 100 years of USA governments who seem to wilfully invade another country, slaughtering innocent people as they see fit. Let's hope.

<u>Day 97</u> – Thursday 22nd January 2009

It has been a cracking day today. We woke at 08:30 and I made us a hearty breakfast of scrambled eggs on toast to set us up for a day at the tennis with Mark even concurring it was awesome. After our respective showers, we collected our sandwiches and drinks we prepared last night and headed for the door, then went to the library to drop off some DVD's we had rented over the past few days. Then, we got on a tram for 5 minutes up to Melbourne Park for 12 hours of tennis.

Upon arrival, I was nearly ejected for the use of my camcorder and some power mad security guard asked me to turn it off. I felt like telling him where to stick it but I did not want to get chucked out after not even 2 minutes in the grounds without even seeing a match. The first match we watched was on showcourt 2, where British girl Elena Baltacha lost 2-1 to the very manly Amelie Mauresmo. It was still a good match to get us in the mood for a day's tennis even if the ladies on show were not the prettiest in the world. After that finished, we went across to the Margaret Court Arena to watch an Australian girl lose in straight sets. We caught the tail end of a Fernando Gonzalez match and we were sat amongst a few hundred Chilean fans, who created a great atmosphere. Chi-chi-chi le-le-le Viva Chile! The Aussies, as you would imagine, really get behind their players and, on the surface, it all seems good fun. Then, we saw the last 4 sets of the 5 set battle of Croatia where Mario Ancic defeated Ivo Karlovic.

After that, we decided to walk around the fan area for a while. Mark wanted to queue up for 1.5 hours at the Garnier stand, all so he could get a free bag with gel and shampoo in it. We nearly argued about it as I refused to give up 1.5 hours of my time to do that. It amazes me what people will queue for to get something for free and, when it boils down to it, it is greedy. We were at the tennis – I wanted to watch the tennis. Mark could not understand it. I cannot understand the human species sometimes and the things it will do to get something for free. It is pure greed. Tell that to Mark and the others in that queue for 1.5 hours. Ridiculous.

But, at 18:00, we settled in front of the big screen outside the Rod Laver arena to watch a night's tennis. We saw Venus Williams lose to Sanchez Navarro, which was a shock. Then we waited for the Andy Murray match. Just as it was getting freezing, and the Andy Murray match had just started, a guy offered us one ticket to go in as he did not need it. Mark snapped it up and ran inside so I was left outside in the cold to watch it, although he did consult with me first and we decided it was not worth both of us sitting outside. About 10 minutes later, two ladies approached me and offered me two more hospitality tickets, which I snapped up straight away. I phoned Mark, who met up with me near the food stalls and we got the choice of seats in a stadium that was emptying apart from the mob of Tartan Army fans. We sat right in the corner, all to ourselves and it was amazing how it turned out. Murray won and was then interviewed on the TV in front of us and the TV cameras pointed right in our face. Mark got a text off Sam and Clare asking if we were at the tennis as they could see us behind Andy Murray on the TV. What an end to a great day. I have caught the sun and I think it has been the best day so far in Melbourne.

Day 98 - Friday 23rd January 2009

Compared to yesterday, today has been uneventful. Mark got a phone call at 16:30 saying he has got a job, which is good. He always seems to have an advantage though as he has an Australian passport meaning he has citizenship. I am not that bothered – I am happy for him (in a way). But, it is funny how, now he has work, he starts giving me advice on what to do with agencies etc. That never happened before. Sneaky fucker!!! Sometimes, what you see is not always what you get! At least one of us has work, which gives hope that there are things out there.

So, tonight, a Friday night has been spent doing nothing. This is not making the most of my time in Melbourne. I sometimes think – what is the point?

Day 99 – Saturday 24th January 2009

Mark and I have just been chatting about people we meet along the road and keeping in touch. It got me thinking – I don't keep in touch with anyone, or they do not with me. It must be something about me that this is not the case. I always remember before I came away people saying 'Oh, you'll make loads of friends. You'll have a great time.' I can't say that after 3 months. Maybe Roger and Siri from Harnas but no exceptional folk – not yet.

Mark gets phone calls from people we meet but I don't. I don't care much as the people ringing him are not the people I wish to be associated with. If people do not want to get in touch, why should I?

But this also got me on to thinking about what friends I actually have. Since leaving school, I went to college but I do not keep in touch with any people from there. Then I went to University and the only person/people I keep in touch with are from Germany. Maybe it's something I am doing wrong. But, the way I see it, I'd rather have 5 exceptional friends than 1 million average friends. Let us be honest, Adam and Chris are 2 of the best guys anyone can be associated with. Mark is not a bad fella. I'm doing well.

Tonight though, after a lot of walking around the city, we went to a Vietnamese restaurant for food. Now, we are back and at the moment I am totally pissed off with Mark for continuously talking down to me in a demeaning manner. He was lucky tonight I did not punch the fucking face right off him. But, he is a mate and that would not be on. Maybe it is time for us to go our separate ways.

Day 100 – Sunday 25th January 2009

Day 100. Not a day that will go down as one of the best since I have been travelling if I am to be honest. Not much has been achieved and I am fairly disappointed by that fact if I am honest. I look back at the past 100 days and think – has it been worth it? Now, don't get me wrong, I have done some amazing things – some things that people will never get the chance to do but now I am thinking what is the point? A feeling of melancholy fills my head, which is hard to hide as other people know something is wrong. I am hard to live with (with people who do not know me). I know that. But, all I have done today (and yesterday come to that) is to think about home and compare my situation now to back there. Nobody takes a chance on me here as they do not there. It is hard to express how I am feeling though. A lost mind in a lost world, unable to speak out about what he sees or what he is feeling. Despair more than anything. If I could, no-one would listen. Just gamble your life away. At least back home, I had some contacts but here no-one knows me. No-one cares. No-one forever.

Day 101 – Monday 26th January 2009 – Australia Day!!

Australia Day. Today has been a beautiful day to celebrate Australia Day. We had a lie in this morning until about 11:00 and we then arranged to meet Meredith in Federation Square at 14:00 after we had something to eat in Hungry Jacks on Swanson Street. Anyway, we met up with Meredith and walked to the park where so many daft things were taking place – very Australian. It did bore me. But, we had a walk over to the shrine in Melbourne, which is a war memorial, which I found to be beautiful. We just do not have the room for these places in Manchester. I could have spent longer but Mark wanted to get back to the river to watch a plastic duck race. None of ours won (but they were never likely to as mine was number (27527). The winner was 00545. Anyway, we headed for a beer to

Young & Jackson's on Federation Square and we heard Andy Murray lost in the tennis, which put a downer on the day and I thought mark still owes me for the ticket at the Australian Open. I, again, slipped Mark $20 on the way there so he had enough to tide him over until we got to a bank. So, we went down to a British pub on Collins Street called the Charles Dickens, where I had a can of Tennants with some British food. After, we moved back to Transport Bar on Federation Square to watch the firework display at 21:15, which was pretty decent. Mark enjoys fireworks more than I do as I do not get it. It was still fun all the same and, after a few beers, we said goodbye to Meredith at Flinders Street station. Mark and I then enjoyed the walk down the side of the Yarra River, past the Crown Casino on our way home. Melbourne at night is one of the most beautiful cities in the world and I want to live here for good.

<u>Day 102</u> – Tuesday 27th January 2009

I awoke this morning and I had to go to the doctors so I could give them $68 for giving me a bit of paper. That was it. The Doctor offered me the chance to have my blood tests done again so I immediately grabbed my opportunity to get my monies worth. It turned out I had to pay Dorevitch Laboratory more money for the tests so, in my greed, I cost myself more money – that serves me right. I don't suppose the tests will tell me anything else. Probably, they'll tell me pretty much the same as these employment agencies who still are not finding me work! I am disconsolate about it now. But I have to keep up hope as, without hope, life is pointless.

Tonight, we went over to the cinema complex at the Crown Casino to watch the movie Gran Torino, which I think is one of the best films I have seen for ages. Clint Eastwood is back to his best and, it is not like me to overhype a movie, but it was quality. If truth be told, I have been feeling pretty down today and I cannot put my finger on it. We went to the gym and, as soon as I got on the exercise bike, my head went and I had to leave and go upstairs for a lie down. I do not know why or what it was. I am just experiencing some emotions that I shouldn't be. In my head are things from the past, which I can't seem to shake. Or maybe it is just because this trip is meant to be achieving something and I can't see me achieving anything here. I'm contemplating hitting the road and perhaps going on a trip to the centre. But I love Melbourne and I want to stay here.

<u>Day 103</u> – Wednesday 28th January 2009

I awoke at 06:30 and proceeded to go across the road to the Casino to catch the West Brom v Manchester United game, played at the Hawthorns. We won easily, 5-0. It was great until about the 70th minute when some dick head came over, sat next to me, and started bullshitting about United. He was obviously a dirty Australian Scouse fan and he totally hated MUFC and what came out of his mouth was not for repeating. Typically, I felt the need to say something as goals rattled in, something to the effect of 'Best Club in the World, FACT.' It did not go down too well with this fool who, naturally, disagreed, but he was left more than angry, when I repeated the fact that we are Premier League Champions,

European Champions and, by the way, World Club Cup Champions. He then threatened to throw me off the balcony in the Casino, to which I offered him the chance and he baulked. When the game was finished, I gave him a pat on the back saying 'that is what your club should strive to be like'. Then I walked off. Maybe this was fanning the flames a bit as he charged after me to the top of a set of stairs in the Casino, above the Sports Bar, where he tried to grab me by the throat and, on doing so, I was forced to push him, causing him to fall into a table and then onto the floor, embarrassed and seething. A security guard came over to quell the animosity and I decided it would be a good idea to walk off, casually chanting Champions, safe in the knowledge we had won 5-0. What a funny start to the day!

Well, it turns out now that Mark is going to head home. Apparently, his old company is going bust and some guys are buying it out and want Mark's help. So, it looks like he is off – once he has a flight sorted out from Flight Centre. It all happened pretty quickly and I would definitely be asking more questions if I were Mark. I mean – why are these guys asking him to go all the way back from Australia to set up a firm? Is he that indispensible or do they just need his money? Also, is it a good deal? It seems like there are too many questions. Mark is exited and, knowing him like I think I do, I'm sure it will work out for him. He seems to know what he is doing and I hope it does work out for him because he has talked about setting up an Audio Visual Business on more than one occasion. But, that life is not for me. All blinded by making more money and much more money. Money can't buy you life. I want my life to be more productive than paper and metal in the bank.

<u>Day 104</u> – Thursday 29th January 2009

Mark is definitely going home! It turns out he'll be going quicker than I thought. He will leave on Saturday night Melbourne and Sunday morning in Sydney. He'll be going just about the time United kick off against Everton. I will miss the guy if I am being honest and not because I will be on my own. Mark is probably the calmer, sensible side of the duo and, in that, I mean he has managed to calm me down a bit. We've come to understand each other more in the past 2 months and I now class him as a dear friend and, whenever I think of travelling the East Coast of Australia, I'll think of Mark too and the awesome time we made of it. What I will not miss, however, is his nit-picking on every $2 I may owe him, when in reality; he owes me a lot more. He has still not paid me back for the Australian Open Tennis Ticket and, when we met Meredith on Australia Day, I slipped him (gave him) another $20 to keep him going. It is not my style to keep a tab of who owes who though – it is just not in my nature. He is a mate and money means nothing compared to that. You can't buy it. I wish some people saw it that way – but they don't and that is the tragedy for them because life must be insignificant when you have to remind someone of $2 because you went to the supermarket to get food.

I did not bother getting up for the Liverpool v Wigan game this morning as I had planned to do so but I wish I had because Wigan scraped a 1-1 draw. The league has got to be ours now!

Day 105 - Friday 30th January 2009

Some things annoy me. Some things really annoy me. Then – some things really piss me off to the point that I want to explode and start punching the fuck out of things. I'll explain the situation to let off a bit of steam. We were on a night out tonight with Meredith and her friend, Phillipa, for Mark's last night in Melbourne. Anyway, before we left, Mark lent me $10 as I only had $130 to pay the rent and it was $140. I explained I would give him this back once we were out. We then proceeded to a Belgian Beer Cafe next to the Eureka Tower to meet Meredith and her friends. As always seems to be the case, I bought us all the first drink for the 4 of us. Mark and I finished off our beautiful Hoegaarden so we wanted another. Mark, in front of everyone, said 'you can buy' this and proceeded to point out exactly what I owe him, totally embarrassing me but neglecting the money for the Australian Open Ticket and the Australia Day cash. He bought me a beer the other night and the $10 for the rent gave him the right to tell me this in front of everyone else. I hate being told to buy a round of beers (being made to look like I am tight) especially when the person doing it owes me around $50. I was fuming and my fist was clenched at being confronted by this situation. In the end, I bought them as it is Mark's last night and I wanted him to have a good time because he is a mate. But then, we all bought a round of beers and the odd round (5th beer) was left to me to buy, which I know I would never see back. Things would get worse.

We went to Transport Bar, where Mark did the same thing. I was fuming but still I relented to speak and, somehow, Mark thought I owed him a drink. So, I left to get money from the bank to buy us a beer and I had to queue for 15 minutes to get back in. Once I got back in, I looked for them where we were before and they had totally disappeared. So, after 15 minutes of searching Transport (which was not overly busy) and not finding them, I was enraged and at boiling point. As I am a proud guy, I left. I've had about 30 calls from them wanting to speak but I do not want to speak to anyone. It is just too much. But, now back at the flat, it seems like it is all my fault and I have voicemails from them laughing etc. It is always my fault, isn't it? But, I am glad Mark is leaving tomorrow as I am sick of being bled dry but, on saying that, it'll be a shame to see the lad go as he has become one of my closest friends but it is time for a fresh start.

Chapter 8 – Goodbye's and Fresh Starts

Day 106 – Saturday 31st January 2009

So, tonight, on the corner opposite the Casino on Clarendon Street, next to the Melbourne Exhibition Centre, with a firm handshake and an 'abrazo' Mark and I parted on our separate ways, with him to return home and, for me, to go into the man I will become. I hope it is not prophetic that I was heading straight into the Casino to watch the football! But, we had some good times and I will miss the guy – I am glad he was with me down the coast. But, time to move on. It's over. We said our goodbye's and now is time for a fresh start.

I sent him on his way with some things to take home for my Mum and Dad – photos etc, which I am sure they will enjoy. After he left, I went into the Casino for Manchester United v Everton, which we won 1-0 so we are now 5 points clear. It is a good position to be in, especially as we have a game in hand over the others. I have just received a text message from Wes, which has perked up my spirits a little bit. He is such a great guy and I wish he was here experiencing this with me. My best mate in the world. You are bound to miss parents on your travels but it is the unspoken people that need a mention. Those people who you can go for a pint and a chat with who know you better than anyone.

Day 107 – Sunday 01st February 2009

So, I watched the United game into the early hours of this morning and then I began to spend my first day alone in Melbourne. I had a phone call from a girl, Janine, who was going to move into the room after Mark, saying she could not move in. I'm not that bothered if truth be told. Anyway, then I had a phone call from Pieter, a Dutch guy who viewed the flat the other night, saying he may still be interested in it.

So, I did my first shop alone and headed home to cook tea. During tea, I had a phone call from Anna, a girl I met in Cape Tribulation, saying her and Ryan (another guy we met there) were at Federation Square ready to watch the Australian Open Tennis Final between Federer and Nadal. So, I headed down to meet them and it turns out that Ryan may want to move in. It would be sound for me if he did as he is a quality bloke – from Leeds but I am not holding it against him. Federation Square was packed with around 5000 fans for the Tennis Final. We were supporting Federer as Anna is from Switzerland, but, unfortunately, he lost in an epic 5 sets to Nadal who is a total beast. Anyway, I have got to stay up to watch the Liverpool v Chelsea game at 03:00am. Come on the draw. It is amazing how sport brings people together from all over the world. It seems to unite, yet divide people, and the passion I have found for sport in Melbourne compares to that of no other city. It is little wonder they call Melbourne the sports capital of the world.

Day 108 - **Monday 02nd February 2009**

So Ryan decided he never wanted the flat today, which is a big disappointment for me as he is a sound guy but never mind. Anyway, Pieter, has just moved in, which will help me to become more patient as we are from different backgrounds. He does not seem to mix with the other Indian lads in our flat, which is a shame and he is very quiet. It would be difficult to live with him for the next few months.

Apart from that, it is hard to put into words what else happened today as it just seems to blend into one void that is not important to my travels. I could be sat at home in the snow!! But, as if I could forget, I visited the neurologist today at St. Vincent's Hospital. He was a sound guy called Dr. Moses, inevitably from Israel. He explained everything in its full context and it turns out that I have epilepsy - as I have now had more than one seizure. I am unsure at the moment how this will affect me in the future as I now have to take this drug, Epilim, 4 times a day for the rest of my life. Why me, was my first reaction.

But, other people have much worse things and I am lucky. Very lucky. You always think that other people get things like this but when you have it, it does not register. You just deal with it and move on. Worse things have happened and, I am sure, will happen. I have no time, or reason, for moaning. The doctor just explained a few precautions like try taking showers instead of baths, do not go swimming alone and try turning on cold taps before hot taps. It all seems common sense.

Day 109 - **Tuesday 03rd February 2009**

I am just sat here in my room in my flat, which has now been vacated by Pieter. He came back from work tonight and told me he wants to find a room for himself - he could only manage one day living with me. I was sound about it and said I understood. But what I cannot understand is why he moved in when he knew the score in the first place. So, he has fucked off and I am going to leave it now. Fuck Mark and his $600. He probably owes me that! I'm not worried if he loses it - so long as I do not lose mine!! Mark will make it back by not buying a pint to those he owes for the next 5 years. But, in a strange way, from what I have seen, people seem to like him for that!

So, I went to the cinema (alone) tonight to watch Valkyrie, which seemed a little bit funny. It is the first time I have seen a film on my own, but I am thinking I better get used to it. I think I have dug myself into a hole with the Meredith situation too. I said to her that, since Mark is leaving, I may give her a call to take her out. I think she took it as 'I'll give you a call' like a bloke says when trying to arrange a date, which I do not really want. Maybe I'll use it as a 999 number - girls you ring in case of an emergency. She's probably 'too nice' to be dealing with me at the moment anyway.

Day 110 – Wednesday 04th February 2009

The fucking shit we have to deal with on a daily basis. I know! I know it really does not matter but, today, for some reason, it does. It is hard to put into words sometimes how you feel – especially when you have no-one to talk to, or nobody understands you, or nobody will listen. I do not like those who moan but sometimes, when writing, it is nice to let off a bit of steam.

I have this interview tomorrow and I am treating it like it is the biggest thing in the world – when it is not, and I know that. Being nice to someone so they can give me a shitty admin job or something, which is not making a difference to the world. It is not the point really. I don't know what the point is. My mind can't seem to focus. I do have a lazy brain I think. Sat in the gym today on the exercise bike, I could not concentrate on the 'getting fit' part of it. My body felt fine doing it, but my mind just got bored until I quit. Distracted. I do get easily distracted or maybe I am lazy or maybe I am a quitter. I don't know. I need to find some routine to give me some focus. Maybe that could happen.

So, as you can tell, the day has been uneventful as the others have been since coming to Melbourne. A month of my travels has been wasted here since the start of the year. Wasted! I should be enjoying this experience but I can't and if I can't do what I came here to do, what do I do?

Day 111 – Thursday 05th February 2009

It has been a positive day on the whole of it. I went to meet Rebecca at Adecco and she seemed really impressed by my Criminology degree and we chatted for ages about it, although I am unsure if she was feigning interest. I think I made a good impression and she will try to find me some work in the field that I want – Youth Crime etc. I doubt she will but she said she would try, which is a plus. She also said that Adecco select the best for interview as times are pretty tough in the job market. Another positive even if she was trying to massage my ego. I may even start some work next week at the Exhibition Centre, which is just over the road from my flat. Great.

I've just had a run-in with my flatmates. They are just moaning about water in the bathroom after I have had a shower, which pissed me off because of all the black hairs and underpants they leave in there, and then they have the nerve to lecture me. Plus all the shit the dirty bastards leave in the kitchen. So, now, they have fallen out with me but they are trying to make amends. I do not want to listen. I'll let them dwell on it. But, like I said, life is too short to worry about these things – that is why I do not moan to them about it. I'll just moan to myself – like always.

I've just texted Meredith seeing if she wants a drink this weekend so looks like we'll head out down Chapel Street. Watch this space.

Day 112 – Friday 06th February 2009

All I could muster doing tonight was to sit in, crack open a beer and watch a DVD alone – the other side of the world. Never mind, I thought. It did cross my mind how ironic things are but that thought soon subsided as I sunk into my inebriation. My flatmate, Kenwar, is desperate to go to the beach tomorrow and go out tomorrow night but I've already arranged to meet Meredith and Rachel. I can't be arsed being put on the spot – even though a few beers on the beach sounds good. I do not want to go out to bars and clubs at all considering my epilepsy and all that. The last thing I want to do is to dance at the moment. I want to sit in a pub and drink beer and forget everything. It is so hot at the moment though. It is the hottest I have been since I arrived in Melbourne and the dry wind that sweeps across the brow does not help to cool me down. I can't get away from it –we have just broke records in Melbourne for 3 consecutive days of +43*C. I keep being informed by the locals that this is dangerous and you do see adverts to put out your cigarette butts. It is bushfire season and, in the UK, we are lucky we do not have to really worry about this. But, in Australia, it is a different matter and can be very serious.

Chapter 9 – Bushfires, Boredom and Unemployment

Day 113 – Saturday 07th February 2009 – BLACK SATURDAY

The Black Saturday bushfires, were a series of bushfires that ignited or were burning across the Australian State of Victoria on and around Saturday 7 February 2009 during extreme bushfire-weather conditions, resulting in Australia's highest ever loss of life from a bushfire. 173 people died as a result of the fires and 414 were injured.

As many as 400 individual fires were recorded on 7 February. Following the events of 7 February 2009, that date has since been referred to as 'Black Saturday'.

You know what? It is funny how you are strong-armed into situations that you do not want to be in, yet, out of fucking politeness, you go along with them.

I awoke this morning to sweltering weather and it was too much to bear. Almost straight away, Kenwar is on my case – when are we going to the beach? So, at 14:00 we went down to St. Kilda beach with an 8 pack of Toohey's. It remained at about 45*C and is one of the hottest days I have experienced. But, the beach was OK – hot, but OK. I got us chatting to a couple of girls who seem keen on meeting up tonight so I took a number. Kenwar wanted to go out just so we could get them back to the flat. He was hopeful but I wasn't. Firstly, it is me and secondly I am not in the mood at the moment. Plus I was meeting Meredith and Rachel – Kenwar insisted on coming. Due to it being so hot, we finished our beers and headed back for a swim in our flat to cool down.

Meredith said she, Rachel and Sarah wanted to meet us at the Belgian Beer Cafe near the Eureka Tower. So, we did. Meredith was late but she finds this funny as 'it is her thing'. I fucking hate lateness. I can't stand it. I let her off as she looked great in a long black dress, which was giving me thoughts. Rachel looked really pretty too but her friend, although nice, had an awful voice, which grated on me. I found the whole situation awkward with Kenwar and I wanted to bail. Meredith didn't seem her usual nice self and was taking the piss more than usual at which I had to bite my tongue. Anyway, all they wanted to do was to dance yet all I fancied was to sit down in a pub. We tried to get into a bar on Queen Street called CQ, but they would only let the girls in as we were not looking familiar (even though Rachel and Sarah have just arrived here from Manchester). It was my get out clause so I fucked off with Kenwar to Transport where I got us stuck into a few beers. It was so difficult with Kenwar as it is another world for him. We met with a load of Irish people but Ken was not interested – or he didn't understand them. Then, the lot of us went to an Irish Pub, PJ O'Brien's on the side of the Yarra and I got Ken a pint of Guinness but it did not go down too well!

But, on arrival back at the flat, news has come in that today has been awful for bushfires about 1 hour away from where we are. It is looking like a bad one with confirmed fatalities. How can I complain when things like this are going on? Things may get worse too.

Day 114 – Sunday 08th February 2009

After we returned to the flat last night and Kenwar went to be, I nipped off out to watch the Liverpool game where the lucky Scousers got 2 late goals to beat Portsmouth 3-2. I was gutted.

I awoke today at around 14:00 after the late night last night and the copious amount of beers I consumed. Dinner consisted of a KFC, which totally drained all the energy out of me. I am now trying to get some sleep as I want to be up for the Spurs v Arsenal game at 01:00 and at 03:00am it is West Ham vs. United. It should be a good night of football. I may squeeze a beer or two in. It looks as though these bushfires are spreading out of control and many deaths are now reported. It is looking like a severe tragedy and everyone I meet around the city appears worried. It is such a sad situation and it just seems to be getting worse. We heard about a newsreader who left it too late to get out of his house and, alongside his wife, they perished in the smoke and unbelievable inferno that is threatening to destroy a large part of this great state. It is so sad.

Day 115 – Monday 09th February 2009

I just want a reason to get out of bed in the mornings!! But I don't have! Rebecca from Adecco was supposed to e-mail me the details for work today but it never came. Always waiting on people to make your life better but it never does get any better – they never make it any better.

So, another day hanging about the city. So much for having a WORK/holiday visa. So much for having qualifications. So much for nothing at the moment.

Day 116 – Tuesday 10th February 2009

You know, it seems ironic to me how, when you are waiting to find a job in an agency, you are reliant on some fool who cannot even do theirs properly. This means, I still have not had an e-mail from Rebecca. I was supposed to have one on Friday and then Monday. Balls to it.

So, nothing to write except the disgusting habits of some of my flatmates. Sunil is the main culprit. He is really beginning to wind me up with his big head and his stupid, immature comments. When he goes into the bathroom in the morning he spends about 30 minutes, aggressively clearing his throat and spitting in the sink. It's enough to wake up a sloth. He is such a dirty bastard and he could turn even the toughest of stomachs.

Day 117 – Wednesday 11th February 2009

You know, over the past few days, when there is nothing to keep my mind occupied, I have been dreaming. Dreaming about things that will probably never happen. I'd love to be able to make a DVD or TV show about travelling but I'm not sure it will ever happen. But to have something you have created or done on the screen for others to see would be pretty cool. So, I've been making a few films of Melbourne and maybe I'll use my other videos to create a DVD when I return.

Anyway, I went out to buy a few items from the supermarket – items which if Mark was still here I could not buy!! Meredith called tonight around 18:00 but I let it ring out as I was not in the mood for talking. Now, I wish I hadn't because that is not like me to ignore someone when they call. All I can do is to shake my head at myself sometimes but, to my credit, I was cooking at the time. She sent me a message, which I did respond to. I also got that e-mail off Rebecca to say that I was not getting that work I hoped for, even though she told me last week that I had it. Liar. It's all downhill at the moment.

Day 118 – Thursday 12th February 2009

God. Times are depressing. Nothing to get up for. It is annoying. If this is what retirement will be like, I don't want to live over 50! I'm in a void. I can't go anywhere due to finances, which is made worse by not having a job! If I get one more response about not having the relevant skills... it's bollocks. Fuck it. Fuck it. Fuck it. It is all bullshit and it is pissing me right off. I've not heard a thing from her at Adecco. Laura from Hayes never responds to me. I'm buggered if I am calling her again. I've even resorted to e-mails but that doesn't seem to work. Then again – she did respond to Mark. So, I have sat around doing fuck all today. Exciting times. Maybe I want to go home. There – for the first time I have said it. The situation is breaking me. Rant over. I am off for a pint!

Day 119 – Friday 13th February 2009

Friday 13th. It is supposed to be bad luck for some people. No good luck occurred for me today, put it that way. I don't do anything with my days at the moment. It is just a blur of what is happening. The only highlight has been a few beers in the flat tonight. I did go to the library today, which turned out to be a waste of time. I wanted to rent some DVD's but I forgot my library card and, when I returned a DVD box it turns out I had forgot the actual DVD. Another wasted effort.

Day 120 – Saturday 14th February 2009

I woke about 13:30 today and have done nothing. Well, I went to PJ O'Brien's on the Yarra about 16:00 where I chatted to a barmaid who had also done Criminology and Law. I don't think she is interested – why would she be in a traveller? So that was that. At about 23:30 I went back to PJ O'Brien's to watch France v Scotland in the Rugby and we lost 22-13.

Day 121 – Sunday 15th February 2009

I went out tonight to PJ O'Brien's to watch the Celtic v Rangers game, which predictably ended in a 0-0 draw. It was one of the worst Old Firm games I have ever seen. I did not get to bed until 07:00 as I went to Urban Central to watch Wales v England in the Rugby. So, I've spent most of today in bed. But, I have only just got home again and it is 05:30. I went to Urban Central again to watch United beat Derby 4-1 in the FA Cup and we are now drawn away to Fulham in the next round. I reckon I'll start watching the games here as it is full of travellers and I can meet people easier here. A funny thing happened – I met a United fan from Preston who was at University at the same time as me and worked in a bar (Roper Hall) I used to frequent. Even stranger, he had a season ticket at United in block N46, row kk, seat 100. Exactly the same block as me, same row, but 50 seats further down. Small world.

<u>Day 122</u> – Monday 16th February 2009

I do not feel as though I have achieved a lot today. I am at the point now where nothing seems worth it. My belief in karma does not seem to go. I did voluntary work in Africa so, on my account, I should do some paid work here! Maybe I do not deserve to be getting any money. Maybe, as Marx put it, I am destined to live a life of exploitation. Never mind though. As long as everyone else is happy. Maybe it is my fault. Maybe I am setting my sights too high. I have said from the start of this trip that I do not deserve this. Why me?

<u>Day 123</u> – Tuesday 17th February 2009

It is here – I am now officially 1/3 way through my travels. At this juncture, I would like to recap on achievements so far and things left to do. Well, for one, the whole visit to Namibia was a total success. My mind will never be able to block out what I saw and experienced there. To sit out at night, under the stars in the Namibian bush and hear the lions roar in the distance is breathtaking. To sleep, next to a Cheetah is, although daunting, just an experience in itself. To be there feeding a lion cub its first bit of meat – heart-warming. Walking with a lion – the single best thing I have ever done or will ever do. Plus, I have proved that I can live outdoors and I am tougher than a lot of people give me credit for.

Secondly, London is not a bad city like I first thought. In fact, each person can find one thing about London they should like. They should, but you can't please all the people all the time!

Thirdly, on my visit to Australia, I think I am the first person in my family to travel this far away from home. I am not too sure where my Uncle Ronnie has been but that would be with the army. Anyway, my trip down the East Coast, although not unique, was still full of adventures, I'll likely not do again. I found peace at Cape Tribulation, which is now lost in the hustle and bustle of Melbourne. Sat on that beach, so far away from civilization, sandwiched between the Rainforest and the Great Barrier Reef, you think about your family and friends and realise what is important in life. The Whitsundays were just paradise. Fraser Island was just a laugh a minute adventure and Magnetic Island is a chill out centre, where I will never forget us watching United v City with a free bar! Amazing.

Yet – I still have not found work. This is why my time in Melbourne is appearing a little fruitless. This is the only reason I am in Melbourne and I can't find it. So, 1/3 away through a trip of a lifetime and I am still not happy, which leads me to think – all these things that I have done, will I ever be happy? That is all we strive for in life – happiness.

<u>Day 124</u> – Wednesday 18th February 2009

For a brief moment today (and I mean a brief moment, mind) I was at ease and I think a smile came across my face like I don't have a care in the world. Don't ask me what I was thinking at the time, but it went quickly. But, it made me think that when I am happy, I am unstoppable. But, when I am down, it's like, do not even talk to me. I do not think it is the job situation (or lack of one) that is annoying me. I am beginning to think it is this flat. I was lying asleep this morning at 08:00 and in walks Sunil to get to the balcony to put out his wet clothes to dry – waking me up! Now, I don't know whether to ignore it this time, then go mental next time so he fucking gets the point. Or, sit him down for a conversation he won't understand and explain it to him. He is a prick now. I've decided.

I had a text from Meredith earlier on and she wants to go out either on Friday or Tuesday. I replied to the question she asked about the job but was non-committal on the going out front. I don't know why. But, that is it. I had tea tonight of ham, eggs, chips and beans. Just what I fancied.

<u>Day 125</u> – Thursday 19th February 2009

The idea of work/travel visa is, besides travel, to work. I thought it would be easy. Maybe my view was too narrow and maybe a bit idealistic. Go travelling, get a job, go South America. Live your dreams. Learn Spanish then go home with a truckload of stories. But, I am getting a reality check at the minute. Maybe it'll be for the best later on but now it is fucking winding me up. All I can do with my days is to go to the library or the gym to fill a bit of time. Happy Days.

<u>Day 126</u> – Friday 20th February 2009

I took Meredith out for a meal down Chapel Street tonight, which is the first time I have been down there. It seems like my type of place – full of nice restaurants, pubs and trendy bars. You can do anything you fancy doing. We settled on a nice little Italian restaurant and, the weather being nice, we sat outside. Meredith chose pasta with pumpkin whereas I plumped for Chicken Cacciatore. Meredith thought it was delicious. Mine was nice but, as always, I compare these things to Nino's. But it was still a pleasant evening all the same and I tried not letting my lack of work ruin it! Even though I am out of work, I still paid the bill. We finished with a little drink in a nice Irish Pub and a kiss before I got on the train to the city and she drove home. She has just sent me a text to let me know she got home OK (on my request. It is just something I do with the ladies to show I care). A nice night has perked up my spirits.

Day 127 – Saturday 21st February 2009

I spent all night in the casino watching football, waiting for United v Blackburn. At 00:00, I watched Villa lose 1-0 at home Chelsea. Then I watched a dour goalless draw between Arsenal and Sunderland. So, at 04:30, United played Blackburn and we managed to win 2-1 and we are now 8 points clear. I watched it with a guy called Darren from Blackburn, who has grown up in Perth since 11. He seemed a decent guy. Football is my only solace in not having a job. Maybe Meredith was right last night when she said I need to get out of the city to do more things. She is quite astute to be honest.

Day 128 – Sunday 22nd February 2009

I didn't get up today until about 14:30 due the fact I did not get in this morning until about 07:00. So, to be honest, I have not ventured out of the building at all today. I did go to the gym about 19:30 and Mum and Dad called me during my sauna, which is the usual routine now on a Sunday night – they usually call about 20:00. It is nice to hear from them each week, even though conversations are a little bit stinted and all we talk about is football. But, I do appreciate the call.

Speaking of football, I have found a channel where I can watch the UEFA Champions League matches in my flat, although the reception is not the best. Plus, this week when the Champions League starts on Wednesday and Thursday, they are showing thee Arsenal and Chelsea games respectively instead of United v Inter Milan – gutting.

Day 129 – Monday 23rd February 2009

So, Liverpool only drew 1-1 with Man City early this morning, which means we are now 7 points clear at the top of the table. It is ours. For once when City scored, I went pretty mental in the casino leading a massive group of Aussie Liverpool fans to assume, because of my accent and I was cheering for City, I must be a City fan. However, I explained to them I was a United fan and that I just hated Liverpool. They did not understand the rivalry between Scousers and United – assuming that because City and United are in the same city, the rivalry must be greater. Mugs. It seems like all I ever do at the moment is to talk about the football. It should not be this way.

Anyway, something mental went on in my brain today as I went to buy a new laptop computer, even though I cannot afford it! I bought an external drive to go with it too. So, that is me here now with my new toy but I doubt it will help me find a job!!

Day 130 – Tuesday 24th February 2009

Meredith and I went to see Ghost Town at the cinema tonight. I was disappointed in it. I found it too slow and not as funny as I expected from Ricky Gervais, who is my favourite comedian. Meredith wanted to sit on the back row, which we did and this got me thinking – it's actually the first time I've sat on the back row of a cinema with a lady, although I tried making it clear we are only friends. I think that is for the best. I'd hate her to get the wrong impression, which has happened before and it can never be a good situation (especially given what went on in Sydney, which she keeps bringing up). Afterwards, we went for a drink to transport and I was showing restraint calling it a night early – there is a first time for everything! Before the film, we saw Nat (Gareth's ex from Holland) who is looking really well and we've arranged to go out next week.

Day 131 – Wednesday 25th February 2009

I awoke this morning at 06:30 so I could try to stream the United v Inter Milan game on my laptop through the internet but it did not really work. It kept sticking so I had to make do with watching Arsenal beat Roma 1-0. We managed a 0-0 draw in the Giuseppe Meazza San Siro. Other than this, I have been pretty lethargic! All I seem to do is talk about football but these journals are based on what is important in my life at a particular time. It may be correct to suggest that, as football is the only thing I write about these days, there is little else important and it is frustrating as I want to find that.

Day 132 – Thursday 26th February 2009

I got up early again today to watch Chelsea beat Juventus 1-0 in the Champions league. Liverpool also won 1-0 in Madrid – those lucky Scouse bastards!!! But my plan of just getting 10 minutes sleep after the football did not work as I ended getting up at 15:30 and the day was wasted so another day has been wasted!

Day 133 – Friday 27th February 2009

Life is poor. All I did was to spend the night tonight watching movies and drinking beer – alone. It is not how I expected my travels to turn out. I need to sort something out in the next week with work or a serious decision is to be made. It just cannot go on like this much longer.

Day 134 – Saturday 28th February 2009

Oh, how I laughed tonight when Liverpool lost 2-0 to Middlesbrough. So, we are now 7 points clear with a game in hand. The bookies should start paying out on us now. I did have a phone call from Danny Smith tonight asking if I fancied moving to Brisbane as there is a spare room at his house and there may be the chance of some work at the place he is working at. I love Melbourne so I am going to give it one more week and, if nothing has changed, I may take him up on the offer. I'd fuck off the bond Hu owes me. We'll give it one more week.

Day 135 – Sunday 01st March 2009

I went out tonight to watch the League Cup Final but we won on penalties so I ended up staying up all night in the casino, drinking with a load of Irish guys and another lad from Irlam. The Paddy's had us on the whisky when Anderson scored the winning penalty then we all piled up to McDonald's for breakfast! We are still on for the quintuple, although we won the charity shield too but, unlike the Scousers, we do not class that as a proper trophy. We still won it though.

Day 136 – Monday 02nd March 2009

I was awoken today at 14:30, hungover, but as it was a private number I chose not to answer it and let it go to voicemail. I listened to the message and it was from Jennifer at Hallis saying they have work for me at Computershare starting tomorrow if I was available. So, I called straight back and she gave me all the details. I'll be on a 3 day training course, which I'll be getting paid for at $20p/h. So, I've just ironed my shirt and trousers so I am ready to start. I am looking forward to working again, which means I can have a bit of money for South America, which is the only reason I came travelling. If this job didn't show up, I would have seriously had to start thinking about returning to the UK, which would have had disastrous consequences.

Chapter 10 – Work and New Friends

Day 137 – Tuesday 03rd March 2009

So, this morning, I awoke at 07:00am, showered and made my way to Flinders Street Station to get the train to Abbotsford (Victoria Park) to start work. It was training day basically, learning about shares etc. It is all money but there is no future in this job. It did feel like back home though as it was raining all day and work just compounded it. I did meet a pretty cool local girl, Edwina, and, at one point there seemed some chemistry between us – especially when we were tied up together during the icebreaker. She is also only here just to earn a bit of cash to go to South America – but the chemistry fizzled when she said she had a boyfriend. Computershare is a huge, open planned office built in an old factory and its sole purpose is to advise people on shares. I notice, as I look around, that there are many travellers here who just want to earn a bit of cash to put them on their way. However, there are a few locals who work here too whose confidence must take a knock by us travellers.

Day 138 – Wednesday 04th March 2009

I went playing 5-a side tonight with a guy called Martin who I met through work. He is from Leeds (Pontefract) and he seems really sound. Anyway, I scored a goal and set 2 up but we lost 5-4. Never mind though, because there are a good few guys playing so it's a good thing to get involved in.

Work was OK today and it is OK getting paid for training. We have a group of really good people doing this thing, which makes it a lot better. Ryan, my other mate from Leeds, has just arrived in Melbourne from Thailand too so I'll catch up with him for a drink this week. Things just seem to be slotting into place both socially and economically. It's getting better.

Day 139 – Thursday 05th March 2009

What was planned for one or two drinks after work turned into a bit of a session as I met Ryan in a pub in the city. We went from bar to bar and, now I've arrived home I have realised I have my first proper day of work tomorrow. Ryan is doing OK and we are on about getting a flat together when Anna arrives back from Switzerland. But, to be fair, we are both pretty pissed tonight and, now, I am not looking forward to tomorrow. The last day of training went OK today and we'll see how long I stick out this job. The whole flat situation is fucked and I have come to the conclusion I need to leave. There is only Nimesh from Nepal in this flat who I actually like.

Day 140 – Friday 06th March 2009

I awoke this morning feeling not too great as I had a few beers last night with Ryan. Anyway, my first morning on the phones was a nightmare due to a problem with the systems although I got paid for it!! But, after they fixed the fault, it went OK. It is a job so I cannot complain. Many more people in the world remain unemployed so I am fortunate. A few of us went to a local pub after work, which is a bit of a tradition on Fridays at Computershare. I had a few pints and headed home where I treated myself to a few beers and watched TV, which is a little routine I should kick into touch but it is OK.

Day 141 – Saturday 04th March 2009

I decided to stay up in Urban Central tonight to watch the United v Fulham FA Cup game in Urban Central. We hammered them 4-0 and are definitely on for the quintuple. Earlier, Ryan and I went out for a few pints to watch the Chelsea game. He is a quality guy and is definitely on my wavelength. We share the banter but appreciate how fortunate we are to be here. The day apart from that was spent lounging about but I cooked a delicious meat pie for tea. Get in!! I'm a lot happier now and things are starting to go for me in Melbourne. I have work, friends and the chance to enjoy a quality city.

Day 142 – Sunday 08th March 2009

I spent the day hanging about the flat, which is a pain because I hate Sunil!! He is one of the Indian's I have to live with and sometime he makes me physically sick. Like I actually want to physically vomit. The thing he does to clear his throat just disgusts me. And the spitting. You know – some people where I am from think of Indian's as dirty. He is the fucking reason why!

I was going to stay up tonight to watch the Arsenal v Burnley game but then I decided I could not be arsed. Steak for tea!! Beautifully cooked. I'm getting good at this.

Day 143 – Monday 09th March 2009

Labour Day in Victoria so I got to have a day off (unpaid). So, most of the morning was spent in bed. This afternoon I decided to go to the gym and a swim along with a sauna. Apart from that – it has been uneventful.

Day 144 – Tuesday 10th March 2009

Back to work today and it did not go too badly to be honest even though it can get repetitive. I lost my temper when I was put on my lunch break at 14:30. So, when I went to the canteen to get some food, they had just closed so I had to walk to the only bakery for about 20 miles, which were just closing and they would not make me anything!! So, I had to walk up to a BP garage and I had to make do with a shitty packaged sandwich. So, I walked all the way back to work, was nearly late and I had to eat the sandwich at my desk, while trying to take calls, which was a pain in the arse.

Other than the eventful lunch, today has passed over as pretty uneventful. Hu called around tonight to say that someone is moving in to my room on Friday, which is another pain in the arse. It was just announced. He is after getting the Indian crew out of the flat and was asking for my advice on how to do it. I played cautiously (not wanting to take sides) but, despite them being dirty fuckers, I could not break my word and advise Hu on what to do to kick them out. That is not fair game and I think I have more compassion than to see a group of guys kicked out on the street. I told Hu I was more honest than that.

<u>Day 145</u> – **Wednesday 11th March 2009**

Work can drag sometimes. It is during these time that you think. About things that mean a lot to you. About friends. I thought a bit about my old mate Andy Bollesty, who is 25 today. Him, me and Wes were best mates back in the day but he seemed to go his own way. But, on my credit, I have forgotten a load of shit that has happened So, I sent him an e-mail just to say that I remember the good times we had as kid's blah blah blah. He seemed to appreciate it. But, as a member of the BMW (Bollesty, Mirfin, Wesolowski) I have a duty to make sure my other 2 best mates are doing OK. I lost a lot of respect for Andy through the company he has gone on to keep and the way he turned his back when I needed him as a mate. I feel differently to Wes as he thinks that Andy still appreciates us both as we went to Stubbins Primary School. He does when it suits and it is pretty much guaranteed none of us will receive an e-mail on our birthdays. Like I say – don't sink to anyone else's low standards. But, a mate is a mate and you have to accept them for their flaws – I know I have them.

<u>Day 146</u> – **Thursday 12th March 2009**

I got up early this morning to watch United beat Inter Milan 2-0 at Old Trafford. We did not play too well to be honest but a win is a win and we are now through to the next round, which is all that counts. I do like the fact that I can watch it before I go to work so a good result can put you in a good mood for the day. But, then as usual, there is always someone there to kick it out of you. But, balls to it. My foot was killing me after 5-a side last night and, my usual 100 miles an hour game does hurt sometimes. I was going in with my usual full force, even when the game was won and the tackle did not even need making! It is all good. I reckon these Aussies are soft though and are pretty scared when I put myself about as I am used to no holds barred games back in Manchester.

<u>Day 147</u> – **Friday 13th March 2009**

I am looking forward to tomorrow when we play Liverpool. These games are always an intense affair and I expect this one to be. It should be good and I think I can say I have never looked forward to a United v Scousers game more in my whole life. Ryan and I are going to the Charles Dickens pub and Collins Street.

We went out after work again for a drink or two, which is nice as it makes us guys feel like part of the team while we are here.

The new guy has moved into the flat today, who'll be sharing the room with me. I have not had a chance to meet him yet but he is German and I tend to get on with all German's. I am just questioning though why Friday 13th is still classed as an unlucky day. Superstitious.

Day 148 – Saturday 14th March 2009

Tonight, I will never recover from.

The worst thing that could happen to me has happened. Worse than losing an arm, a leg. Answer? We lost, at home, to Liverpool. Bu this was not just any old loss. We lost badly. W lost 4-1.

Ryan and I went to the Charles Dickens Tavern on Collins Street. It was a mixed crowd but it was packed. It is funny – I looked forward to this match for as long as I can remember and now we've got beat. I chatted to an Australian Scouse fan who mocked me for supporting United and being from Manchester. Naturally, he got the piss taken out of him. Even worse when I spoke to an Aussie United fan who asked me who I supported and when I pointed to the picture of George Best on my t-shirt he asked 'Who is that?' I felt I needed to be around people I knew and who felt the same way as me. With Wes, Dave and the others from the Dogs. Even Ryan, the Leeds fan, laughed at the result.

It is funny how you never hear from friends for ages and then they call (or text) to take the piss out of you when they know you will be extremely pissed off. I have to learn to take it on the chin but, when you get beat 4-1 at home to the Scousers, it is so, so hard to take.

Day 149 – Sunday 15th March 2009

I cannot talk about how angry I am today. As soon as I woke up (hungover and bear in mind what happened yesterday) Sunil is accusing me of not washing a pan from when I got in pissed up last night. Apparently, they could not make tea until it was cleaned. They waited until I woke up at 13:30. He kept going on so I told him forcefully to fuckoff and slammed my bedroom door right in his face. Then, he called Hu the landlord to let him know. Hu called me later on saying they are small people to which I told Hu I don't really give a shit as it is nothing to do with him. He is not a counsellor. Florian, my new roommate, could not believe how petty it was. Needless to say all the dirty Indian's took Sunil's side. A big argument ensued tonight but I refused to address Sunil. I'll get him before I leave – don't worry about that. He is one of the dirtiest little rats I have ever met. I am annoyed with his older brother Satish too because he isn't bringing Sunil to book about it and as an older brother, he should.

Day 150 – Monday 16th March 2009

And so begins my first full week of work in Melbourne. I am pretty much settled in now if truth be told. A job is a job is the way I see it. The flat situation is becoming unbearable. It is just too full but the habits of some of the Indian guys are awful – and then the cheeky c***s have the nerve to complain about mine.

Day 151 – Tuesday 17th March 2009

Another day of repetitive boredom that is only relieved by the odd coffee break. I hate jobs like this because Big Brother is always watching. George Orwell had it spot on. He would have a field day writing 1984 where I work. I logged in 2 minutes early today and no-one said anything. But, when I logged out at 17:29 (I finish at 17:30) I was immediately brought to book. The way I see it – they owe me a minute! Plus, I hate registered breaks. Different breaks every day. It must be someone's job to organise them for everyone in the place. Why not just do one for everyone and we can have the same time every day? At least then we know where we all stand. Maybe it is just because I am used to having a coffee while carrying on working and being flexible.

Day 152 – Wednesday 18th March 2009

Another day rolling into one. I am still thinking of Saturday's result and it can get me down!! I did order my Formula 1 ticket today for the 29th march so that should be a good day. I'm going down with Ryan and we are planning to have a few beers so that is something to look forward to. Basically, all I am doing at the minute is getting my head down, earning money and saving for my dream trip to Latin America. If I didn't have to go there, I would definitely find a way of staying in Melbourne as I am beginning to love the place. But, Latin America is the greatest continent on earth for those who have any sort of a brain and it cannot come soon enough!

Day 153 - Thursday 19th March 2009

Work is work. Life is life in this town. I like Melbourne and Melbourne likes me. I seem to fit in around here. At first I said I would be prepared to sacrifice my Latin America trip but now I am not sure. That is my dream. Melbourne is great but not that great to sacrifice one of the best trips around so I am looking at booking my trip to Machu Picchu while I can. I want to do some form of the Inca Trail but I am not too sure if I want to do the actual Inca trail where all you see are ruins. I want to mix mine up a bit and meet people along the way – much in the same way as Che Guevara and Alberto Granado did in the Motorcycle Diaries.

Day 154 – Friday 20th March 2009

Well my first full weeks work in Melbourne is over. Working in Namibia was far more rewarding than this as I actually felt some sense of achievement. All I do here is advise people on money and shares so they can try to get that bit more cash, which they do not need. I hate the whole notion of the share market and I see it as just another part of the system that makes rich people richer and poor people poorer. After work, I headed to the supermarket to buy my usual pack of Miller and then I watched a DVD tonight.

Anyway, I do have a nice little routine going. I get paid on Friday and after work I buy my food for the week and I make sure I have an extra nice dish on a Friday and Saturday. Also, on Friday's, I buy my weekly train ticket and ensure there are beers in the fridge for weekends. Who says I am not organised?

Day 155 – Saturday 21st March 2009

Another useful result for the greatest football club in the world. We lost 2-0 at Fulham tonight, which is our second consecutive defeat. We just can't lose this lead to the Scousers!

I had a walk around the city this afternoon and collected my F1 ticket from Ticketek on Exhibition Street. There was a huge Greek Festival on Lonsdale Street so I walked down there and participated in the festivities. Melbourne has a large Greek population and they all seem out for a good time. It was buzzing and a nice way to spend the afternoon. On my walk back to my apartment I stopped and reflected at the side of the Yarra River, on Southbank at what an amazing city Melbourne is. When the sun catches the water and you see Flinders Street Station in the background, the buildings not too excessive as in Sydney, it is a really beautiful sight. Living right on the riverside is a plus that I can take away with me forever.

Day 156 – Sunday 22nd March 2009

I awoke today at mid-day and I had to wait around for 2 hours for the dirty Indian's to finish cooking one of their 30 meals a day, which always seems to be japati and chutney. I only wanted to cook myself a fry-up. It is one of these little things that tips me over the edge. They are just a filthy bunch of fools who need a wash. I am not joking either. Anyway, the day has been fairly uneventful. My weekdays are more exiting I think.

Day 157 – Monday 23rd March 2009

I got in to work today and turned on my computer straight away to find out how Liverpool got on against Aston Villa. I was, slightly, hopeful Villa could pull something off. I was disappointed. It was 5-0 to the Scousers. Shit. But, from then, the day went OK. Usual miserable people who think they can talk to you how they want. I got a few of these calls today but I can handle them OK – for now. I wonder how much longer it will be when I stop biting my tongue and say how I feel!

Day 158 - Tuesday 24th March 2009

"The weak can never forgive. Forgiveness is an attribute of the strong" Mahatma Gandhi

I spoke to Stewart tonight for the first time in a long, long while. It is his 28th birthday you see. We fell out before I left due to him being a selfish bastard but life is too short. I am not one of these low life's who hold grudges and I think I have a higher moral code to turn the other cheek rather than ignore people that you should care about . It doesn't matter who is

at fault as long as we learn our lessons and have the ability to forgive. Life is too short to dwell on our quarrels. He said it has made his day that I called. So, that was one good deed done for the day.

I have just found out too that I have forgotten to change my flight details from Venezuela to Miami and from Miami to LA. Now the flights have expired. So, Flight Centre would not sort it out for me and I have to contact American Airlines myself. So, I called them and it is such a pain in the arse. One person tells me one thing and another tells me another thing. But, as it stands, my flights may expire on 11th April – one year from the purchase of ticket so it looks as though I may be fucked.

Day 159 - Wednesday 25th March 2009

A day that has passed by the same as all the other working days recently. I have a routine back in my days now. A routine that has not existed since the days back home, although this routine makes me a lot happier as you don't have to listen to a huge load of pricks telling you this or that or thinking for a minute they can have an opinion on how you decide to live your life. It's personal freedom that is important. I have a life here that could be how I want to live – except the flat situation. It is a pain, which is a negative I should not dwell on. I need to suppress all feelings of negativity, which I will work on. Even though this job is not what I want to do, it is still a job and the people are all great to work with.

Day 160 – Thursday 26th March 2009

My mind, sometimes, does wander to back home. I often think about people back home and if they think of me. Am I missed? I am not too sure. I have not heard from Wes for ages. He has not e-mailed me for ages to see how I am and sometimes I think if my best mate can't, then who can? But, I mainly think about people's lives back home and when they will take the bull by the horn and live life how it is meant to be lived by getting out of the door and to see the world around us while they can. To meet people of this world and to learn. To see what is out there. To have something worthwhile to say for a life, which is supposed to have meaning.

Day 161 – Friday 27th March 2009

I stayed in tonight because I am off to the F1 on Sunday so I watched a DVD, had a few beers and arranged with Ryan the plan for Sunday. I have not heard from Meredith in a while but fuck it. I can't be bothered making the effort with her. Hu, my landlord, never showed up to collect the rent tonight. If he turns up tomorrow, I won't be here – simple as that. I am making it my goal to not be here tomorrow. He is a dick though. He has this notion in his head that he can just show up when he pleases and we will all be in and always have $140 for the rent. Well – balls to him. For now though, I am just trying to save cash for the next stage of my adventure. Hopefully, I can save up $2000 or close to it. It'll never happen!!

<u>Day 162</u> – Saturday 28th March 2009

A dull Saturday where I ventured into the city to buy a set of shin pads for 5-a side on Wednesday nights. It is compulsory to wear shin pads and, since I started, a couple of us have been forced to wear 'travellers shinnies', which are 2 pieces of card, retrieved from an outside bin, shoved down our socks to fool the referee into thinking we have shinnies. It worked well. Although, I always like to play like Faustino Asprilla with my socks around my ankles, no shin pads and, first time I played, I got reprimanded!!

I had shit news today. My IPod has been officially confirmed as 'fucked' as the hard drive is buggered. I took it to an Apple shop right across the street from where I live and those were the words they used (good customer service saying it as it is). So, now, I have no music for the rest of my trip. What pissed me off tonight was Hu showing up at 01:30am. I was just about asleep and he knocks on my door to wake me up. Not only for the rent but to have a go at me. He put a screw to stop the shower door opening outwards, which I thought was stupid as we had to really squeeze to get into the shower as a result and it was even more difficult to turn the shower on. So, with my knife, I unscrewed it and tossed it over the balcony! It needs a magnetic closing device to stop the door opening when people take showers. To wake me up at that time was a big no no. So, I was fuming and I told him 'Hu, do that again and it'll be the last thing you do', putting the frighteners on him. He got the point and skulked off.

Chapter 11 – Boys Will Be Boys

Day 163 – Sunday 29th March 2009 – Formula 1 Melbourne Grand Prix

What a day it has been today. I was going to get up at 07:00am to watch the Holland v Scotland game but I decided against it because I had a long day planned at the F1. It was just as well because we lost 3-0. So, I got up a bit later, had a sausage and egg sandwich and went to meet Ryan in Young and Jackson's opposite Flinders Street Station for a couple of beers. We then went to Transport bar for one and made our way on the tram down to Albert Park. Upon arrival, I bought a programme and we then needed to find a good spot. Naturally, it was in a beer garden. This was where we spent a couple of hours chatting to two old boys, Barry and Alan, from Manchester. We had a few beers and food and then we went to watch the race. Jenson Button started on pole and won. I felt, for once, proud to be British. At the end of the race, during the celebrations, we went down the pit lane and I even saw Richard Branson, which was funny. We then went to watch The Who, who were amazing. My Dad, I hate to say it, was right. Such a good live band. Ryan and I headed back to the city for a few beers and, now, I am home, all tanned and ready for work tomorrow!!

Day 164 – Monday 30th March 2009

This morning I woke with a slight hangover from yesterday but I still managed to make it into work unlike a couple of blokes who had obviously had one too many beers at the F1 yesterday and called in sick. However, on getting into work, we were told that it is expected we will be quiet tomorrow so not all staff will be required. Naturally, as everyone wants the money, no-one volunteered to take time off. So, names were pulled out of the hat (not in public I will say) and what do you know? My name was one of the unfortunate 4. Shite. So I now lose a day's wages tomorrow. At least I can have a lie in and the weather should be nice so that is a positive so I am planning on taking a walk down to the MCG and chill out on the side of the Yarra River in what I now call my 2nd city (after Manchester of course).

Day 165 – Tuesday 31st March 2009

Well, even though I did have a day off today I decided I better make the most of it. So I decided to take a wander down the side of the river, past the MCG and back upon myself again. I found a nice little spot near to the sailing club on the riverbank and I just lay there for an hour or so in the crisp, Melbourne sunshine. It was delightful to lie there, with a book, and let the world go by. It was at this time of peace that I was rudely interrupted by American Airlines saying my flight from Caracas to Miami cannot be changed after 10th April 2009. So, now I have had to cancel it but, luckily it is refundable. But, my flight from Miami to LA has been lost, with no refund. So, now, I am stuck in Venezuela it would seem. I need to somehow get to LA to get my return flight home. Maybe I will do a trip through Central America, which would be more fun anyway, passing through Colombia to Guatemala, Nicaragua through Mexico to the so called 'friend to the North'. So, that is what

I am doing now - trying to sort this mess out. Typical Americans. But Central America is appealing unlike the Yankee Town, which I imagine is appalling. I fancy going to Guatemala to learn about what happened in 1954 when the CIA illegally overthrew Jacobo Arbenz. That may have to wait though.

Day 166 – Wednesday 01st April 2009 – April Fool's Day

I feel like the only fool these days. Going into Computershare always to get mucked about with my hours. They just keep chopping and changing everything and no-one knows where they stand.

That is the beauty of agencies though. Those with security in their jobs seem to think they have control over your life. Like they can pick and choose how they want to use you. "Workers of the world unite". But it seems it will never happen as they have turned it into a dog eat dog world where it is every man for himself. No-one will ever get together to make a difference. So long as I live, I will never let this happen. I am nobody's fool.

Day 167 – Thursday 02nd April 2009

I didn't bother getting up this morning to watch the Scotland v Iceland game. I don't think anywhere would show it – especially not over the England game and I would rather watch paint dry than watch that bunch of hooligan's play, with that incessant brass band droning on in the background. Maybe I'm turning into a guy called ABE (Anyone But England). But, we won 2-1 all the same, which is a good result on the face of it. I had to go into work, which was a little bit draining but I still managed to play 5-a side tonight. This is the first week I have played and not scored a goal. We concurred that my form has dropped a little. At least I've made some decent mates out of playing football. Martin from Leeds, Rob from Melbourne and John Ho from Melbourne (although I think he has Korean roots). I wish I could live here – I think I will (once South America is out of the way) make an effort to get my visa to live here full time. Melbourne is amazing.

E-Mail:

Hello everyone.

Just a quick update regarding my travel situation. Things have hit a little bit of a snag - basically because the Yankees don't know their arses from their elbows. I've had to surrender two flights on my round the world flight tickets (the only two that were with American Airlines). The flights I've had to let go are from Caracas, Venezuela-Miami, USA and from Miami, USA-Los Angeles, USA. American Airlines gave me this crap about not being able to change the flights after one year of purchase (which was 10th April 2008) even though every other airline I've been through can. Luckily, the Caracas-Miami one is refundable at

$331 so, providing my guy at flight centre gets off his arse and requests a refund, I'll get it sorted by the 10th April 2009. However, I've lost my flight from Miami-LA.

But, you'll probably notice I've now no flight out of Venezuela at the end of October. I'm looking into getting another one sorted via Trinidad and Tobago. If I can get on this (for US$430), I'll have to make my own way from Miami all across the USA to LA, which may turn out to be quite fun. But, honestly (I'm saying this sober now), the less time I have to spend in the US the better. I'm considering doing a trip instead through Central America (Guatemala, El Salvador, Mexico etc) in order to get my return flight from LA which I'd much prefer to do anyway. I'm making those plans now. At least countries in Central America aren't the cause of 99.9% of the world's problems!! Some people laughed at me before I came away when I said the US was the place I least wanted to see. I can't find one redeeming feature the States have to offer for me wanting to go - so many better countries in South America.

Rant over!! I had an awesome time at the GP at the weekend. I'm really happy that Jenson Button won over Lewis Hamilton (I've always thought he was the better driver anyway - just needed a decent car).The Who were amazing in the gig after the race! But, it was a decent day and me and my mate from Leeds managed to tuck a few beers away in the process. Work is good, although I'm not too sure how it will last. I love Melbourne - I want to live here but saying that I can't wait to move and start travelling again. I'm so looking forward to South America. The finances may be a bit tight to do a trip to Ayers Rock and the Inca trail. If I had to choose, the Inca Trail would win every time!

Hope everyone is OK back home and I'm not being missed (fat chance of that)!! I'll be back in touch soon when those annoying Yanks haven't wound me up as much!!

Take it easy,

Alistair

Day 168 – Friday 03rd April 2009

For a change, I decided to stay in tonight. I managed to find Kraft Cheesy Macaroni, which I cooked for my tea. I used to eat that as a kid quite a lot (even though it is probably laced with chemicals). I only cooked it tonight as I could not be arsed buying (or cooking for that matter) anything else. I didn't even buy any beers! Shock! Work was OK. At least I did a full day and got through it with relatively little hassle, which is all I can ask for these days.

Day 169 – Saturday 04th April 2009

I went to the gym for a considerable amount of today, which left me feeling invigorated and ready for a night on the beer. I was basically waiting for the football tonight, which has restarted after an international break. Chelsea did over Newcastle 2-0 at St. James' Park. I was really out to see the Scousers play Fulham at Craven Cottage. I was sat having a few beers in the casino sports bar amongst a huge group of Liverpool fans and the more beers I had, the more vocal I became for Fulham. Liverpool battered Fulham all game, hitting the bar god knows how many times but it wasn't going in. I did let me guard slip that I was supporting Fulham, not actually as a Fulham fan but as a United fan. Then came the taunts by the Scousers – not that they have much to taunt about. Anyway, Liverpool battered them until, 91 minutes, when my hopes of a Fulham point were nearly realised. The ball rolled to Jew Yossi Benayoun in the box and I was left fuming as he drilled a shot into the net. 1-0. Surrounded by Scouse dick heads going wild saying 'that's how you win leagues' and 'we're going to do it. We're going to do it'. I made a hasty exit. Not so hasty as it was obvious I wanted to punch a hole in the wall because I do have my pride. But, they were right in only one respect. That is how you win Championships because I have seen us do it enough times. I asked god tonight for one more.

<u>Day 170</u> – Sunday 05th April 2009

After a frustrating week, god answered me tonight and his answer was 'Fuck Liverpool'. Officially!! Get in is all I can say about tonight. The day has dragged and dragged and nothing seemed to be going right. I managed to fuck up my tea and I was struggling at the gym plus I wandered around the city centre streets aimlessly all day, achieving nothing.

So, by the time I went over to the casino to watch United v Villa I was a little pissed off. Normally, all the big screens in the Sports Bar work with no problems. Tonight, one didn't and, it just so happened, it was the TV showing United. So, me and one other 17 year old Aussie lad supporting United had to walk over to an upstairs bar in the casino and it was on a shitty plasma screen TV. We missed the first 2 goals (when we got there it was 1-1). The bar was closed and I could not get a beer and the bartenders were clearing up as people brushed passed me to go outside for a smoke, some stopping briefly to cheer on Villa as they knew I was so into this match and up for it. An American girl who was clearing up was pissing me off singing stupid songs and, generally, being the most annoying person I have ever heard. When one of her colleagues approached to ask the score I said to him 'Gonna ask her to shut up? It's getting annoying now.' He did too. Then, she went 100% worse and said 'I'm going to support A Villa now.' I just said 'Well, can you do it fucking quietly please.' We were playing shite too and not looking like scoring, which made matters worse. Even worse came on 60 minutes when Villa went 2-1 up and the bar staff were laughing and the smokers coming and going were happy. Only me and this 17 year old kid wanted United to win – although his knowledge about the club was minimal. 82 minutes, Ronaldo scored and I let off a huge sigh of relief, going a little mad. The 2-2 score and the noise I made then attracted some Scousers who were desperate for Villa to hang on. They were confident that, if Villa held on for the draw, they had won the league as they told me an infinite amount of times. However, 92 minutes Federico Macheda scored one of the goals of the season to make it 3-2 United. I nearly ripped the roof off the Crown Casino and wild celebrations ensued, running around the casino. I didn't know what to do. I missed my buddies from Manchester. I walked up to this 17 year old kid watching it with me and picked him up and hugged him as if he was my best mate. I uttered a quote I heard last night 'That's how you win leagues. United top of the league'. Get in. I love it. I've got to get up for work at 07:00 – it is now about 03:30. Never mind. It was worth it.

Day 171 – Monday 06th April 2009

Work always feel better when:

You are starting mid-afternoon

Your team has won at the weekend

The only problem was that they are cutting the hours so it means less money is coming up. But, the group of people are sound. Tonight, I have just been knocking about and it's a routine similar to back home. It does seem dull and I feel I should be achieving more but all I do is think about the next stage of my adventure. You cannot travel all the time without a bit of work in between. That is the stage I am at.

Day 172 – Tuesday 07th April 2009

I had a full day at work today, which is decent. Nothing much else to report. I am going to get an early night tonight because I have to get up at 04:30am in the morning to watch United v Porto in the UEFA Champions League.

Day 173 – Wednesday 08th April 2009

What a shocking game that has been today. I got up early, made breakfast consisting of scrambled eggs on toast and coffee. After 6 minutes Porto scored. We then scored 2, with our second coming on 86 minutes. Job done you think. But, 91 minutes, Porto popped one in. I was cursing the TV. So, I went back to be as I didn't have to be in work until 15:00. I took my 5-a side gear with me and dropped it off at Martin's on the way as he lives over the road from work.

Anyway, we turned up to play football and, if we won our game, we got to play for the Championship in the next game. We did and we won 6-1, thanks to a hat-trick from yours truly. But the second game was against a Japanese team we have lost to twice this season, with the first occurrence being on my debut. Technically, they are a better team but we defended really well and Martin managed to knick a goal for us on half-time – 1-0. We couldn't believe it. After playing the first game for 40 minutes, this game was scheduled to last 60 minutes and to keep a clean sheet for the whole first half in 5-a side was an achievement. Second half, Martin scored again followed by a great goal on the volley from them. 2-1. Then came the moment of luck I asked for as they got tired and we, due to my

Scottish grit, got stronger. The ball was kicked against me, which sent the ball ricocheting into the bottom corner of the net. I was then booked (again) as I lost the ball to a guy in a Liverpool shirt and I went in hard to tackle him after losing the ball. The ref said I was too aggressive in trying to win it back. Subconsciously I think I did it as he had a Scouse shirt on! To make up for it, I found a spot on the wing, skipped past one player and curled a shot into the far corner – Dennis Bergkamp –esque. It broke their spirits and we won the championship 4-1. Great news. We are having a weekend in Torquay to celebrate.

Day 174 – Thursday 09th April 2009

I think I have done something tonight I shouldn't have. Me and my pal Mark, the Irish lad from work, went out after work on a pub crawl to celebrate Easter as everything is shut tomorrow. Anyway, his girlfriend joined us and it was fine. We all went back, pissed up, to their house near the MCG and Mark passed out after too much weed. Me and his girlfriend were sat out the back and one thing led to another so to speak. I am not sure who initiated it. All I can remember is having to leave in a hurry with the rest being a blur. I am not even too sure how I got home but I think the Eureka Tower acted as a beacon for me to guide me home but I was outside the MCG for a while. It is funny how we conveniently forget things from a night out when we have done something wrong. Like the time at University I woke up and a huge road blockade was in my hallway. The way I see it – if I can't remember it, it didn't happen.

Day 175 – Friday 10th April 2009

Good Friday. I do miss Good Friday back home. It is the one day of the year everyone seems up for going out. It is worse today, considering I have got a huge hangover, which has led to the day being a write off, apart from nipping to McDonald's on Clarendon Street, next to my flat to get a hangover cure. I even ordered a pizza for tea as I could not be arsed cooking anything. My mind is wandering to back home, wondering what my family and friends are doing today. I'm also thinking about last night and my misdemeanours.

Day 176 – Saturday 11th April 2009

A night again spent in the casino, watching the football. I am sick of Liverpool fans. Anyway, they were on first and won 4-0 against Blackburn. When United came on afterwards v Sunderland, I was the only one there supporting United. So, when Sunderland equalized at the start of the second half, they were all up for it. But, 80 minutes, Macheda did it again and it cued over the top celebrations in the middle of the sports bar again. Get in.

Day 177 – Sunday 12th April 2009

Well... I am lying here on Easter Sunday listening to The Courteeners and wondering how my money will last for the rest of my travels. I am going to be fucked if they keep messing up my hours. I am relying on a tax rebate from work and have got Mum on the case. My guy at Flight Centre has been trying to get me a refund for the wrong flight from Caracas to Miami. That needs sorting! So, as it stands, I have no way of getting out of Venezuela at the moment. It is bullshit how different conglomerates affect your lives in so many ways and we just have to lie back and take it, rolling over like the dogs we keep as pets. Since I came to Australia, I have relented a little on my Anti-Capitalist stance but that is not to say it is still not in me. I am fully aware that my journal entries are less critical than they used to be. Just because that is the case, it does not mean I have lost my Socialist roots. As long as there remains injustice, these views will stay with me. As it is Easter Sunday, this is an appropriate phrase to use - 'I'll resurrect them when I get to South America.' Because that is the place, at the moment, where I want to be - to learn.

Day 178 – Monday 13th April 2009 – Easter Monday

I have been thinking a lot today about my dream of seeing Machu Picchu and if it falls within my monetary situation. Now, I could use my money I have in my ISA, which would do the job. That is what I have been thinking today. What's the point in it being in a savings account? Live today as if it were your last. What's the point in having money if you are not going to spend it? Going to Machu Picchu has been my dream ever since I read about Che Guevara going there on his Latin American journey, and then subsequently seeing it on The Motorcycle Diaries. Fulfilling dreams is important in life. I have never had many dreams. I just go along with things. But, on doing this trip, I am realising it is important to have them. Not just plans, but dreams. Things you wish to do before you die. No-one shares these ideas with me though. They just sit, listen and say 'I wish I could do something like that'. No-one will be there by my side to experience the beauty of a dream coming true. So, it is with a heavy heart I write a dream will come true, but it is a lonely one.

Day 179 – Tuesday 14th April 2009

A full day at work today, which, if I'm honest, is all I have to report. I am going to get up for the Chelsea v Liverpool game at 04:30am (supporting Chelsea obviously) and then go to work straight after. Mark has not returned to work since last Thursday – I hope it wasn't caused by my actions. I can see how an argument may have occurred between them two though.

Day 180 – Wednesday 15th April 2009

I did manage to get up for the football this morning and what a game it was. Chelsea 4-4 Liverpool. Now, usually I do not give the Scousers any credit because I hate their guts but they did their club and fans proud today. The 96 fans tragically killed at Hillsborough 20 years ago were not forgotten. As a United fan, all I can say is well done to the Scousers and their efforts deserved better. But, as always, I am glad they are out. Speaking of football, I played tonight and those Australian guys do not like how physical I play. They are so soft. The referees agree with them. But, I am not changing the way I play. Every ball has to be won and I give 100% - even if tonight was a friendly. Try getting some of these Aussies to play with some of the lads I have played with in Manchester. They'd have no chance. United v Porto in Portugal in the morning.

<u>Day 181</u> – Thursday 16th April 2009

United are the team for me. We did it. We beat Porto in Porto and became the first British club to win there. It was worth getting up at 04:30. Ronaldo scored the only goal from 40 yards. Probably the best he has ever scored. But, as usual when you are happy, some bastard tries ruining it for you. At the final whistle, Kenwar came in the lounge moaning. He got short shrift and I think he was put out when I told him it would only get worse when we play Arsenal in the semi-finals.

After that, I went to work and we were really busy today. No-one was going to bring me down today and I was on cloud 9. The flat situation is shit but I really do not care. I'm happy. I'm looking forward to South America. I want to travel forever.

<u>Day 182</u> – Friday 17th April 2009

What an eventful night it has been tonight. I went out to meet Ryan and Anna in Urban Central next door as a girl they met, Diana, when we were in Cairns is back over from Germany. At first, I thought that they were trying to set us up but I don't know if they were. Anyway, we did a few bars in town and Ryan and Anna went home leaving me and Diana out. So, we could only get in one place called The Joint at the bottom of Elizabeth Street. It all seemed friendly enough until Diana had to wait ages to go out for a smoke. The bouncer was letting other people out ahead of her and, because it was not a busy bar, I found this out of order. So, from the bar, I went over to where we were stood upstairs to have a polite word. To go out for a smoke, the bouncer had to unclip a rope for people to walk out onto the balcony. On asking, this prick who was smaller than me, refused. Then, being a gentleman, I unclipped the rope offering Diana to go outside. At this, the bouncer tried grabbing me by the throat and when that did not work, he called for backup. 3 huge bouncers grabbed me from behind and dragged me down the stairs, ripping my Politik shirt in the process. Outside, I thought the heavy handed tactics were over but another 2 large Indian guys jumped on top of me, dragging me to the ground and started putting the boot in. The coppers then showed up and whacked ME in handcuffs!! ME! This is the first time I've ever had handcuffs on me. I was fuming with the police asking why they put me in handcuffs when I was getting my head filled in. They said they were trying to restrain me as I looked agitated. I said to them 'that is the biggest bullshit I have heard. 4 guys are beating me up; I am bound to seem a little agitated'. Diana came outside to give a statement along with a group of guys who were in the bar and they all said that what happened to me was a disgrace, with one guy (a journalist) demanding that the coppers took the handcuffs off me. I thought about my Mum as this was happening. What would she think? That is what annoyed me. I was upset too when I saw my reflection in the shop window and I had blood running down my face. At first I thought it was from me and I was gutted as I was far too good looking for this. However, once the handcuffs were removed, it turned out to be the blood of someone else, which makes me feel a bit better. However, I have made a friend in Diana and we bought some beers and came back to my place.

Day 183 – **Saturday 18th April 2009**

I awoke today at 14:00 and proceeded to the police station opposite Melbourne City Library to make another statement and a complaint about the coppers on duty last night. I had one girl taking my statement who didn't know what to do (fair enough, she was new and people have got to start somewhere). But, the other lady giving help did not want to listen to a word I was saying. She kept telling me to tell her what happened in my own words, but proceeded to interrupt me all the time. The statement was typed up on a Word Document. It seemed so unprofessional and the girl doing it could not even spell (throat was a particular one she struggled with). Perhaps my attitude was a bit off but they really did take the piss out of me and I felt powerless to do anything about it.

Anyway, I met up with Diana tonight and we went for a meal up Brunswick Street with Anna and Ryan. We all agreed it was shit – poor service and poor food. My problem is that I compare every Italian to Nino's. Once we finished there and stopped off at a bar across the street, we made our way to Windsor to meet a group of lads who we met last night (when I got my head kicked in). It was one of their birthday parties and a whole bar was hosting it. They are such sound guys and they were really happy Diana and I made the effort. Ryan and Anna left after 2 drinks but Diana and I joined the birthday celebrations in a bar called Electric Lady Lounge on Chapel Street and we partied all night. At about 03:30am we got a taxi back to Urban Central but the two of us were by no means ready for bed. All that was open was a place called The Pit just around the corner, who at first wanted to charge us $15 to enter but, when we relented to pay, they let us in for free as it was now going on 04:30. We got a few pints in each and sat there watching Guns 'n' Roses Wembley gig on a large screen. Whenever I hear November Rain, Paradise City, Sweet Child 'o' Mine and Knockin On Heaven's Door, I will think of Diana. We seem to click and get on really well.

Day 184 – **Sunday 19th April 2009 – Meet Constantine**

This afternoon Florian and I went to a bar where he works at Port Melbourne to watch the F1. Naturally, I wanted Button to win and Flo, being a German guy, wanted Vettel to win. Vettel did win and we enjoyed it with a platter of tapas food and a few beers. It was nice to sit by the port overlooking the ships coming and going. Maybe I will get on one of them to Visit Tasmania or Penguin island (Phillip Island). Anyway, I was then on the beer for the day! We got knocked out of the FA Cup tonight at Wembley by Everton after a 0-0 draw. I watched it with Diana in her hostel and she introduced me to her friend she met in Cairns – Constantine. He is a quality guy and so funny, to the point I nearly cried. Even though he is not a big fan of football, he stayed up to watch the game, which I thought was nice. He is a Greek fella and is absolutely mental so I'm glad I've made a new mate.

Day 185 – Monday 20th April 2009

What food we feasted upon tonight. Constantine took Diana and I to a little Greek restaurant on Johnston Street (not too far from where I work) called Jim's Greek Tavern, where we ate course after course of probably the best food I have tasted. Dips, lamb, calamari, octopus, scallops. Some of the finest food I have tasted and I am glad I've met a mate who is into his food as much as I am. What a guy he is. I didn't make it into work as I was done in from last night but I got a phone call from the copper who whacked me in handcuffs on Friday and he said they won't be charging anyone.

Day 186 – Tuesday 21st April 2009

Back to work today and it has felt like quite a long day. I have not achieved much at all. I am off to bed early now as I am getting up to watch the football in the casino. Liverpool v Arsenal. Still no sign of my workmate Mark – I think he has left. Oh dear. My fault? Maybe.

Day 187 – Wednesday 22nd April 2009

I awoke very early to go to the casino to watch the match and what a classic. It was another 4-4 draw involving the Scousers and I have to give them credit. Arsenal too for that matter – especially Andrei Arshavin who scored all Arsenal's 4 goals. The most important match takes place tomorrow. We play Portsmouth at home and need to win.

Work was work and I am getting sick of these callers who phone up and treat you like a piece of shit they have just stepped in. It is happened a lot and all I wonder is where has the decency gone in the world. OK, the job I am doing may not be as important as some jobs, but I deserve to be spoken to with respect. Balls to them.

Day 188 – Thursday 23rd April 2009

I got up ridiculously early for the match but we won 2-0 so we are back to the top of the league. The day into tonight remained largely uneventful. It is only 20:30 and I am going to go to bed because I am shot.

Day 189 – Friday 24th April 2009

After work, I went out to a Vietnamese restaurant with Sarah from work and we are pretty close but we both called it a night early after one drink in a bar before things could lead anywhere. I think we agreed there may be far too many complications even though we both wanted to. I spoke to Hu when I got home shortly before midnight and I convinced him that the hole in the wall was not me. This hole appeared last week and no-one is taking responsibility although I think it was Sunil as Hu told me Nimesh mentioned something to him. I am going to bed now. I enjoyed my meal with Sarah and I think we'll hook up before I leave Melbourne.

<u>Day 190</u> – Saturday 25th April 2009

Oh no! It has happened again. I had another seizure today.

I got a call from Constantine about 15:00 asking if I fancied going out for some food in town. So, we went to a little Vietnamese place on Swanson Street – which is the main street in Melbourne running down to federation Square and Flinders Street Station. Constantine went to order some rice cakes as we were still hungry after our Vermicelli but realised he had no cash and he nipped out to get some as they would not accept card payment. By the time he came back, I was lying on the couch with a nurse with me (who had been in the restaurant at the time). The ambulance had blocked the main street in Melbourne and a huge commotion was caused as a result. If you are going to cause a scene, at least make it a good one. Lucky. I knew nothing of this until I came around in hospital about 30 minutes later. The paramedics asked me questions like what year it is and what month to which I could not answer. However, I guessed at the date and got it right! Constantine said that I was trying to chat up the 40 year old paramedic – even in my state of unconsciousness I never stop. Anyway, Constantine was great and he stayed with me at the hospital until 22:00 when I was discharged. We sat there for about 5 hours chatting up the nurses and at this point we really seemed to bond. I was wrecked though and my Epilim levels in my blood were quite low indicating I have forgotten to take my medication, which is true. Epilepsy is something I never thought I would have but it is times at this you want to be at home. At the same time, worse things could've happened to me and I am glad Constantine knew about my condition (luckily I told him last week). Anyway, I was gutted it happened again and we headed back to see Diana at Urban Central. They advised me to go to bed but I wanted a beer and I wanted to watch the football, which was not on until about 04:00am. We were playing Spurs at Old Trafford. I'll admit I was stupid and stayed up with Constantine and Diana. It looked like things were getting worse when we were 2-0 down at half-time but we clawed it back in the second half and won 5-2. I then went to bed even though I could not muster up much energy to celebrate this excellent result and an excellent game.

<u>Day 191</u> – Sunday 26th April 2009

I spoke to Mum tonight to let her know of thee seizure. She was worried, as is to be expected but she was insisting, as were the Doctor's, that I take my medication.

Anyway, I went out tonight to do a couple of bars with Diana, Ryan, Anna Constantine and a mutual friend of ours, Giovanni from Milan. It was a multi-national affair and probably the greatest rivalry came from Ryan and me as we argued between Leeds and Manchester. Naturally the Leeds side of the argument did not have a leg to stand on! But it was all good fun and Ryan is probably my best mate here in Melbourne.

Day 192 – Monday 27th April 2009

We have started part-time hours at work this week, which is a total ball-ache because we all need the money. But, part-time is better than no time. I am feeling really tired at the moment due to my seizure the other day. This one has whacked me more than the others did but I will not succumb to this. So, in that frame of mind, tonight I joined Constantine, Flo, Chris (Flo's mate) and Diana for a quiz night next door in Urban Central but we were awful and still Stephen Hawkings Football Boots does not win a prize for best name - again!! It was all good fun.

Day 193 – Tuesday 28th April 2009

So, Diana has gone over to Auckland, New Zealand today and I am fucking glad because having her around has tired me out!! I am obviously only joking as I love her to bits and she is a really nice girl. We will definitely keep in touch. I do not know what it is about German people but I seem to get on with them really well. First, the German girls from Hamburg at University who I still speak to, Flo my German flatmate and now Diana. I wish I could say the same for the guys from India.

I was shattered tonight so I decided to take an early night. I have got to get up early for the Doctor's tomorrow to go over my epilepsy problems.

Day 194 – Wednesday 29th April 2009

So, I went to the Doctor's this morning and it still annoys me that in Australia we have to pay $68 for seeing the Doctor (every visit). It is something we take for granted so much in the UK – the right to a free visit to the Doctor. Anyway – for the 5 minutes it lasted, he told me it was probably due to me not taking my medication. Amazing – 6 years of medical school and $68 to tell me something I already know.

But, afterwards, I treated myself to a KFC and felt like a fat Yankee afterwards. I could not play football tonight due to work commitments and Martin and I agreed over the phone that the team will probably fall apart without me! I am off to bed now because I need to get up early for United v Arsenal in the Champions League Semi-final at 04:30am.

Day 195 – Thursday 30th April 2009

Flo and I woke this morning at 04:00am for the match. I decided to cook us both a sausage and egg sandwich to put us on for it. However, cooking the fried egg proved a little tricky as someone in the flat has hidden the frying pan. Look at the daft idiots I have to live with. Undeterred, I improvised with a hot plate those Indian's use to make Japati's on and we were cooking on gas – literally!! We then went to the casino to meet my mate Ian from football but, unfortunately for him, he is an Arsenal fan. We couldn't decide whether to get a pint in but decided to do the drinking in the second leg. He was good natured, especially considering his team was shit and we ran out easy 1-0 winners. We should have won by more but a win with a clean sheet at this stage is important.

So, that was that and then I headed to work for my 4 hour shift. I don't know how much longer it will last if I am honest. But, I am grateful for money coming in at the moment. The night was just spent chilling out and I am off to bed – early!!

Day 196 – Friday 01st May 2009

I'm feeling melancholic at the moment. It is as if I am questioning why I have come away and, if it existed, the motivation I had when I first started travelling. I did have these idyllic dreams when I first came away. I am not too sure what I thought I was going to achieve. I wanted my trip to be different. To be a changing experience. In a way it is. But, in another it is just the same as the other people's trips and it is not different at all – even though it is. I have seemed to have lost that force that was driving me all along – the need to make a change. All I seem to be doing here at the moment is acting like all the other people – that is doing anything to survive. So, I do not know how I feel at the moment. But, now I look around, I see I am just the same as everyone else.

Day 197 – Saturday 02nd May 2009

I had another one of my moments today where I decided I needed to buy something – a camera this time. So, off I ventured into town and bought one, which happened to be the same as the one that was stolen from me in Sydney. I only paid $50 for it so I can now take photos of the rest of my trip.

Tonight, I went to watch the Middlesbrough v United match at the casino and we ran out easy 2-0 winners and took a step closer to the title. For a guy on his own, I was naturally full of it in the casino sports bar but many Aussies (in there for AFL) liked this as I showed balls and a lot of passion for my team so we got drunk on Carlton beer and had a good time.

Day 198 – Sunday 03rd May 2009

I cannot believe my laptop is wrecked. It is totally done in. Hu tried to repair it on Friday but all he did was to update it with a shit version of Windows. So, now, I think I'll have to take it to a laptop repair shop on Clarendon Street to see what they can make of it. My meagre budget is taking another hammering.

Me and an Indian lad, Gary, went to join Constantine for pool tonight. Now, when I first met this lad and he told me his name it reminded me of the Only Fools and Horses Episode when they managed to find an asylum seeker in their truck and called him 'Gary.' How I kept my face from breaking out with laugher I will never know. It was on the tip of a very long day drinking for me and Constantine, as he phoned about 10:45am saying he was off to watch the Ricky Hatton v Manny Pacquaio boxing fight. Anyway, I met him in town and he was with 2 lads – one called Mark from Crewe who is a quality lad and some other lad called Graham from the Wirral. However, nowhere was showing it. Anyway, we were tipped of that a place in Port Melbourne would be showing it so, after nipping into a pokies to put a bet on, the 4 of us jumped in a cab to a pub called The Local. I had Ricky Hatton to win in either round 9 or round 11, which served me really well in Cairns. I was confident. I was only going to have one pint but that went downhill straight after Ricky got knocked out in Round 2. A lot of Filipino's were in the bar cheering on the Pac-Man and we had no argument. Constantine's consoling words of 'you're boy got smashed' didn't do much to cheer me up. I really like Ricky Hatton but he has gone too far now. He can't live with these boys. However, Graham and I were happy to be in a boozer selling pints after Mark went home complaining of a hangover. Graham was trying to kill time until he went to Cairns tonight so the 3 of us stayed out on a session. We headed to Transport Bar on Federation Square and the 3 of us took a liking to the lead singer of a live band who was playing. She was cute and, naturally when they stopped for a break, the 3 of us made our moves. Funnily enough, she took a liking to yours truly more than the other two, much to the annoyance of Constantine who sees himself as a ladies man even though he is about 2ft tall! The lad from Greece also tried his best at keeping up with Graham and I in the drinking stakes, but, bless him, he couldn't. It was a good day.

Day 199 – Monday 04th May 2009

I took a day off work today due to my activities yesterday. It wasn't my fault as work never informed me had hours for today, although the agency apparently tried calling me 7 times and left 3 voicemail messages to tell me what time I needed to start. However, my phone was conveniently on silent and when I stirred out of my pit at mid-day I found the messages. So, I called Jenny at Hallis and charmed her into believing my tale and I have full hours for this week – starting tomorrow!! I have taken to not worrying about money (yet) but it may be getting near that stage. I'm enjoying it too much.

Day 200 – Tuesday 05th May 2009

Not a day that will particularly inspire the emotions. I remember one person saying to me that they feel they have achieved nothing in comparison to what I am doing but, as yet, I do not feel I have achieved anything. Maybe, on returning to my homeland, one day I will sit back and reflect but the journey is not nearly at an end. Every man wants to inspire others but what is the point if he cannot inspire himself?

Day 201 – Wednesday 06th May 2009

I got up at 04:30am and made my way over to the casino to meet Ian to watch United v Arsenal UEFA Champions League semi-final second leg. For an Arsenal fan, Ian was optimistic. We ran out easy 3-1 winners and won 4-1 on aggregate. We were 2-0 up in 20 minutes and, maybe I should've showed more decorum in front of my mate, but I went crazy! I stopped short at taunting him but it was unbelievable. I bought a beer or two as well and, Ian who was up for a pint before the match started, didn't bother as he sank deeper into his chair. But, at work today after the game, I started to miss home. I started thinking about my family and friends back in Manchester making plans to watch the Final on the 27th May and I want to be there!! Last year's final in Manchester was one of the best nights of my life and any United fan who was in Manchester that night would totally agree!

Day 202 – Thursday 07th May 2009

I think I slept about 13 hours last night. I went to bed about 20:00 I think as I was completely exhausted. I even forgot about 5-a side but, at work today, Martin told me they lost for the second week in a row. Is it a coincidence that I am not playing?

But, I found out today that the European Cup Final will be contested between us and Barcelona who knocked out Chelsea with a last minute goal today. A bit lucky I heard but that is football. I was sprightlier at work today than yesterday. Sarah from work has asked me around to her flat (again) and a man can do little but imagine what for. Any other time, I would be there but the stories of bed bugs that are infesting her flat are putting me off slightly!!! Not a good way to seduce a man.

Day 203 – Friday 08th May 2009

Flo had the night off work tonight so I took him on a pub crawl around Melbourne. Anyway, we were sat in PJ O'Brien's on the side of the Yarra when I got chatted up by a 50 year old woman who talked constantly about her Grandchildren and the fact that 'she hadn't had a bit since November?' This revelation nearly caused me to vomit profusely although being as diplomatic as ever, I said 'November? What? Grandchildren? Bye-bye'. Needless to say, Flo and I made a hasty exit and I went on the hunt for younger prey and, preferably, someone who doesn't need to take out their false teeth before going to sleep.

When we returned, we found Hu the landlord has not been again to collect the rent. I am losing patience with that guy, I really am. He thinks he can just turn up when he wants to but balls to it. Work was its usual self. I was left in until 19:00 with a mate of Sarah's – another Irish girl called Ashleigh. Turns out me and her are going for a drink tomorrow so I am not too sure how Sarah will take that but I told Ashleigh not to mention it.

Day 204 – Saturday 09th May 2009

I have not really achieved much today, which is a bit of a disappointment. At least my laptop is fixed now, although it did cost me $115. But, after a few drinks tonight, which I mentioned yesterday, I slipped away to check on the Celtic v Rangers game and Celtic lost 1-0. I went over to the Charles Dickens to meet my mate Martin from work who was watching Leeds lose 1-0 to Millwall in the play-offs. I was trying to watch the Celtic game, which was also on but I was stood amongst 100 pissed-up Leeds fans that were getting aggressive. They sang the disgusting chants about Munich and Martin knew this annoyed me (even though he didn't sing the songs). I didn't say anything for fear of getting my head kicked in although, when Millwall scored and it was 1-0 I did have a huge smile and the attention was directed away from me and onto the 4 Millwall fans at the front of the pub who went crazy. A riot nearly ensued.

Day 205 – Sunday 10th May 2009

What a night. I headed to the Charles Dickens Tavern on Collins Street with Martin, Ian and Constantine to watch the Manchester Derby. Finding a pub this time was not as eventful as on Magnetic Island. Before we left, Constantine and I shared a jug of beer in Urban Central and then we went to meet Martin and Ian. They wanted City to win, just to wind me up but it was all good humoured. Constantine had to stop for food (naturally) and then once the match started he had never seen anything like it. As soon as I got there and got us a pint in, I knew the place needed a kick up the arse. So, I stood up and started singing, which didn't go down too well with the bitters and the scousers wanting City to win but it did with the United fans and, from there, the atmosphere was electric. It was a great night and we ran out 2-0 winners.

This afternoon, I met Ryan and Anna at Transport Bar for a few drinks and they are a really nice couple. I am glad to have made 2 nice friends. Ryan wanted to come out tonight, but Anna was against it so he had to keep her sweet.

Day 206 – Monday 11th May 2009

It is Wes' birthday today so I sent him an e-mail with my birthday wishes. I was in work today from 12:30-19:00 and I want more hours.

Tonight, I am just chilling out in my flat thinking about the days gone by and what I have achieved. It makes you reflect on how lucky you are – or how lucky I am.

Day 207 – Tuesday 12th May 2009

Flo and I went to watch the film Defiance tonight. It is about a group of Belarusian people who fight back in the forests against the Nazi's in WWII. It was strange to watch it with Flo who is German. Not in a bad way, but it was interesting sitting down for a coffee afterwards and hearing his account of things. He had ancestors who suffered greatly too. That is the thing that escapes a lot of people – a lot of German's died and suffered too during that war, caused by fascist pigs. I am just happy to be on the left-wing, socialist side of the divide.

On having a coffee in the gold-star lounge at the cinema (which do good Latte's), the Barista took a shining to me, actually remembering what I usually have and the fact that I am from Manchester in UK. We got chatting but, short at asking her out, she seemed a little young for me. I told Flo to fill his boots as she is the perfect age for him but that was dead in the water.

Day 208 - Wednesday 13th May 2009

"Some people make money, others make history" Tony Wilson

I have just returned from playing football and I managed to grab a brace. Not to be big-headed but I am the only one holding that team together!

I had a disastrous piece of news tonight. Dad phoned me up, before I left for football, to say that they had received an invoice for me for $900 for the ambulance ride from the Vietnamese Noodle House, 5 minutes up the road to St. Vincent's Hospital. That is absolutely ridiculous. I can't afford it – simple as that, so the insurance will have to cover it. But, like I have said for years, we take the NHS for granted so much in the UK. I'll never pay privately. It is something I will take from 'Mr. Manchester' himself – the late Tony Wilson. The NHS is one of the best services in the world and it is something, as British people, we should be proud of - at least when they are providing the right services instead of purely cosmetic services. At least we, in the UK, are not like the US where they check your wallet before they check your pulse.

Day 209 - Thursday 14th May 2009

I had a chat with Nicole at work, who is from Chicago, US and she echoed my sentiments about the US healthcare system saying that you are pretty much fucked if you do not have health insurance. She was pretty impressed by my knowledge of American Politics and told me if I ever went to Chicago, I should give her a call and she'll show me around. I'll bear that in mind. It's a pity her boyfriend is knocking about because she's hot. She's got the whole Latin Vibe going on with her surname being Suarez and that seems to appeal to me. Anyway, we have a cracking group at work. Nicole seems to get it rough from the customers when they hear her accent but it is to be expected. I told her as much – "Nicole, the reason people have a go at you more than the rest of us, is because you have a Yankee accent." She took no off offence to this, laughed and agreed with me.

I was awoken awfully early today as I had to go to the Casino to watch United v Wigan at the JJB. After we went, 1-0 down, our nerves were frayed. The other guys from Manchester were as nervous as me.

However, we won 2-1 with a late Michael Carrick goal sealing it. Cue mayhem between me and 2 other lads from Manchester – we'd never met before but that is what football does. That is the league in the bag now. All we need is a point against Arsenal on Saturday night. I can't wait. So, I have been buzzing my head off all day at work as a result of the football. It's brilliant but I miss home all the same.

Day 210 – Friday 15th May 2009

God. It all kicked off tonight. Well, I'll tell the story. I left for work this morning at 09:30 and, before I left, I made sure the kitchen was tidy – spotless. Friday's are my cleaning up day so fair enough. Everything was perfect and that was it I thought. No problems. After work, I picked up some beers and headed around to Constantine's where we enjoyed a civilized evening eating pasta, followed by cheese and wine, forgetting completely about my beers. It was nice and we had a good chat about things. He is one of the best guys I have ever met. At one point, however, it was a bit too girly as he was sat there practicing on a Manikin dolls head, doing some sort of blow wave hair style because he is a hairdresser (or) 'stylist' as he puts it!! I told him to put it away and we got onto talking about past conquests etc.

So, it came to 00:15 and I had to leave Constantine's who lived 2 minutes away, and return to my flat to give Hu his rent. So, with a hug for Constantine for the wine, cheese and pasta I headed home, happy and my belly full after a civilized night. Upon arriving home, Hu was stood in the kitchen with his family, and all the Indian lad's were knocking about. I gave him the money and he said 'Alistair. You haven't cleaned.' The kitchen was full of bin bags etc and curry and loads of shit scattered over the floor. It was like a bomb had hit it. Sunil and Bobby (a specky twat) just stood there smirking. They had obviously done it to set me up. I was raging. It is a good job I only had a little drink tonight as I would've bitten somebody's nose off I was that angry! So, I told Hu, forcefully, I did clean up this morning before I went to work. Then I stormed off for a walk around the block for 10 minutes to clear my head and the angry thoughts. I came back and Hu had a quiet word telling me to explain what happened. I said I do not need to explain myself to you. I know it is that specky Indian lad Bobby's fault. If I am still mad in the morning, I will smack him for sure. He's overstepped the mark now and some people just need to learn a lesson.

Day 211 - Saturday 16th May 2009

I confronted Bobby today and warned him not to piss me about. I pushed him into the fridge and then I grabbed him and pulled him to give him a punch but he fell helplessly to the ground. As I stood over him, ready to give him a smack, I saw the helplessness in his eyes and the fear on his face and, for the first time in my life, I knew what it was like to show mercy. I was ready for giving him a kicking but I took the moral high ground and let him off with a warning, storming off out to find peace in the city.

I do not want to dwell on him anyway because we won the Premier League tonight after we got the point we needed against Arsenal – we drew 0-0. We celebrated in the Charles Dickens Tavern and, for a second for me and my mate Mark, we could've been back in Manchester, all enjoying it together. A load of us from Manchester are going to also meet up for the Champions League Final next week. I am looking forward to that.

To celebrate, me, Mark and a few other strangers headed down Chapel Street to find some skirt. However, our chances were scuppered hugely by the consumption of beer and our singing of United songs, which only seemed to attract the wrong sort!

Day 212 – Sunday 17th May 2009

I went around to Constantine's about 16:30 as it his birthday. We sat and ate some cheese, drank wine and decided upon what to do. I bought him a card and he seemed to appreciate it as he hasn't had one this year. Anyway, around 19:00 we decided to head into the city for a few drinks. We went to some really cool bars we know – places you would not know existed, tucked away down some piss alleyway where you just see a random door and, for a moment, the world does not exist. We sat atop a rooftop bar called Cookie, and all that looked down on us were the tops of a few skyscrapers. It was cool and I enjoyed it. It's what makes Melbourne different and, for me anyway, the greatest Westernised City in the world.

Day 213 – Monday 18th May 2009

I think I missed my Neurology appointment this morning. Too bad. Not the best thing to miss as St. Vincent's Hospital is only a ride away on the 112 tram, which passes my apartment. I can't believe it has been 2 years since I had my first seizure.

So, I got into work for 11:00 and have had the usual calls and all the nonsense that involves. People ask me what I would do if I was them concerning their shares. Although I can't answer, I want to say 'Sell them. Go and do something worthwhile like volunteering in a developing nation. Don't accumulate more money than what you need. A man only needs so much and the rest is for showing off'. But I can't say that... or can I?

Day 214 – Tuesday 19th May 2009

I am just thinking about that comment yesterday – 2 years since my first seizure. If it wasn't for that seizure, I would not be sat here in Melbourne writing this. I would not have been to Namibia, walked with lions, slept out with Cheetah's, walked baboons, scuba dived the Great Barrier Reef. So, when people say to me 'are you bothered you have epilepsy? I say 'No. Because this condition has forced me to do things that some people do not get the chance to do'. Life is too short. I am now grateful for every minute. It is crazy in a way how something like that can make you start living.

Tonight, Flo and I went to the cinema to watch Angels & Demons. I still think the barista serving me my Latte fancies me as she remembers my name, flirted a lot and was really interested tonight in Manchester. She is a nice enough looking girl but, as I said a week or two ago, a little young for me.

Day 215 – Wednesday 20th May 2009

7 Days to go until the Champions League Final. I wish I was back in Manchester for it – just for one night then come back here to Melbourne because I could live here. Hopefully, it'll be good over here all the same.I played 5-a side tonight and we won 8-4 thanks to another hat-trick from me. A girl called Jan who comes to watch us is pretty hot and it seems to inspire me. I've taken a shine to her and I think the feelings are mutual and we've planned the weekend away to Torquay this weekend so, if she is there, we'll see how it progresses. She is my type – black hair, pretty face etc. She is a friend of my mate John Ho's girlfriend, unattached, so we'll watch this space.

Day 216 – Thursday 21st May 2009

Tonight has been quite an eventful night if I am honest. I worked until 19:00 and by the time I got home, cooked a meal and washed up, it was nearly 21:00. So, then Constantine calls me saying today was his 'name day'. Greeks have a name day apparently. But I thought it was any excuse to have a beer but he assured me it wasn't!! So, we met up and headed into the city. We headed to our favourite bar called Section 8. We were hitting the Peroni's and enjoying how it felt to sit on a barrel under the patio heaters in this back street bar we loved. So, a girl takes a shine to Constantine and we got chatting, with me sat next to her mate (an obnoxious 20 year old art student). Anyway, Constantine and her mate got on pretty well but this other one just turned to me and said 'by the way, if you think anything is going to happen, I am a lesbian'. What could you say to that? Well, I said 'What makes you think I am interested in you darling?' She didn't like that, probably because she was a feminist. She rated 2 points higher on the feminist index than Germaine Greer.

Conversation at this point was stinted. I had to go one step further and said 'I do not like girls with tattoos anyway' as she had one on her back saying Tyson. She told me that was a depressing story why she had the tattoo to which I, clearly not interested now as it was going nowhere, said 'OK. Don't tell me then.' She then proceeded to tell me anyway how it was about her dead friend who had died 6 months ago, which went on for 30 minutes (probably to get shot of her as a mate). I needed to leave and, when it came to chucking out time, this was it. I was shooting off home ASAP but the others tried blagging me to go to a bar – especially Constantine as he wanted to get lucky tonight. I informed him that if I did, I would end up killing myself as this girl is a raging nutter. We parted and I came home.But, about 10 minutes into arriving home, I got a call from Constantine who went on to another bar with them. After I left, he found out (in his words) 'what a dickhead' she was and he ditched them too by saying he was going to the bathroom but running out of a fire exit. He said I must have the patience of a saint for putting up with her for 30 minutes.

Day 217 – Friday 22nd May 2009

We had a fun night tonight at my mate Rob's beach house in Torquay – a quaint little seaside town on the Southeast Coast of Australia. He picked me up from work and, along with Martin, Ian and Mike, we made our way down to the beach house around 19:00pm. By the time we arrived everyone was already there so we spent the night drinking and I managed to meet a few more decent Aussies. In particular I found the time to make my move with Jan, the girl I like who comes to watch us play football. I like her and she likes me – for sure.

Martin had a few too many glasses of goon and was, let's say, ill in the sink downstairs throwing up the goon he'd consumed. So Jan helped put him to bed to which he said to her 'If you ever get tired later, there's plenty of room in here'. She agreed she'd had better offers and we all took a laugh at Martin's expense. Everyone seemed to drift off to bed early, leaving the window open for me and Jan to stay up having a 'good time'. Apparently, her and her family are off to the MCG tomorrow to watch the AFL and she invited me along. I said 'thanks,' gave her my number but I won't be going – I don't do parents!! We concluded that Rob's house is smashing for a weekend away.

Day 218 – Saturday 23rd May 2009

We all woke this morning and I was surprised at how many people were ill last night. I wasn't one of them, however. A couple of guys went for a surf but I remained in bed as it was far more appealing. But, when we all got up, the job was to get a shower, have breakfast and then to clear up. Martin did the scrambled eggs with a hangover and Emma did the rest. It was OK and the worst part, as with all parties, was the tidying up. After that was done, a game of football was organised – Pommies v Aussies. The Aussies had 1 more than us at first but when the teams were levelled after the first half with scores at 4-1 to them, we took control thanks to a superb solo goal by me, which was started by a little Cruyff turn on the line, a nutmeg and a cool finish. We then recovered and won an absorbing game 5-4 with Martin knocking in the winning goal – taking it off my foot. We celebrated together on defeating the Aussies!!

As most people were hungover, we headed back and Rob dropped me off at my flat around 16:30. I put a pizza in the oven and basically stayed in the flat until 23:00. Nimesh has stated his surprise that tonight, on a Saturday night, I am actually in and not out as always. Football season has ended!

Day 219 – Sunday 24th May 2009

Flo and I went to the Charles Dickens Tavern tonight to watch the last day of the season in the Scottish Premier League and the Monaco Grand Prix. Rangers won the league and Jenson Button won the F1. Anyway, it turns out that this pub is showing the Champions League Final on Wednesday night so that is where I will end up.

Apart from that, today has been uneventful. I managed to muster enough effort to go to the gym though.

Day 220 – Monday 25th May 2009

One more down before the Champions League Final. I managed to get up Ok this morning but for what? All the stupid calls? People do not listen. They ring up for advice and then interrupt you through your part of the conversation. It is a really rude thing these Aussie's have going on.

Day 221 – Tuesday 26th May 2009

It would have been Sir Matt Busby's 100th birthday today and what a fitting way for us to be in the Champions League Final. The fridge is stocked up with our beer and we are looking forward to it. It is going to be a great night but I wish I was back home in Manchester for one night only!! With family and friends watching the match together.

Day 222 – Wednesday 27th May 2009

Well – work seemed to take ages to finish today but, once it did, I rushed home to make tea and then went out to play football. The other team didn't show, giving us a 3-0 victory by default. But, all this was just delaying time until the Champions League Final. So, I went to Safeway to get some nibbles. Most people I know are going to get up for it but Flo and I were staying up drinking beer! At 01:00am we went to the hostel next door to play pool and enjoy a few beers with Marc from Crewe. At about 02:00 we went to the casino for a beer and then I said we should whack $40 on red at the roulette table. We did, and won but Flo pocketed the money!! Cheeky. But, that paid for our beers and then we walked over to the Charles Dickens pub but it was too full and we were turned away at the door. So, we headed back to the casino and the bouncer nearly didn't let me in as my t-shirt said 'That is Jesus. He just thinks he is George Best.' The bouncer said it could cause offence and everyone agreed he was being a dickhead.

So, the match started with us pretty tanked up on rocket fuel by this time and we did not turn up. We were outplayed for most of it and lost 2-0. The thing that annoyed me more was all the foreign United fans who do not know a thing about the club or its history, then proceed to slag us off because Barcelona are world class. I am gutted.

Day 223 – Thursday 28th May 2009

The day was a washout after last night's result. I am still gutted we did not turn up. I got up at 16:30 and headed to KFC, which was unhealthy. Then, tonight, I needed a milkshake so I went to the BP garage to get one. That is about as eventful as it got apart from people calling me to wind me up about the result.

Day 224 – Friday 29th May 2009

I am glad I am finished for the weekend and I have the whole flat to myself tonight. I asked Sarah around for a bit and I told Hu that I am moving out on the 24th June 2009. I actually went after work to book a flight to Sydney but the JetStar system at Flight Centre on Clarendon Street was down – so I'll go back tomorrow. I also need to get some contact lenses tomorrow too and some extra writing material. Work seemed to go pretty quickly today and I cannot believe I only have 3 weeks left here in the great city of Melbourne. I have just settled and found a nice work/social life balance. Maybe today went quick because all I did was try to book hostels and I did manage to find a decent one in Santiago. I stay at the wake-up hostel in Sydney and then I booked one in the bohemian area of Santiago de Chile called Bella Vista. I am looking forward to the next step now.

Day 225 – Saturday 30th May 2009

I had a rush of blood to the head today and I decided it would be a good idea to spend nearly all my money. But, it was not on frivolous items as would happen back home. Firstly, I bought a flight to Sydney on 24th June 2009 for just before I go to Chile. It needed to be bought so now is the best time of any to do it and it cost me $108. I then walked into the city, via the beautiful Yarra River to an optician where I needed contact lenses. The girl told me they could not sell me contact lenses as they needed to test my eyes. Not wanting to waste money on an eye test, I charmed her into letting me buy the lenses I needed without an eye test. She took mercy on my story about travelling and let me have my purchase. Tonight, my friend Martin was having a party for his birthday at his house. However, it would have been a little tricky as Jan would be in attendance and a repeat visit is not on the cards so I chose to conveniently lose my phone for the night.

Day 226 – Sunday 31st May 2009

I had to lie to a friend today, which is not something I like. It was Martin's birthday last night but, like I said, I could not be arsed going so I told Martin today I got waylaid in town, even though I just stayed in and had an early night. Anyhow, I went out early evening with Ryan, Constantine, Anna and Flo. We just whipped the froth off a few beers and went back to the flat. I do not fancy work tomorrow but it is only going to last another 2 weeks, then I will be living my dream in South America. I think even as a child it was always my dream to visit South America. When you see that continent represented on films, it always looked so colourful and vibrant. The scare stories American media will have you believe just make it seem all the more appealing.

Day 227 – Monday 01st June 2009

1 day to go until my birthday and it is the first time I will be away from home. But, today, I felt a little bit done in, perhaps due to the activities of yesterday evening. I am getting really sick and tired of work now and I just keep looking forward to getting back on the road. I am just kicking my heels here now. I am apprehensive of the next move but that is only natural – I was the same before I went to Africa. But, what separates me from others, is that I know what I am doing is right.

Chapter 12 – Welcome to a Quarter of a Century

Day 228 – Tuesday 02nd June 2009

25 today. It is my first birthday I have spent away from home – away from my family and friends. It feels a little strange if truth be told. The day started by getting up early for work and Nimesh, from Nepal, gave me a handshake and a hug. I opened the card from Mum and Dad whilst eating my breakfast. It did make me realise how important family is and, also, people seem to still be asking about me, which is nice. It is always nice to know you have not been forgotten. Anyway, I took my card into work and placed it on my desk while I worked. Sarah came over to wish me Happy Birthday and the day went OK.

Once I got home with a 6 pack of beer, I made myself steak & chips for my tea. Flo and I then went to Urban Central to meet Constantine in the bar. Marc, my mate from Crewe, bought me a black sambuca as a birthday present, which reminded me of my 21st birthday in Manchester (5 of us drank 3 bottles of the stuff). We went to meet the rest of my mates in Transport Bar on Federation Square. We got there at 20:35 and waiting there were Ryan and Anna – and Martin. Meredith showed up at 21:30 with her friend, (even though we arranged to meet around 20:30). She stayed for a drink and then fucked off. She hardly said a word to the group and informed me she hadn't been in touch because she thought I was angry with her. I haven't spoken to her in a while as I thought she was off travelling. Anyway, she left without making an effort with any of my friends so balls to it. Just before she left, my friend Giovanni from Milan arrived and stayed out with us. We proceeded to a bar called The Lounge and then everyone decided to call it a night. Constantine and I went to Urban Central bar for a last pint and then we called it a night.

Day 229 – Wednesday 03rd June 2009

I felt OK this morning when I got up for work so I didn't mind going in. However, over the course of the day, I gradually felt worse and became drained more and more. By the end of it, I could not wait to leave. An early night was in store for me! I do not know why I drink sometimes. People all over the world find new and exotic ways of inebriation but I still do not know why. Maybe it's to forget or to change into another person they want to be. Whatever the reason, I am no good at work after a night on the booze. It's just something I have to face up to.

Day 230 –Thursday 04th June 2009

I was going to go to the gym tonight but instead I just sat around and watched T.V. It is amazing how I only have 20 days left in Melbourne and I would definitely find a way of staying here if I was not moving on to South America. It does not seem 2 minutes ago since I arrived with Mark at Southern Cross Station on the Greyhound Bus but, on reflection, it has been 6 months. 6 months!! Melbourne is a cool city but I am ready to leave now. The time is right for South America.

Day 231 – Friday 05th June 2009

I did not really want to go out tonight but Marc said he was just going to enjoy a box of goon at his hostel next door so I called around there and spent around $30 on beer as well as the goon. It was fun and, for the night, we seemed to rule the bar. We put Manchester tunes on the jukebox and it seemed to remind us both of back home on a Friday night down a local boozer. That is what sometimes used to happen and I think that is my idea of a good night. A few beers, some good music with good mates and a laugh. We now have a long Bank Holiday Weekend here in Australia as it is the Queen's Birthday. It is amazing they celebrate the Queen's Birthday but we do not in Britain. Amazing. My dream is to celebrate the day we become a Republic and not a Monarchy. I have been slated in the past for saying this and those fools who claim that the Royal Family bring in a lot of money to the British Economy are wrong. They take far more out than they put in. One can only dream about a republic – for now.

Day 232 – Saturday 06th June 2009

I woke up a little rough today following last night's activities so I made a monster fry-up. Flo is laid up pretty bad with the flu thing he has had and he even went for tests yesterday for swine flu. To give him some peace and quiet, I nipped out for a few hours to take in Melbourne in a new context. I visited the Melbourne Shrine – a memorial for those who lost their lives in past conflicts and then I headed to Melbourne Art Gallery. I know, me at an Art Gallery!! But it was very interesting to find out about the history of Asian ceramics and the old utensils from ancient China. It tells of a civilization that, although not as technologically advanced as we, still was far advance for their time. I now want to reach out and touch the Inca Culture.

Day 233 – Sunday 07th June 2009

I decided to stay in tonight – even though it is a Bank holiday Weekend. Why do I want to celebrate the birth of a monarch who doesn't represent me? Especially when I support Republicanism for the United Kingdom movement, seeking to remove the British monarchy and replace it with a republic that has a non-hereditary head of state, much in the same way the likes of Tony Benn, Morrissey and Will Self advocate for Republicanism. That is all I have to say on that subject. Many would call me anti-establishment. I wouldn't. I would call me anti anything that subjugates one group of people, whilst another is born into a lifetime of privilege and wealth.

Day 234 – Monday 08th June 2009

It was Flo's last day today so we went out for a little drink but, on thinking about it, he is very young compared to me and Constantine. He just sat there in silence without much to say, although for his credit he has been ill over the past few days.

Anyway, Hu turned up before we left for a beer to show 2 people around and sort out Flo's bond. He then disappeared to see off the other guys and he came back 10 minutes later with a bank statement saying the machine had swallowed his card – I wouldn't be surprised if he did it on purpose to get out of paying Flo his money. He only had $250 on him and Flo's bond was $700. He was trying to rip off Flo and I saw this so I challenged Hu to think quickly before the situation got serious. Raj, our other flatmate, lent Hu $150 for Flo while I paid Flo $300 while specifying to Hu not to mess me about. He says he'll call around tomorrow with it. He is a cheeky bastard. I told him in no uncertain terms that this will not go on when I am moving out. I want my bond at least 4 days before I leave.

<u>E-Mail:</u>

Hey,

Just a quick e-mail to say thanks for all the birthday wishes everyone sent last week (for those that forgot, I'm sure you had a good reason - just kidding)!! It is not the same when you get to 25. Me and a few mates went out for a few drinks on Tuesday night in Melbourne, but I had to work all day (unfortunately).

I've only got another 2 weeks or so left in Melbourne before I head back to Sydney. I go on the 24/06/2009 and spend 3 days in Sydney, where I can tie up a few loose ends there doing things I should have done either when I first arrived, or over Christmas. Then, on 27/06/2009, I head off to Santiago, Chile for 7 days. I'm not looking forward to the 16 hour flight. I'm making plans to visit a city called Valparaiso (to the West of Santiago), which looks pretty cool. I've also just booked my Inca Trail Trip for July. Leaving it until the last minute (which is what I've done) has meant that all the permits for July have been sold. However, I've booked on an alternative trek, which takes in all the Indigenous communities along the way, where I spend a night there. Ultimately, I get to spend the night in Aguas Calientes and then visit Machu Picchu. This trip lasts 7 days and it sounds like a physical challenge.

Anyway - I'm on a day off from work today as it is the Queen's birthday weekend so its a bank holiday. It's amazing how the Aussies celebrate this, but we don't back in Britain!

<u>Day 235</u> – Tuesday 09th June 2009

Tonight, I have made an effort to stay in and enjoy time in my room by myself without Flo. Just enjoying a bit of room because I know for sure it is not going to last long. That swine Hu will try to cram as many people in as possible. I say swine – he has not been a total prick but it is just the way he goes about things. He does not seem to think things through yet he seems a peaceful enough guy who would not harm a fly. I just hope, for his sake, that he does not try anything on in regards to conning me out of my bond when I move out.

Anyway, work is a big pain in the arse and I do not know what it is about old Australian people – the rudest people in the world. Old people in Britain can (at times) be rude but they are far more patient than their Australian counterparts. I am sick of being talked down to like I am a piece of shit because I am younger. It is probably a jealousy thing as they have achieved bugger all in their lives and now it is too late. I am saying this out of frustration and my feelings will change by tomorrow.

Day 236 - Wednesday 10th June 2009

I only have 2 weeks left of being in Melbourne and I am going to miss it. I have made a lot of friends here. Friends I want to keep in touch with, which means a greater effort on my part to do so. In fact, I think some of the mates here are better than some I have got back home. More genuine and I will be sorry to say goodbye to Computershare and my workmates there. It has got to be one of the most soul destroying jobs I have ever had. But, it has allowed me to have a regular income and meet some good people. And it is the meeting people that inspires me.

Day 237 – Thursday 11th June 2009

Constantine and I headed out to the casino for a few beers tonight and to try our luck with any girls that would listen to our tales of adventure. Needless to say it turned into a late one and we were chatting to 3 women from Adelaide for a good part of the night and we all headed down to another bar in the casino. We were going to head back to Constantine's for a 'party' but one girl who was left out in the group baulked at this prospect and the other 2 then had to, reluctantly, leave. Constantine and I were left gutted as we both saw it as a good few hours wasted as we both put our time and efforts and, eventually got nowhere –not even a number. He has to be one of my best mates here – yet we are totally opposite people. Physically, he is short and dark yet I am tall and blond. Our personalities are different. He is the fiery Greek having all the characteristics of a typical Mediterranean yet I am more of a thinker and pacifist. We do not have the same interests at all but that does not seem to matter. What unites us is that we are both open minded and determined to enjoy life to its fullest and we'd both do anything for our friends. Anyway, at 03:30 we called it a night.

Day 238 – Friday 12th June 2009

I got up for work OK this morning, had a shower and got changed fine. Then I had a lie down before I left but getting back up proved too difficult so I called in sick, which now I am totally ashamed of. I just got really tired and my motivation to go in to Computershare, to a job where I was not making a difference was not there. I awoke at 14:00 having a day off work. Never mind – even though I could do with the money. I know many people will judge me for this but I am not a bit interested in what they say. When they start thinking on a higher level other than money, I will maybe start thinking about listening.

At around 18:00 I was sat watching television when the intercom went in the flat. I answered it and I didn't recognise the face or the voice. A Glaswegian lad called Stuart says 'Hi. We're moving in today.' Hu never told us!! So, in they came on the premonition they were getting my room and thought I had moved out. Naturally they were mortified and didn't want me to move out. They are a really nice couple called Stuart and Lorna from East Glasgow and when we were chatting in the flat, I made them a brew and a glass of Irn-Bru each to remind them of the good country. No-one had any idea but it turns out that Bobby and Raj are moving out tomorrow. Hu wants me to move in with Nimesh. If it was anyone else I would have said 'no' but Nimesh is OK. Plus, if this couple were not Scottish, I may have said 'no.' But, after I went for a few beers with Constantine, I thought: why have 2 more people suffering? I called Stuart to let him know I would move my things into the other room and him and Lorna were really grateful. The true Scottish spirit shone through. They are spending tonight at Urban Central and moving in tomorrow. It is typical – now I am moving out, two people are moving in I actually get on with. Where is the justice?

Day 239 - Saturday 13th June 2009

OK. I had 2 options today. Any of which would have given me a chance with a member from the opposite sex. Firstly, I could've gone out with Sarah from work to a party up Brunswick or with Nat from Holland, a girl I know from Sydney. She was going up Brunswick too. Whatever, my chances of getting some were hopeful. What did I decide to do? I went out with Ryan and Anna early afternoon to the Elephant & Wheelbarrow as Anna had friends over from Switzerland. One girl, Yvonne, was really hot so I decided to make a day of it with them and put all my eggs in one basket. I thought I stood a chance with this Yvonne. We drank beer all afternoon then headed out to Chapel Street where I nearly lost my life to a tram as I was crossing the road. I looked the wrong way and, by the time I turned around, a tram was heading directly towards me about 10 meters away. Quickly moving out of the way, I pretended like nothing had happened to save face – but it was a scary moment. We all headed to a Nepalese Restaurant for a meal, where I devoured a scallop curry and Yvonne and I were sharing a bottle of wine. I decided to ignore the calls from Sarah, asking why I wasn't at the party. Shortly after the meal, Yvonne informed me she was engaged much to my annoyance as it was neglectful on my part not to spot a bloody ring – rookie mistake!!! This is happening all too much with me. By this time it was too late to attend the other party up Brunswick and I could see myself being left up the creek without a paddle.

After the meal, we headed to a bar over the road called The Lucky Coq, where Ryan and I seemed to drink ourselves silly. With this, any chances of romance were blown out of the window and I got a train back to Southern Cross – alone. I did call in to see Marc for one last beer at Urban Central but, by this time, it was time for bed.

Day 240 – Sunday 14th June 2009

Not much happened today if I am being honest. I am going to miss Melbourne when I leave next week. It has become my home and I have met some decent friends. Friends I hope to keep for a long time. I just hope I keep up the effort to keep in touch. I have done so far with Roger and Siri who I met in Namibia.

I texted Sarah to say sorry for making the party and asking if she fancied a drink in PJ O'Brien's tonight. No reply came. Make of that what you will. Maybe I deserved that. It is looking like the one that got away – another to add to the list.

<u>Day 241</u> – Monday 15th June 2009

Constantine and I went to see a movie called State of Play tonight and he thinks I should give the barista a try! He would. I thought it was a good film – a well acted piece with a good storyline. I bumped into a guy who goes to my gym downstairs who said he'd give me a few pointers this week because he trains with the AFL players. 'That'd be good because I am letting myself go a bit' I said to him.

Work was fine and my last week started pretty well. The staff at Computershare all know the score and it is littered with travellers just wanting to earn a bit of money as they pass on through. I feel a bit sorry for those staff that are doing it as an actual job, whereas, if I am honest, our commitment is not at 100%.

<u>Day 242</u> – Tuesday 16th June 2009

Another dull day today at Computershare and I am just counting down the days until I go. I can't actually believe I have managed to work there since the start of March. But it has been a decent job and I have met some decent people since I started here, which can offset the boredom of the work. It ha served it's purpose as I now have money to carry on travelling and fulfil my dreams of visiting Machu Picchu.

<u>Day 243</u> – Wednesday 17th June 2009

I can't believe today that I am into my last week in Melbourne. It is pretty weird to think I have lived here now for nearly 7 months. It has become my second city and a part of me. But, time to leave on the 24th so no regrets. I won't be shedding a tear even though I will leave a bit of my heart in Melbourne. I'll take a memory of every street with me, wherever I go, wherever I end up. I went out tonight with Constantine and Giovanni to a place we have been known to frequent in the past – a place called Shanghai Dumpling House and then next door to Section 8. The Dumpling House is amazing even if the staff are horrendously rude! Giovanni is leaving tomorrow to go back to Milan for a few weeks and I probably will not see him again. He is a cool guy. Before we left from Constantine's, we sat and enjoyed some fine Gorgonzola, some Greek Cheese and a bit of stilton I had managed to acquire with Turkish bread, drinking wine. Constantine cut our hair respectively having a go at me whilst doing mine for moving too much!!

Day 244 – Thursday 18th June 2009

I got a shock today when I looked at my wage in the bank. It is a lot less than I expected it to be but I don't know why considering I had 2 days off last week! It annoys me how few rights agency staff have in relation to sick leave or anything like that although I do not deserve it when mine is as a result of going out getting pissed!!! I cannot complain at all really.

I felt a little melancholy on the train journey home as, after tomorrow, I will not be doing it anymore. Victoria Park to Southern Cross station has become my usual route and, looking out of the window as I passed the great MCG, I contemplated if this would be one of the last times I would ever see this sight. I do hope not.

Day 245 - Friday 19th June 2009

Yes! It was my last day at work today, which is great. I managed to achieve practically nothing, not least in part to a cold I seem to have acquired, meaning my nose has been running all day. When I was leaving, Sara, a Team Leader, came over and said thanks for everything. Then, Sarah from Ireland, gave me a kiss and a hug that meant more than it signified. We have arranged to hook up on Sunday night I think. Dave Johns, another Team Leader, then saw me out and shook my hand when I left. He is a nice guy and I hope he moves on from Computershare because I think he can achieve more. It has some cool people working there but the job is shit and we all know it. Anyway, Constantine and I went out for an eventful night. We headed to the Elephant & Wheelbarrow on Bourke/Exhibition Street where we ended up gate crashing a shit 21st birthday party upstairs. We were chased out of the pub for trying to pull a girl who was the girlfriend of the guy whose birthday it was. She secretly knew the party was rubbish and I think she was tempted to come out with Constantine and me to a few more bars. Our protestations fell on deaf ears especially when Constantine was caught with food from the buffet, stuffing it into his mouth as we made a quick retreat down the stairs, clearly having pissed off all in attendance.

Tomorrow... I go to the Great Ocean Road with Ryan and Anna – meaning I have to get up early and I am not too well if truth be told!

Day 246 – Saturday 20th June 2009

I had to wake up at a stupidly early time (for a Saturday) at 07:30 to meet Ryan and Anna at McDonald's on Clarendon Street so we could pick up the car from over the road. Anyway – I am not feeling too great today if truth be told. I have got the chills and a general feeling of shitness. Anna started to do my head in with her Swiss timing as everything was so regimented and she panicked about the daftest things. So, we went to pick up the car and I have lost my driving licence. I couldn't believe it. The only time I needed it for the past 8 months and I have lost it. I had it yesterday but I believe I may have lost it upon making the hasty retreat last night from the Elephant and Wheelbarrow. The Dalai Lama would tell you that is Karma. I would say it is bad fucking luck. Ryan thought it was because I wanted a few beers and let him do the driving! I took this on board and did have a few beers. Anyhow, we set off on The Great Ocean Road, with Ryan struggling to navigate us out of Melbourne City Centre. The first stop of any note was at Spilt Point where 'Round the Twist' kids TV show was filmed. I remember watching that as a kid with my brother. We had a tour of the lighthouse and the Australian lady conducting the tour spun us a few yarns to which we listened intently, taking each with a pinch of salt. Atop the lighthouse, it was blustery and not for one with Acrophobia (fear of heights).

The next stop was the 12 Apostles where Anna insisted on taking 100 photos – of rocks sticking out of water! They were beautiful but you can only have so many photos of one thing. Then she started moaning at Ryan and I drinking beer etc. It was obviously my fault even though Ryan was encouraging me! But the sunset over the 12 Apostles signified my time in Australia is coming to an end. I saw the sun set in the distance behind the 12 Apostles, and the sparkles from the sea seemed prophetic that, on the remotest of coasts here in Australia, as the sun set, a new dawn was rising. I thought about the weeks ahead and I could already taste the empanadas of Chile. Smell the sweet fragrance of a Venezuelan Beauty Queen. Feel the clouds of Machu Picchu cool my cheeks! The sunset was the last amazing thing I will see here and I stood there, reminiscing about all the amazing things I have done here.

Tonight, I am not good. I am freezing cold when everyone else is hot. A load of drunken Irish girls turned up at our hostel to ruin my peace and then my head nearly split. So noisy and unfeminine and I cannot stand that. I do not know what the Irish obsession is with the pub but even though they have boxes of beer knocking about, they still have to go to the local.

Day 247 – Sunday 21st June 2009

Anna woke me up at 06:30am to see if I wanted to go with them to watch the sunrise but I was still ill, unfortunately, so I stayed in bed. Anyway, 2 hours later they returned to wake me up and they had made breakfast. Ryan's poached eggs were not as good as he had made out after a recommendation from Masterchef Australia. However, he put it down to there being no oil. To cook the eggs wrapped in cling film does seem, to me, too much bother but Ryan and Anna swear by it. On the way back, we stopped off at a few spots – the most notable was Apollo Bay for Fish & Chips, which I have not eaten for ages. I could not finish mine as I am still ill. We then went to Lorne to take a look at a beautiful waterfall, 30m high. I thought if this waterfall is this nice, how is Angel Falls in Venezuela going to be? We then went to Teddy's lookout, which was simply beautiful and I was shocked at how beautiful. It was probably the best thing I have seen so far on The Great Ocean Road. It is just Ocean for as far as the eye can see, then, as you look back, dense forest. On arriving back to Melbourne, we went to a Vietnamese Restaurant. Anna complained about the lack of vegetarian meals and was afraid of getting a ticket when we parked the car. She is a nice girl but too Swiss. She is the complete opposite to Ryan who, let it be said, is a bit of a rogue – a loveable rogue. I also forgot to ring Sarah to meet up tonight but I think I am too ill for any physical contact.

Day 248 – Monday 22nd June 2009

I got up early today to sort out a few last things in Melbourne. I had to go to get a last payslip from Hallis and post my Medical Form back to the Gap year Company who have organised my Inca Trail/Lares Trek. Anyway, I went over to Constantine's about 16:30, where we ate cheese, drank wine and watched a movie. Then we headed to the Belgian Beer Cafe near the Eureka Tower, where we stayed for a few hours and the Hoegarden went down really well. After stuffing our faces on Antipasti we went to the casino for a final beer (or 2). Constantine is a mate I will miss when I leave. He is such a cool guy and I have made a good mate.

Day 249 – Tuesday 23rd June 2009

I can't believe this is my last day/night here in Melbourne. It has gone so quickly, considering when I first got here at Southern Cross Station with Mark in January. I have met some good people. Today, I had to get a Medicare refund and then get my tablets for my epilepsy, which will last for the rest of my trip – my bag is now stocked up like a pharmacy.

I nipped around to Constantine's to give him a stereo I had and to show him how to download music from the internet. Anyway, we headed out to meet Ryan and Anna for a curry off Queen Street, which was nice. Then we headed to a pub over the road called The Mitre, where we tucked into a few beers. It was my last night and meant to be as all the music on the stereo in the pub consisted of Oasis. Happy Days. I bid farewell to Ryan and Anna on the corner of Queen/Elizabeth Street, then Constantine and I went to The Lounge. We were joined playing pool by a sexy girl from Perth who then joined us at Cookie. Constantine and I fought for her affections. At first, I thought she was into him more but as we were stood at the bar on the rooftop of Cookie, she leant against me holding onto my hand. Give Constantine his credit, he never gave up and kept on trying to prise her away but she returned to the sanctuary of leaning against me at the bar, holding my hand. When it was time to leave, I had a little kiss and called it a night. Constantine and I headed to the casino for a last pint. He said I must keep his North Face jacket he lent me tonight as a farewell gift. What a bloke. We parted on Clarendon Street with a hug and vowed to keep in contact.

Chapter 13 – Farewell to the Land Down Under

Day 250 – Wednesday 24th June 2009

I got up early today to pack away a few remaining things. I waited for Hu to show up to give me my bond back. Naturally, he tried to con me out of my money, saying he could only give me back $250. I said to him "Fuck that." He refused to budge so I just warned him not to fuck about. There were only the two of us in the flat and I reminded him what a predicament he was in. I was on the verge of laying into him when he seemed to panic, apologised and paid me what he owed me. We departed on acrimonious terns but I am glad I won't have to see him again. I then got on the bus outside Urban Central, to the airport and said a fond goodbye to Melbourne – for now at least.

The flight to Sydney was all on time and I arrived in Sydney around 13:30. I got to the wake-up hostel an hour later via a transit bus outside the airport. I had a brief sleep this afternoon and then went for a $2 steak at the Shark Hotel, where me and Mark used to frequent. I sent him a text message in the process. Nothing much has changed in Sydney. I had a walk down to Circular Quay tonight and sat outside the Opera House, overlooking the bridge and the harbour. It is such an amazing place. I seemed to sit there, on my own in silence for what seemed an eternity looking as the light hit the water on the harbour, then at the cars going from North Sydney over the harbour bridge into the city and I thought: this is simply amazing. I can't believe my days in Australia are coming to a close.

Day 251 – Thursday 25th June 2009

I awoke early this morning as I had to get a few things done. Firstly, I had to go to get breakfast and then I was ready for the day. I nipped into the Westpac Bank at 275 George Street where I closed my account and I ordered some US Dollars and Chilean pesos. That is me all set for going on my next trip. I also went to look into climbing the Harbour Bridge today – one last special thing to do before leaving. Anyway, due to medical reasons I couldn't as on the Health Questionnaire it says 'Have you had a seizure in the past 6 months.' Upon answering yes, I was told I couldn't participate in the climb. If only I would have done it when I was first in Sydney – but I planned on leaving it as something special to do on my last day. No regrets, is what I say but at least it leaves me an excuse to return one day. This is the first time my epilepsy has affected me doing something though.

Tonight, I went for a lot of drinks with the guys from my room at the wake-up. I was totally wrecked and had everyone on the old sambuca/redbull concoction Mark and I invented way back when, so that got us started. We met this weirdo from Queensland who came back to the Wake-Up for a drink and, sat outside, the fucker pulled out a knife on me after a brief argument. He wouldn't have used it as I think he was just making a point and, without it, I would've battered him. However, I asked 'what the fuck are you carrying a knife for?' Then I took it off him and explained that it is fucked up to carry knives. I then went to bed safe in the knowledge there is one less knife on the street.

Day 252 - Friday 26th June 2009

My last day in Australia was spent with a raging hangover due to last night's activities – those jager-bombs don't do much to help the situation. It must've been a good night as I woke up with more money than I went out with as I couldn't have gone to the bank as my account is closed. It is strange and I can't remember how it happened! Anyway, I needed to go to the library for free Wi-Fi as I am a traveller who needs it. Anyway, I was woken up over the tannoy at the Wake-Up saying Michael Jackson has died today in LA. I didn't believe it at first but it turns out to be true. The remainder of my time has generally been spent walking around Sydney, thinking of what I am leaving behind. Sat outside the Opera House, I will have fond memories of this country and I may return one day. Unfortunately, I didn't get to Ayers Rock but I know I will have made the right choice when I get to Machu Picchu. I'd much prefer to see that than some big rock.

Day 253 - Saturday 27th June 2009

I awoke at 05:50am in order to get the flight to Chile. Anyway, on arrival at the airport, it turned out I now needed a printed itinerary, which I did not have. So, I had to walk about the airport with 26.6kgs on my back trying to find somewhere to print it off. Once I had it, I could now get my flight to Auckland, New Zealand.

Sydney – Auckland

The flight to Auckland went off without a hitch. There was one Air Stewardess there who was the most beautiful girl I have ever seen, which always makes the flight a bit better. New Zealand is a lot further away from Australia than I first thought but, considering all the travelling I have done of the past few months, it seems like only a short journey.

Chapter 14 – The Spine of Latin America

Auckland – Santiago

How much turbulence does there need to be on a flight? Fuck man! At one point the screens went off and, I'll admit it, it was a bit scary. But it was quality. I sat next to 3 ladies from the Sunshine Coast in Australia, with the one sat next to me being the cutest. They were all mid-thirties, but that wouldn't stop me!!

On arrival in Santiago, I was immediately struck by how much I would need to speak Spanish. The lady at Passport Control asked me 'Numero de vuelo,' which on a given day I would know how to answer. However, maybe it was due to the 16 hour flight, but I was left flummoxed. All she wanted to know was the flight number. I then made my way to Hostel Bella Vista, which is in a dodgy part of town apparently – maybe due to its bohemian character. On travelling away from the airport, we drove through some barrios to drop off a couple of locals and we could see the majestic Andes in the distance, with their snow capped peaks acting as the spine of this fine continent, full of history and revolution.

Upon arrival in the hostel, I started using the free Wi-Fi and got chatting to an Irish guy, James. At 14:40 we decided straight away to catch a Universidad de Chile football game, which was due to kick off at 15:00. So, we hopped in a taxi who told me it would be 30 minutes to 'El estadio'. We told him to stop and he wouldn't so we jumped out in the middle of a rough barrio, making a run for it to the nearest local pub, where we were greeted by the magnificent Chilean hospitality. I have to speak all the Spanish as James doesn't know a word. Anyway, upon talking about working in Melbourne with James, it turns out that Sarah, the girl I worked with, was practically a neighbour of James' from back in Dublin, they went to college together and they frequently go to the same local pub. It is such a small world. After a couple of beers with some local guys, I needed some sleep so we went back to the hostel after climbing a mountain to see the statue of the Virgin Mary of Santiago. The statue of the Virgen Mary stands atop San Cristóbal and looks out over the city of Santiago. The statue is partly the work of French sculptor Bartholdi, of the US Statue of Liberty fame.

At 20:00, we headed out on the town in Bella Vista where we ate food and did a few bars. We really stood out as the Gringo's in the Chilean Bars. We went to a Sports bar, where we were the talk of the place. 3 people were immediately onto us, drinking our beer and wanting us to go dancing with them. I was apprehensive of the 2 girls so I said 'maybe later.' They got the point and buggered off. However, we met a group from Santiago who asked us to join them and the 2 girls, Camilla and Karen, took a big liking to me so we arranged to hook up tomorrow. The bars around here are very dirty, with the toilets in an unimaginable state, full of shit and other things I cannot go into for fear of vomiting up the meal I consumed earlier. However, I found a guy like me can do well out here amongst the ladies, whose reputation as being 'the friendliest on the continent' has proven right and I have only been here 10 hours or so. James and I were escorted by the owner of the sports bar to a 'private club' around the corner, which was tucked away down a little back street. He had a word with the security who let us in and it was awash with Chileans dancing. We were given cans of Heineken and I got up on the stage to join a group of women dancing. At one point I was doing the Full Monty 'Leave Your Hat On', flirting outrageously with a 30 year old native. I did well to say the least especially once she heard my Spanish upstairs. However, a short time later, James was found not to be doing so well. Dancing on the stage, he was trying his best with a lady who was married and her husband was watching on from below. Naturally, the Latin American's are hot-headed at the best of times and James' actions did not go down too well. As he didn't speak Spanish, this lady literally had to point to her wedding ring and then the husband below who was about ready to pull a gun on the two of us (or so it seemed)!!! So, James (panic stricken), and I, headed upstairs to the bathroom and made a plan of action to leave. Time was called at that bar and we headed to another few bars on our first night. We called it a night when, at one point, I needed to use the bathroom and they had no doors on the cubicles. Needs must. Chile is awesome and my Spanish is better than I thought.

Santiago

Santiago, sandwiched in between the Andes and the Pacific, is a city rich in revolution, turbulence and betrayal by the so called "Friend to the North". The dictator from 1830 to 1837, Diego Portales, fought a war with Peru from 1836–1839 that expanded Chilean territory. Chile fought the War of the Pacific with Peru and Bolivia from 1879 to 1883, winning Antofagasta, Bolivia's only outlet to the sea, and extensive areas from Peru, and the two nations have a rivalry to this day. Pedro Montt led a revolt that overthrew José Balmaceda in 1891 and established a parliamentary dictatorship lasting until a new constitution was adopted in 1925. Industrialization began before World War I and led to the formation of Marxist groups. Juan Antonio Ríos, president during World War II, was originally pro-Nazi but in 1944 led his country into the war on the side of the Allies.

However, in 1970, Salvador Allende became the first president in a non-Communist country democratically and freely elected on a Marxist program. Allende quickly established relations with Cuba and the People's Republic of China, introduced Marxist economic and social reforms, and nationalized many private companies, including U.S owned ones. However, this was no good for Uncle Sam who still wanted to control Chile's resources, keeping it as a banana republic. Therefore, on 11th September, 1973 (what I like to call the real 9/11 atrocity), Allende was overthrown and killed in a military coup covertly sponsored by the CIA, ending a 46-year era of constitutional government in Chile. General Pinochet, instead, replaced Allende with USA approval. These events did not change history as on 9/11/2001- they were far too normal an occurrence in these parts. A government report in 2004 indicated that almost 28,000 people had been tortured during Pinochet's rule, and at least 3,200 murders and disappearances had taken place. This was freely endorsed by the Thatcher regime in the UK and the Reagan regime in the US.

Day 254 – Sunday 28th June 2009

I did arrange to wake and speak to Camilla online at 12:00 but, due to my phone not going off, my flight from Australia and the amount James and I put away last night, it was never likely to happen. But we did catch up online later.

James and I took a wander downtown today to central Santiago, where we enjoyed a 'Coffee with legs,' which is something unique to Chile. These came recommended but, basically, it is a place where you get coffee, while some old tart in a tight fitting red dress up to her arse makes you coffee and you drink it stood up. To be fair, the girl on the front counter looked cute but my attempts at banter fell on deaf ears. It was a different experience from Starbucks all the same. You can visit an X-Rated coffee bar in Chile where a girl serves you coffee in only a Nun's veil, where you get a little more than sugar with your coffee.

We went to an Italian restaurant in Bella Vista tonight, where I ate a delicious meal of Lasagne with crabmeat. I had arranged to meet with one of the girls from last night in an Irish Bar but it turned out to be too far from where she lives. Anyway, James and I went all the same and it turned into a crazy experience. We were sat watching the TV and a news report came on saying how a young lad had died last night – it just so happened it was outside the bar we were sat in, around the corner from our hostel in Bella Vista. We wondered why people were lighting candles outside. James thought it was for Michael Jackson. I came up with a more plausible reason that it may be for the national holiday for St. Peter and St. Paul, which is tomorrow. We were both wrong.

Anyway, on getting home, I arranged to meet Camilla tomorrow outside the Cathedral on the Plaza de Armas. I am not too great with Spanish at the moment and her English is non-existent. It will be a good experience for me to practice my Spanish anyway.

Day 255 – Monday 29th June 2009

What a great day it has been today. I got up at 11:30 and met James downstairs. We headed out for some Chilean Empanadas and a little drink. After saying goodbye to our hunger we bid each other farewell as he is off to Mendoza this afternoon and my remaining time will be spent between Santiago, Valparaiso and Vina del Mar. I headed off at 13:30 to meet Camilla outside the Cathedral. At first it was slightly difficult due to the language barrier but the notion that Chilean's are the most daring on this vast continent proved true. We soon seemed to overcome the language barrier as I got more and more confident and began to remember what basic Spanish I already knew. She also helped me develop upon my existing vocabulary. We had a walk around Santiago and it is such a beautiful city. As today is a national holiday, everything seemed to be closed so we headed to Bella Vista where we shared a coffee and then a couple of beers. We were joined by her friend Karen and her friend Jorje. At times, I could not understand a word but we overcame it. It felt nice to sit and converse with the locals, rather than sticking to my own people. I think they appreciated it.

Karen and Jorje then left after a couple of hours and I went to get something to eat in a restaurant with Camilla. The food was a huge disappointment and I was really annoyed at the mess that was served me. We decided to leave and go for a walk. We shared a kiss at the side of the Rio Mapocho with the Andes towering over us and then again on the Plaza de Armas outside the Cathedral, under the moonlight. It was, if I say, quite beautiful. She gave me a poncho (to keep me warm), which 'I must keep as a present (regalo).' On chatting to this girl, I find she has never left Chile and, instead, the only holiday she gets is maybe to the south of the country, which is supposed to be very beautiful. I won't get a chance to see the south like Patagonia due to it being inaccessible at this time of year due to the weather. This got me thinking about the disparity between someone from the UK and someone from Chile. I get the opportunity to travel the whole world, walk with lions in Africa and scuba dive the Great Barrier Reef, whereas an average person in Chile cannot even leave their own country. It is not fair and the financial systems that are in place to maintain the Status Quo need to be permanently abolished to give everyone a fair chance, to promote the freedom they tell us exists. Anyone who thinks that the 'Westernized world' at present is free and democratic is a fool. If you look at yourself the way I have looked at myself, you'll come to this conclusion.

However, the Chileans seem happy enough all the same and they are by far the friendliest people I have met since travelling the world. Shyness is not an adjective I would use to describe them, put it that way. Anyway, I walked her to get her bus home and she insisted I take a taxi home as it is 'muy pelegroso esta noche (very dangerous at night).' So I said I would. On walking to find a taxi, it did not really seem that bad so I walked home. On crossing the street, an old chap virtually stopped, mouth wide open staring at me as I walked by. It was as if I was a person from another planet and he had never seen a white man before. I let on and a smile broke on his charcoaled face, filled with lines marking the age of time, which showed bits of broken and discoloured teeth. I carried on by, feeling safe in this city as if I was in my own.

<u>E-Mail:</u>

Hola de Chile!!

What an amazing country I am in!! I have only been here for one day but I am having such an amazing time.

Yesterday was pretty weird because I arrived from Australia yet I managed to fit so much in. I checked into the hostel around 15;00 and then it was decided that I was going to a football game in the estadio nacional. It turns out, the Irish guy I was going with was best friends with a girl I used to go out a few times with in Melbourne (but we didn´t find this out until we were having a beer last night in Santiago). Anyway, we never saw the football in the end as the stadium was too far away and the taxi driver was trying to pull a fast one. So we climbed a mountain to visit a statue of the Holy Mary, overlooking the city similar to the Christ redeemer statue in Rio, Brazil.

Last night I went out to a few Chilean bars in my Barrio (neighbourhood) where I tried the Chilean food and beer etc. It is amazing. So, I went to a few Chilean bars where I stood out like a sore thumb with my blond hair ´él rubio´!!! Anyway, the Chilean people are so friendly - especially the ladies (ATTENTION English girls: you can learn a lot from Chilean girls)!! Anyway, on leaving the bathroom a

Chilean girl grabbed me and started talking to me as Gringo's do not normally visit their bars. So we got chatting with their group and my Spanish is better than I thought. The guy I was with could not speak a word but with my Spanish and their (limited) English, we had a quality night. One of the girls also had an Oasis song on her phone, which made my night! So then we did a club and had a great night!

Tonight, I went out with one of the girls from last night and, although my Spanish is by no means perfect and her English is by no means perfect, we seem to get on and really understand each other. It is crazy!!

But, I'd give a word of warning - don't come to places like this if you can't speak any Spanish. The Irish guy I met can't speak a word and its a struggle for him. Luckily, I can speak Spanish well enough to get by and at least hold a conversation!

I'm off to bed now. I can get my head around how yesterday I was 9 hours ahead and today I am 5 hours behind!!

Day 256 – Tuesday 30th June 2009

I decided to not visit Valparaiso today as I think I had better see as much as Santiago has to offer first. At first, I visited the Cathedral on the Plaza de Armas and sat for 20 minutes taking it all in. It really is the most beautiful building I have ever seen. It beats anything in Britain. It amazed me how people went there during their lunch hours to have a pray. Praying to who I do not know. Praying for what I do not know. But maybe it is to pray for something better than the shit people have to see, day in, day out. Outside the cathedral, I bought a set of Rosary Beads from an old, Gypsy lady who was being largely ignored by the passersby. She grabbed both my cheeks between the palms of her hands and blessed me in the sign of the cross, with a beaming smile as she did it.

I then proceeded to a cafe on the Plaza, where I ate a Spanish Omelette – harking back to the days of Colonial past. On the television, we all watched the news where a coup has just taken place in Honduras to overthrow the left-wing government of Manuel Zelaya. From what I gathered from a local gentleman, Zelaya has recently formed an alliance with Hugo Chavez in Venezuela and a military coup is now deposing him. All the guys in the cafe seemed to be interested in this revelation and it interested me too.

Tonight, I came back to the hostel in Bella Vista and I decided to have a few beers. It was OK as a few people gathered. Apart from 3 (one in particular) public schoolboys from West London, who are just stuck up arseholes, with that poncey Southern accent I really detest. Tonight, I think I hate it more than the scouse accent. This one guy was a dick (called Tim or something like that). He is proud that he is travelling South America knowing only 6 words of Spanish and that he can get by without interacting much with the locals. When people were playing shots at pool, he was up putting his bollocks over the pocket. This annoyed me as there were women about from continental Europe (Germany, Switzerland etc) and they were embarrassed. I apologised for him and said to them 'don't judge us Brits like this'. This guy is a stuck up, public schoolboy who is so ignorant of the world and everyone in it. The only reason he travels is because Mummy and Daddy pay for it and to show off to his mates that he has been to a particular place. Not to learn anything about the country. Not to give anything back. Tossers – the lot of them. They wouldn't last 2 minutes where I am from. They wanted me to go out for a beer with them and onto a club. I just said 'no.' I went to bed safe in the knowledge that tomorrow I will be going to Valparaiso and I will not have to see their smarmy, public schoolboy faces ever again.

Valparaiso (valpo)

Valparaiso (or simply Valpo) became the main harbour for the nascent Chilean navy, and opened to international trade, which had been limited to commerce with Spain and its other colonies. Valparaiso soon became a required stopover for ships crossing between the Atlantic and Pacific oceans via the Strait of Magellan and Cape Horn, and gained particular importance supporting and supplying the California Gold Rush (1848-1858). Valparaiso was declared a World Heritage Site in 2003, thanks to its historical importance, natural beauty (large number of hills surrounding a picturesque harbour), and unique architecture (particularly, a mix of 19th century styles of housing).Valparaiso is the birthplace of many historically significant figures, including Augusto Pinochet and Salvador Allende. It has also been the residence of many artists like Pablo Neruda and Nicaraguan poet Rubén Dario. Valparaiso is famous for its nightlife, especially its bohemian pubs and bars where poets, writers, tango aficionados, sailors, university students, and just about everyone else spend hours drinking, dancing, and socializing well into the early morning hours. In fact, most restaurants and bars do not adhere to a set closing hour, but instead close "when the candles burn down."

The bohemian nature of Valpo really struck a chord with me and I literally had to be dragged away from its streets as I wanted to take it all in. It really is a place for the traveller and one can find contentment amongst its people who live simple lives. This simplicity is something I wish to take with me for the rest of my days and, as much as I have left a piece of my heart in most places I have visited, Valparaiso and its people, has left its mark on me.

<u>Day 257</u> – **Wednesday 01st July 2009**

I got up early this morning due to those southern fuckers arriving home late and two of them decided to have a heart to heart in the dorm as the rest of us all tried to sleep. This is how inconsiderate they are. One was crying at one point and I was raging. Then, at one point, another started talking in his sleep.

Over breakfast, me and this Aussie fella (who is off to Colombia this morning) were talking about how pissed off we were with the situation. He said he nearly said something at one point – if I was made to get up things could have turned nasty. Anyway, Camilla showed up at my hostel at 09:50 (20 minutes later than she said she would've been but I let her off). We walked to the bus station for me to get my bus to Valparaiso and she headed off to University.

Valparaiso was amazing. I arrived shortly after 13:00 and I walked around the city for a while. It is so different to any other city I have visited. Built on a hillside, all the houses live on top of each other. In the bustling city at the bottom, people line the streets, selling whatever trinkets they can, to get by, to live. It is a strange atmosphere and I noticed I was the only white man walking the streets, standing out like a sore thumb. After visiting the markets and speaking with a man on a fish stall, wanting to taste some free food and getting nowhere with my haggling skills, I took a taxi to La Sebastiana, the house of Pablo Neruda, Chilean poet, writer and politician. Pablo Neruda is considered one of the greatest and most influential poets of the 20th century. Reading such poems as the United Fruit Company, There Is No Forgetting and The Heights Of Machu Picchu, I can see why. He was an amazing man who had an amazing life.

Upon arrival at La Sebastiana at 14:10 it turned out to be closed for the afternoon siesta. So, I had a walk around the local barrios on the hillside and it was really a beautiful scene. I ventured into a local restaurant, Oda Pacifico, overlooking Valparaiso, Vina del Mar and the Pacific Ocean. It truly was a beautiful sight. The chef came out and made his recommendations and I opted for Mahi-Mahi, topped with caviar on a bed of wild mushrooms and peppers. It has to be one of the best meals I have ever tasted although it did not fit in with the bohemian life I am currently living. Homemade bread with blueberry butter was an amazing touch too.

After that, I went back to La Sebastiana. This gave me a greater insight into the magnificent poet and how he lived his life. It all seemed to make sense how he defended the proletariat over the world and how he had proletarian sympathies. I also learned how he was a denouncer of the US during the Cuban Missile Crisis. I bought a book on a selection of

Neruda's poems, which has Spanish and an English version. The language used is very inspiring. I will take this book wherever I go in South America.

Anyway, I luckily managed to get my bus at 17:45 back to Santiago. I say lucky, as I walked back from La Sebastiana through the barrio's of Valparaiso, getting lost and taking a tour of Vina del Mar. I returned to my hostel around 20:00 and spent a bit of time catching up with things online. This Chilean girl I met is getting on my nerves a bit now. She is getting too full on – it is actually annoying to be honest. I am going to have to cool it down. Someone did warn me though that Latina's are quite possessive. Anyway, I am off to bed now as I have walked about a lot today.

Day 258 – Thursday 02nd July 2009

"Tengo fe en Chile y su destino"
Last words of Salvador Allende Gossens, 11/09/1973

I spent today roaming Santiago, learning about the history of this fine city, running parallel with the Andean mountains. I again visited the Cathedral as it is one of the most beautiful things I have seen. I sat there myself and, for once, I had a little pray. Do not ask me what for, but I prayed.

Visiting the Presidential Palace, I learned more about the history of Chile. It really amazes me how countries, notably the USA and Spain, have asserted their influence on Chile over the years, much to the chagrin of the Chilean people - especially towards the USA who backed a vicious military coup in 1973 to oust the democratically elected president Salvador Allende from power. Allende made his last stand in the Chilean Presidential Palace on 11/09/1973 as it was under siege by a Military Coup. He had a few remaining loyalists but, in his office on that fateful day, he gave a historic speech on radio broadcast, explaining how proud he was of the Chilean people and declared the prophetic phrase that is scrawled across his statue in front of the Presidential Palace today "tengo fe en Chile y su destino (I have faith in Chile and it's destiny)." He uttered these words before putting a gun to his head, pulling the trigger and blowing his brains out. It sickens me that the USA was in cooperation with the military junta – especially when you consider the fascist dictator they replaced Allende with – a certain General Pinochet, who proceeded to disappear 3000 people, torture 31000 and track down Chilean nationalists in other nations, helped by President Nixon in the USA. These unfortunate souls, who had leftwing sympathies much as me, are thought of as brave comrades, said to be no longer with us, floating somewhere at the bottom of the sea. USA foreign policy dictates that anything is 'better than a leftie' even a fascist dictator like Pinochet.

I spoke with 2 students on the street of Santiago who were campaigning for free education as, apparently, it costs too much for the average person to afford. They told me how much they hate Margaret Thatcher for supporting Pinochet during her regime. I agreed and shared my mutual disgust for (if you can call her) a lady that tried to ruin the working class struggle in Britain. Pinochet regularly visited Thatcher for 'tea' and she, as much as him, is as responsible for the deaths of those brave people that mysteriously disappeared under his regime. For those reading this that still maintain Thatcher did a good job, in the words of these students, I say this – 'you are a selfish fool who do not care who your regimes support so long as you are OK.' In essence, all these students want, and the rest of Chile for that matter, is to be left alone, without outside influence from the superpowers who try to control minds, bodies and souls. All they want is what USA preaches – freedom and national independence. Is that too much to ask?

Day 259 – Friday 03rd July 2009

Over breakfast this morning, I met a girl, Abby from Dorset, who is doing the same thing as me in Peru and we are on the same flight tomorrow so it'll be good to have some company.

After breakfast, I went to watch the Andy Murray tennis match at the Irish Bar in Bella Vista. Anyway, typically he lost in the semi-final to Andy Roddick so that was a bit annoying. I then went to meet Camilla in front of the statue of Salvador Allende at the Presidential Palace. On my walk down there, there was a protest and some demonstrations occurring. Now, I had been warned to avoid such circumstances in South America as, at times they can turn violent. However, if you listen to what other people do, you stop living your own life. So, I looked in at what was going on. It was a protest against the government due to the extortionate tuition fees. I headed on my way after finding out what was going on, naturally on the side of the students. As well as healthcare, I believe education should be free to all – not just those who can afford to pay for it.

Upon waiting at the Statue of Salvador Allende, a stray dog came over and put his head on my knee, obviously wanting some attention. So I sat there stroking it while I waited and he would not leave me alone. He was a scruffy, German Shepherd I called Salvador after the great man himself. Chile has a problem with stray dogs, which I have noticed. Owners get them and then find they cannot cope and let them run free, all over the city. It is such a shame to see dogs, lying at the side of the road with no food and nowhere to go. Camilla and I walked around Santiago for the day and into the night. We went to a nice, quiet little spot and made out, which was nice. After that, we headed to a fountain where she asked me to stay in Chile (well she'd been asking all day to be fair) but she finally asked 'si o no?' I bluntly said 'no.' It is not possible for me to stay in one place because one girl asks me. I said to her 'I'll walk you to the station.' At the station, she started to cry and I gave her a hug saying the usual bullshit like 'there are plenty of better guys in Santiago for you' and 'there are more fish in the sea.' Usual bollocks but translated into Spanish it doesn't seem to work. She gave me a letter she wrote for me saying she wished I could stay in Santiago and that I need to return to live in Chile. Tears rolled down her cheek as I said goodbye. It was getting a little too serious for me as I do not do serious relationships so I walked away. On the return walk back to my hostel, I did something I said I would never do – I bought food from a street vendor. It was the national dish of Chile – a hotdog. It was quality. Now, I am all packed up and ready to leave for Lima.

Chapter 15 – The Land of the Incas

Day 260 – Saturday 04th July 2009

So, I awoke at 03:30am this morning to get my flight to Lima, Peru. I filled my ravenous appetite with toast and cereal from the hostel, had a freezing cold shower and proceeded to the airport through the black morning streets of Santiago, with Abby. Once we arrived at the airport, there was a problem with my e-ticket, which nearly made me miss the flight. They had my records but no reservation number. So, with 30 minutes before my flight, I was sat in some back office in the bowels of the airport at TACA Airlines chatting away with this lady who spoke no English and it was a test for my Spanish – especially at that time in the morning when I was understandably grouchy. We sorted it out and then we had to rush to check in, going through security with the pilots etc. I made it just on time and Abby was stood there with a sandwich and a drink for me, which I devoured in no time.

On arrival in Lima, we had to wait around 15 minutes for our transport to show up. He was a cool guy called Merino and he drove us the 40 minute drive to Miraflores district, which is very touristy. Anyway, my Spanish held up very well and we had a talk about Peru and, of course, football.

Lima does look very poor (in some parts) but the place I stay, Miraflores, is not too bad. It is not like being in Peru – or how I imagined. We are by the coast and ignorant American's fill the streets with their stupid, loud conversations. On arrival at the hotel, I needed an adaptor for my Australian computer and for my camera. So, a little Peruvian chap went out and bought one for me. After, I sat a listened to his stories about work, his family and his general life in Peru. He currently works as an odd-job man here at the hotel, which pay's pretty well in comparison to some jobs he could be doing. At least his family can eat well but there looks no prospect of retirement for this chap before his final resting place. He was happy to talk as much as I was happy to listen. He told me he doesn't get much chance to speak with us foreigners as either they do not speak Spanish or they do not want to listen. Tonight, Abby and I went to a restaurant in an open air mall and ate at a shitty Frankie & Bennie's style place – *puta de mierda*. I do not enjoy being in Miraflores. It doesn't seem real and I can't wait to get to Cusco tomorrow – to visit the real Peru.

E-mail:

Hola a todos!

Today, I am off to Lima. I take a flight at 06¨40am and it is now 03;50am and I am heading for the airport. Last night, I said farewell to my friends in Chile, who actually asked me to not go to Peru and spend the next 5 weeks here. But, like I told them, I need to travel further. Chile is an amazing place (probably the best I've been to so far) and I am not too happy to be leaving. On saying that, Peru will be amazing. Over breakfast yesterday, I met a girl who is taking the same flight as me to Peru and doing the exact same projects so that's OK - a bit of company on the flight etc.

Anyway, I'll let everyone know how Lima is - I am there for 1 day so I'll make the most of it.

Day 261 – Sunday 05th July 2009

We awoke in Lima early this morning and were collected by Luis Calderon who took us to the airport for our respective flights to Cusco. I flew with Star Peru, while Abby was with LAN. My flight was fairly uneventful apart from some fool behind me nearly taking my head off each time she pushed on my headrest to get up to see out of the window. At one point, I just said 'for fucks sake' and, to get the message across, I said 'Hijo de puta' in Spanish.

Upon arrival in Cusco, I was met by a Peruvian band in the traditional dress, playing the panpipes as I was collecting my luggage. It was really beautiful and I took time out to listen to one or two of their songs even though I could not purchase a CD. I then made my way out of the airport and I was met by Belinda, part of the host family I will live with for the next 2 weeks, who had a sign with my name on it. She gave me a kiss on the right cheek, which is customary in Peru so I will have to bear this in mind in the future. We then proceeded back to her house in a taxi, which is in the region of San Borja in Cusco. It is a quite beautiful house and immediately you are welcomed by religious artefacts. The house is located about a 10 minute walk from the school and 15 minutes away from the Plaza de Armas. We speak Spanish all the time and my Spanish is really improving now. All those people in Britain who scoffed when I said I could get by in a Spanish speaking country – look now!!

Belinda made me a cup of coca tea, which is really meant to help with the high altitude as Cusco is 3,400m above sea level. I was also introduced to her 17 year old son who is currently studying administration although, after this, I needed a sleep as I was shattered. Lunch was served up at 13:00, which consisted of chicken, vegetables etc. Belinda's son-in-law also introduced himself who seems like a nice guy; although for much of the week he has to work in another city so misses his family etc.

After lunch, I decided to take a walk into Cusco, to find the Spanish school and to go to the Plaza de Armas to see what this city has to offer. The Plaza is really the most beautiful and romantic place in the world. The Cathedral overlooks it in all its beauty and I actually cannot believe I am here. It has taken a while to arrive but here I am in the heart of the America's.

Tea was spent eating the leftovers of dinner. It is not a big thing in Cusco due to the high altitude. Apparently, having a large dinner here in the evenings can play havoc with your digestive system. I met the man of the house, Caesar after tea. He is a polite chap who welcomed me officially into their home saying 'bienvenido'. He didn't say much more as I think he was tired after a full day at work, which did not bother me as I was interested in sleep. I can see I will enjoy my time here. I have found a place to which I feel I belong.

Cusco

The Watanay Valley (the place where the Cusco is located) was part of a gigantic glacial lake called the "Ballivian Lake", which covered all the southern zone of Peru. Therefore this land is very fertile. Because of it, the first inhabitants chose this wonderful territory to live. The first nomadic tribes of shepherds arrived to this land 10000 years ago.The first cultures that developed in this valley were the Marcavalle and the Chanapata. These ancient societies had a profound control of the agriculture and the ecology, which were based in the solidarity and the respect to the Earth.

Between V and VIII centuries, the Wari, one of the most important Peruvian cultures before the Incas, dominated this zone. The Wari built the city of Pikillaqta a great city of stone located to 30 Km far Cusco city, which one of the most important Pre-Incan archaeological centres in Peru.

The first Incas arrived to Cusco around XII century. There are two myths that explain the origin of the Inca people. The first is the myth of "Manco Capac and Mama Ocllo"; this myth says that these mythological personages surface the Titicaca Lake in Puno. They were sent to earth by their father "the Sun" to bring culture to the barbarous world. From the Lake, they began a slow quest (around 500 Km if they took the shortest route over the Raya pass), which ended in a valley far to the north, at the spot where Manco Capac probed with his golden staff, and it disappeared into the ground, in the Huanacaure hill. They founded their civilization in this place, the actual City of Cusco.

Another myth of the Inca origins, concerns to the four Ayar brother and their wives. They emerged from caves of the Tamputoco hill in the Paruro province at south of Cusco. One of the brothers, Ayar Cachi, was so violent and wild that he destroyed entire mountains with his sling-shots. For safety's sake the rest of the family lured him back into his cave and entombed him there.

There, he remains to this day, causing occasional earthquakes with his struggles. Of the remaining brothers, one grew wings and flew off into the sun, another turned into stone on the mountain of Huanacaure, which became one of the most sacred Inca Apus (former Andean Gods), and the last, Ayar Manco (Manco Capac) inherited all the wives and reached Cusco to found the Inca Empire.

The most important Inca was the great Pachacuteq, whose name means "he who moves the Earth". After the escape of Wiracocha, his father, Pachacuteq conquered to the "Chancas" (inhabitants of the actual Apurimac region) who were the main enemies of the Incas. During his reign the Tahuantinsuyo (the original name of the great Inca Empire) began its expansion. Pachacuteq was a great statesman and architect; he organized all the empire and built the main Inca cities and monuments like Machu Picchu, Sacsayhuaman, Tambomachay, Tipon or the Coricancha.

But, the son of Pachacuteq, Tupac Inca Yupanqui was who made the main conquests. During its reign the Empire covered all the actual Peru, Bolivia, Ecuador, Colombia, Chile and Argentina. The empire reached its major splendour during the reign of Huayna Capac the son of Tupac Inca Yupanqui in the XV century. The Incas built their amazing Empire only during 100 years between the reign of Pachacuteq and the reign of Huayna Capac.

Later the empire was divided by a civil war amongst Huascar and Atahualpa, both sons of Huayna Capac. During this war occurred the arrival of the Spanish invaders who sacked and destroyed Cusco. In 1536 Manco Inca began a long and bloody war against the Spanish invaders having a siege of 8 months over the city. Finally in 1572, after a war that lasted 36 years, Tupac Amaru I, the last king of the Incan dynasty was defeated, captured and executed cutting his head off in the Huacaypata (the Plaza de Armas in Cusco).

In 1650 the city was seriously affected by a violent earthquake that destroyed almost every colonial building. The history says that this earthquake stopped only when the "Señor de los Temblores" (the Christ of the earthquakes) left to the streets; since this date the "Señor de los Temblores" is the Patron of the city. Later in 1780 the city was again scene of a social-quake: the Tupac Amaru II rebellion, one of the most important rebellions in America. He fought for the Peruvian emancipation but unfortunately was betrayed, defeated and then killed as well as his whole family and followers in the "Huacaypata".

In 1821 Peru got finally its independence from Spain thanks to the Argentine general Jose de San Martin. In 1933 the 25th Congress of Americanists in "Ciudad de la Plata", Argentina, declared Cusco City as the "Archaeological Capital of South America". In 1950 another great earthquake of 7* on the Richter Scale in the Mercalli scale, shook the city destroying 75% of the buildings. In 1978 the 7th Convention of Mayors of the World Great Cities, performed in Milan, Italy, declared Cusco as "Cultural Heritage of the World". In Paris, on December 9, 1983, the UNESCO declared Cusco as "Cultural Patrimony of Humanity". In 1990s, the city was embellished during the municipal government of the mayor and famous Cusqueño leader Daniel Estrada Perez who constructed many new monuments and beautiful water fonts like the monument in honour to Pachacuteq, the Pumaqchupan font, etc. It was also during this time that the Coricancha was recuperated and restored.

Today, Cusco is the capital of the region of the same name and the Historical Capital of Peru, according the Peruvian Constitution. Cusco is now the main tourist destination of the country and one of the most important cities in Latin America. It is the symbol of the Peruvian Culture and the greatness of the Andean man. I would recommend anyone, before they die, to visit this place but I doubt many of my family and friends will bother their time. That is a tragedy.

<u>Day 262</u> – Monday 06th July 2009

Sweet dreams my little amigo, Barefoot and homeless in Rio De Janiero
Sleeping on the step of a church, Whose doors are locked
Living in a cardboard box, Inside at the shrine, The Priest sips fine wine
Dines on fine food and looks for a sign
No mother no father, No shoes nor a bed
No place to relax and rest his weary head, Where his next meal will come from
Nobody knows: But everyone can see the church is covered in gold
Ian Brown: Street Children

I slept for ages last night, which was just as well considering all the travelling I have done. It is so cold here at nights, which is why I wore my socks, shorts and a body warmer to bed alongside being wrapped up by 3 Alpaca blankets. I woke at 07:00am and proceeded to take a shower. I managed to get some hot water, although it was only a trickle, but it didn't bother me. I went for breakfast in the kitchen consisting of bread, juice, jam and butter.

After breakfast was finished, I went back to school. I met Abby who informed me she had missed her flight from Lima as they had no record of her so she had to pay $450 for another one. We then had to take a test to judge our Spanish levels but I am not too sure how I got on as they never told us the results. I am sure I did fine though. During orientation, we all had to introduce ourselves. One girl, Marina introduced herself saying she is from Luxembourg. An American prodded me asking 'Where is Luxembourg?' Upon answering where it was, she questioned my judgment 'are you sure?'

A Peruvian chap who works at the school then gave us a very informative and interesting tour around Cusco. How the Inca's constructed some of these buildings with the size of the stones they used, I will never know. How the Spanish Conquistadores sacked Cusco as the Capital and made Lima the modern Capital, I will never know.

Maybe one day, I'll marry an Incan descendent of Pachacuteq (**Pachacuteq means 'he who remakes the world')** and create revolution in these parts, but as has been said before and we all know, without guns, it'll never work. That word 'revolution' is constantly in the air around Latin America – all the time. It is as if everyone is asking 'When is the revolution going to happen?'

I went back to the house for lunch, where Belinda and I ate Brocolli soup and some sort of a steak, with rice and an orange puree (although politeness forbade me from asking what it was). I washed the dishes and this seemed to please Belinda who thanked me profusely for doing so, and even made a point of mentioning it to Caesar this evening.

This afternoon, I went for another walk around this majestic city. I am amazed by the amount of people trying to sell things here – basically trying to survive. Being a blond haired traveller, I stand out more than anyone else so I am an easy target to be approached. Indeed, as I made my way up to Plaza san Blas, I was followed by a young child who couldn't have been more than 10 years old, whose name has escaped me. He tried selling little trinkets and I said I could not buy them off him. He said to me 'but you have money. I have nothing.' It was heartbreaking to see as I crossed the road, leaving that child behind on the corner as I headed to San Blas. This is what befalls the children in this area. Poverty exists a lot around here and, amongst the children especially, it should not be. I wonder where they go at night, when it is cold, when I have a warm bed to sleep in. When I have given up so much to live this life as a wanderer – is it right?

I headed to the Cathedral and paid the 25 nuevo soles to enter. It is a spectacular sight and I had a pray while I was there. Again, I am not too sure what for but maybe it was for the children, aimlessly walking the streets. I asked god why children are starving and got no response. Am I finding Jesus in South America? No. It is a very religious place and the churches are by far the most impressive I have seen. It always makes me question why religion is always so important to those people who live in poor countries. Maybe they have to believe in something better than the shit they see every day. What sickens me is the crassness of the Catholic Church here. Roofs are covered in gold and the amount the Catholic Church wastes on frivolous matters and such when I can see children lying on the floor outside, starving and hungry, without a bed. It is my belief that many people in the Western World believe in God to absolve them of their sins – their sins of their blind ignorance to humanity. It is in my opinion that the Church merely acts as another repressive institution, much in the same way as Parliament does or the monarchy does. It is designed to pull the wool over people's eyes, making them believe in a system that simply doesn't work. It is as if people assume there would be anarchy if the corrupt church was not there to uphold morals. I do not need some hypocritical priest to tell me about right and wrong. What's right is right and what's wrong is wrong. And it is wrong that so much money gets ploughed into the church when kids on the street starve outside. It also reminds me of a film I watched called 'El baño del Papa (the Pope's toilet)'. It's a film based on a visir by the 'holy father' to a town in Uruguay, which was supposed to bring wealth and prosperity to the poor citizens of the area yet ultimately ended up costing the citizens more than they prayed for. Beto (the central character) thought he found an ingenious idea to devise 'The Pope's Toilet' where the supposed thousands of visitors could relieve themselves (at a small cost). In order to fund this Project he used his daughter's collage fund to finance the scheme. However, the large crowds never materialised and Beto was left broke. It is an interesting film about the Catholic Church and South America. The Catholic Church is revered in South America but the question I ask is – why?

I then met Abby and her friend from back in Dorset, Graham who sounds and looks like a stoner (self-admitted too) but he is OK. I am not a fan of guys who are proud of that. Abby and I then went for food in a cool bar in San Blas overlooking Cusco, with the lights sparkling it really was beautiful. I made Abby eat something with me (even though she wasn't hungry) as I did not want to eat alone so I tucked into a sandwich and she had a fruit salad. I then made sure she got safely into a cab and I walked through the barrios for

20 minutes back to where I live. What I do notice about South America, which I noticed in Chile but neglected to say, are the sanitary facilities. You are not allowed to flush toilet paper, or any other paper product for that matter, down the toilet. Instead, you need to place the item in a dustbin situated next to the toilet for your convenience. However, this has escaped my attention quite a few times and it is something I will have to keep in mind. It is these basic conveniences we take for granted in the Western World – things I will never take for granted again.

<u>Day 263</u> – **Tuesday 07th July 2009**

I got up for my first lesson today at 07:00am. I had a freezing cold shower, had breakfast and then headed to school, which is pretty cool. I like the layout as all the classrooms are off a central courtyard where you can sit out and enjoy a coffee and mix with people from a variety of countries although, predominantly, people come from USA. I am in a class with a French guy, Laurent, and a girl, Amber, from the States. Our teacher is a cool guy called Erwin and I think he finds the Manchester humour funny. Mornings here are spent learning Spanish but afternoon's we have as free time to visit the city and need to practice our Spanish. I wanted to take everything in Cusco had to offer.

I arranged to meet Edwina, my friend from Melbourne who is currently travelling South America. As I waited on the Plaza de Armas for Ed, I was approached by 2 local girls who couldn't have been more than 10. They were selling trinkets but I couldn't buy them. I asked the where their parents were and they said they do not know. I asked why they were on the street at this time and they said to work. They need to or they do not eat and if they do not eat, they do not live. Anyway, It's funny how Ed and I worked together over in Melbourne and now we are both here. We met up tonight and headed to a Peruvian place for dinner around 21:00 where I had the traditional Andean meal – Cuy (Guinea Pig). Cuy, alternately called *Cobayo* or *conejillo de indias* is a guinea pig or cavy. The taste is compared to rabbit, thought delicious, and though difficult to accept for people in other countries who regard guinea pigs as pets, the *cuy* is a staple of Andean cuisine. A local guy told me they are called "cuy" for the sound they make *cuy, cuy.* The cuy has a place in pre-Colombian Inca tradition, consumed only by the nobility or used as a sacrifice and a means of foretelling the future via the entrails. Cuys are today raised commercially and form a nutritious part of the Andean diet. An important part of the *Novoandina* cuisine, cuys are prepared in various ways according to the region, but in Peru, they are usually served with potatoes or rice and a savoury, spicy sauce. In the **Huancayo** region, the cuy is preferred fried with a sauce of pepper and achiote. In **Arequipa**, it is prepared baked as *cuy chaktado* and in **Cusco**, it is baked whole, as a small suckling pig, with a hot pepper in its mouth.

We then headed to a little bar, the size of a living area, on Plaza San Blas where a live band were playing and we joined a local guy in his birthday celebrations – being allowed to push his face in a plate of cake. It was a tiny place – so small in fact I was sat right next to the singer of the group and a jamming session ensued. He sang Bob Marley and Stevie Wonder songs, which I really enjoyed with the highlight being Get Up Stand Up, my favourite Bob

Marley song – it seems to epitomise what I stand for. He also sang Kingston Town, which was poignant for me as it was my Grandad's final song at his funeral. It felt as if the big man was in the room with us.

Cusco is such a cool city but, at 02:30, I decided to call it a night and get a taxi as I have done enough walking today. With a kiss goodnight for Ed, we parted and I walked back through the supposedly dodgy San Blas area, through the winding back streets and alleyways, all the way home with no problems. I am just so happy to be here and I think every day how lucky I am. Most people do not get these chances.

<u>Day 264</u> – Wednesday 08th July 2009

I awoke this morning slightly tired after last night's antics with Ed but I was OK for school. I feel I am learning a lot and I am surprised by how much Spanish I actually know. But, it is a good thing that I can converse in Spanish with my host family and it means a lot to them too.

So, school is great and the teacher Erwin seems a cool guy. I get afternoons off as I said yesterday, so this afternoon I had a wander to the cathedral again, which is very nice but not as nice as the one in Santiago de Chile. I did not like the fact that we had to pay 25 soles to enter a church but it seems they are cashing in on tourism.

Tonight, I went out with Ed again and we ate out in a restaurant with 2 of her mates. It turns out, after I left last night, they stayed up until about 06:30 so, naturally, they were pretty knackered tonight. But, I love the whole Latin vibe here in Cusco. Outside the bars there are guys offering cocaine at will but you just have to be polite and say 'no gracias' like you would to those trying to sell you clothes, pictures or other artefacts. Personally, I take no offence to being asked if I want to buy drugs. Many foreigners sole purpose is to come here to sample the purity of the cocaine on offer so those selling it are not aware if I am here for the culture or the Charlie.

<u>Day 265</u> – Thursday 09th July 2009

I actually feel I am learning a lot from this Spanish school and it is a rewarding experience. Especially when I wander around the narrow streets of Cusco, speaking with the people of this fine country, it is amazing how much I am taking in about Inca Culture and modern Peru.

The only negative I would say of this beautiful city is that it is very touristy – for me anyway. Like I have said before, I am part of the problem. All the Yankee tourists have as much right to be here as I do but it is not to say I do not enjoy it. But, on saying that, I have more respect for those who try to learn the language and assimilate themselves, than those who don't. I'd like to feel I am a little different from the hundreds of tourists as I try to meet the locals and listen to their stories.

Tonight, I stayed in with the family for the evening meal, which is usually the same as what we have at lunch – but less. They eat less in the evenings due to the high altitude, but I find that I am starving all the time, which is not unusual. As a mark of respect, I eat everything I am given. Not just as a mark of respect to the family, but to those people who do not get the chance to sit down for a meal. The food is more unusual than the food I'd get in the UK, but it is nice enough all the same. I do miss my Mum's cooking though.

Day 266 – Friday 10th July 2009

It turned into a bit of a mad night tonight as a lot of us from the school went out for a night out. We were due to meet the American girls (both called Amber) at 19:00 but, rudely, they never showed. I was slightly annoyed as I fancied my chances with one of them – even though she does have a boyfriend in the States (and she is only 18). However, the rest of us headed for food (my curry was shit) and then headed out to a few bars on the Plaza de Armas. The group broke away leaving me, a guy from Durham called Mike, a Brazilian girl called Marina and a German girl called Theresa. Anyway, the cocktails were going down really well and the Brazilian girl had me on Caipirinha's in Mythology and we danced salsa (or tried to). In Mama Africa's, Mike was sick after a few too many Mojito's and Pisco Sours (Pisco Sours are the National Drink of Peru) so I piled him off in a taxi and went back upstairs to dance the night away. Anyway, I got the Brazilian girl to teach me a few dances from Brazil, which we affectionately called 'The Manchester' after my inability to pick it up. She said to me 'I think you should kiss me now,' so I gave her a peck on the cheek. Then she went in for the whole lot and I baulked at this, moving away. She then got upset when she saw me with another girl from the school and the German girl, Theresa, had to send her home in a taxi. Theresa then returned and I suggested we go to a bar in San Blas to watch a band I knew who were playing, so that's where we headed. On return to the Plaza de Armas we stopped by the Cathedral for a kiss. She then invited me back to where her host family lived, to which we had to be very quiet as we are not allowed to take guests back to our host families for risk of being thrown out of the school. I have always said German girls are very difficult to break and rarely 'put out.' However, Theresa proved me wrong. There are a lot of decent people in Cusco and I am making a few friends.

Day 267 – Saturday 11th June 2009

> ***"Don't lie, don't steal, don't be lazy."*** Cornerstone of Inca law

I was knackered when I got up this morning but I had to go to change some American Dollars and then there was an excursion planned to Saqsaywaman with the school (it can be pronounced Sexy Woman). So, I got to the school and, for the people involved last night, I acted as if nothing had happened. On the bus, I sat next to Amber who said she was gutted she missed me last night and that we should definitely go out tonight. From what I've heard, she seems to like me. After picking up the tourists, we made our first stop at the Coricancha, in the heart of Cusco, which original name is Inti Kancha.

It was far too touristy for Laurent and I so we decided it would be a good idea to sack it off as there were about 30 people in one group and it was not personal enough. We agreed that there were too many distractions. So, we'll go later on our own.

Upon sacking the group off, Laurent and I headed to the Museo Inka, where we had a 3 hour personal tour immersing ourselves in the fine culture of the Inca's. The building was once the palace of Admiral Francisco Aldrete Maldonado, hence its common designation as the Palacio del Almirante (Admiral's Palace). The palace itself is one of Cusco's finest colonial mansions, with a superbly ornate portal indicating the importance of its owner. The mansion was built on top of an Inca palace at the beginning of the 17th century. The main draw of this archaeological museum is its collection of Inca mummies, but the entire facility is Cusco's best introduction to pre-Columbian Andean culture, including the rich cultures that thrived before the Incas. The museum's exhibits include ceramics, textiles, vases, jewellery, architectural models, and an interesting collection (reputed to be the world's largest) of Inca drinking vessels (*qeros*) carved out of wood, many meticulously painted. In the courtyard is a studio of women weaving traditional textiles. It is amazing. The Inca's knew brain surgery, astronomy and, more importantly, poverty did not exist in Incan society. There was no poverty, nor hunger, thanks to some of the most sophisticated farming methods in the world. The Incas brought us potatoes (hundreds of varieties) and maize. This poverty did not exist until Pizarro and the Conquistadores arrived from Spain. Pizarro did not adopt the 'Don't lie, don't steal and don't be lazy' morality that held Inca's in such high esteem. Accompanied by an army of 200, the Spanish were met by 6000 Inca defenders. However, the Spanish had guns and heavy cavalry. Pizarro tricked Atahualpa (the last Inca Emperor) into entering an enclosed courtyard accompanied only by his nobles. Atahualpa was no match for Pizzaro's army of guns and cavalry. Pleading for mercy, Atahualpa filled his 'ransom room' with gold and silver, to give to the Spanish, the majority of which was taken from the Coricancha. Once the Spanish had pilfered all they could, Atahualpa was put to death, and with it the Inca Empire crumbled.

After the extensive tour was complete, we headed back to the Coricancha, where we had initially started the day. Laurent and I enjoyed our own personal tour through the various Inca Temples and heard the stories of how they were destroyed when the Spanish arrived – all in the name of gold and excess. It really is heartbreaking. The Coricancha was one of the most revered temples of Cusco and you can see the areas where the Spanish have decimated the walls, which were once decorated in the jewels Atahualpa used as an attempt to save his own life – proving in vain.

<u>Day 268</u> – Sunday 12th July 2009

I awoke at 07:50 today and proceeded to the school to meet Laurent as we were heading to visit Tambomachay and walk the 12km back into Cusco, visiting the sights of Puka-Pukara, Q'enqo and Saqsaywaman. We bought some bread and ham so we could stop on the walk back for lunch and even bought some water as the altitude can affect things slightly.

We got in a taxi, which drove us up to Tambomachay. At Tambomachay, we both stopped to chat with a woman selling various Inca Artefacts who told us an alternate local name for Tambomachay is *El Baño del Inca*, "The Bath of the Inca." The function of the site is uncertain: it may have served as a military outpost guarding the approaches to Cusco, as a spa resort for the Incan political elite, or both. Upon chatting to this pleasant woman, we were persuaded to buy a jumper made of baby alpaca wool. I tried my best to haggle and she asked me 'Que quieres pagar (what do you want to pay?)'. I responded 'Nada. Es gratis no (Nothing. Is it not free?). We laughed and I ended up being charged 80 soles for this although, as her and her husband didn't look busy, I gave 100 soles and I was blessed by this lady who, as happened in Santiago, placed both palms of her hands on my cheeks and wished me well.

Laurent and I then headed to Puka-Pukara. Puka-Pukara had many functions in its time. It used to contain fountains, canals, baths, various rooms, and towers. Due to this, it was thought that Puka-Pukara was used as a sort of hunting lodge or resting place for travellers. Here, weary travellers could stop off to rest, eat, or drink. Another function of Puka-Pukara is that it may have been used as a fortress. In fact, the name Puka-Pukara comes from two Quechua words meaning red fort. In its day the fort may have been an impressive red colour since the limestone contained iron. The location of the fort is strategic as it overlooks the Cusco valley and it looks down at Tambomachay.

Further down the road, we stopped off at a pleasant spot, on the hillside, to the side of the road, overlooking Cusco and we decided it would be a good idea to have some lunch. We both sat there in awe of this scenery we were witnessing and, French or British, it was something that could unite the whole world. It is a pity the Colonialists didn't feel the same.

Our bellies full, we proceeded on the 8km walk down to Q'enqo and Saqsaywaman. However, on the road down we were stopped by a group of local men who asked us to join in a game of football. I went on one team, taking up my role in central midfield, while Laurent played in goal for the other team. Football is a great thing – it unites people around the world, for those who show an interest in it. It is a pity economics doesn't. I managed to score 2 goals and set up 2, with Laurent being hopeless in goal. A few decent flicks here and there managed to get the attention of a couple of local girls who were looking on, applauding my every move and I greased the attention for all it was worth. Laurent and I only agreed to stay for 5 minutes, but we ended up playing for nearly 1 hour, only stopping as the altitude really began to affect us, debilitating me to the extent I was crippled up on all fours breathing heavily. This brought great humour to my teammates and the local women, who were laughing at 'el rubio' (the blond one). The locals really took to us and we all shared an embrace as Laurent and I headed further down to see the ruins.

At Saqsaywaman, we had our own personal tour guide, called Maria. She took us around the great fort and we understood most of what she told us. The Incas called it the House of the Sun and the Spaniards called it a fortress because of its zigzag shape and the 1536 revolution. The construction, which is made up of three platforms one on top of the other, was one of the most important religious complexes of its time. Some scholars believe the walls were a form of fortification whereas some believe it has been constructed to form the head of a puma (like that at Ollantaytambo, which forms a llama). There still remains a lot unknown about how the walls were constructed. The stones are so closely spaced that a single piece of paper will not fit between many of the stones. This precision, combined with the rounded corners of the limestone blocks, the variety of their interlocking shapes, and the way the walls lean inward, is thought to have helped the ruins survive devastating earthquakes in Cuzco. The longest of three walls is about 400 meters. They are about 6 meters tall having an estimated volume of stone is over 6,000 cubic meters. Whatever the purpose, the Inca's show modern day engineers how to do things.

After Saqsaywaman, we realised we had missed Q'enqo so had to walk back. Maria took us there and guided us around. It was really interesting and she told us that human sacrifices did exist in Inca time, as well as sacrificing animals. Q'enqo is on top of the Socorro Hill and was used by the Incas as a religious spot although many actually believe that Q'enqo had an astronomical function.

After that, we headed to the Cristo Blanco next to Saqsaywaman, overlooking the city of Cusco. It was unbelievably beautiful, demonstrating how Catholicism has taken over the religious beliefs of this area – just as Manco Inka said the Spanish would try to do. We proceeded on the walk back to Cusco, through an area we were told was dangerous at night. One old gentleman asked if we wanted a drink. Laurent was wary of this, but I decided to trust this old chap and took a seat beside him. We shared an Inka Cola and he informed us of his life, working the lands and how opportunities to make money are getting restricted as he is getting older and his wife could not work due to ill health. I asked if the government would do anything to assist, to which he looked up at the sky, let out a deep, deflating sigh, then looked at the ground with a shake of the head to suggest that this government does nothing to assist its poor people. This gentleman, whose name we did not get, seemed exacerbated that he had worked hard all his life, never asking for help from anyone and now, when he needs help, it is nowhere to be found. He also told me that every day, he offers people a drink as they walk the winding road back to Cusco from Saqsaywaman and we were the only folk to have stopped to talk – to listen. We offered money for the Inka Cola's to which he seemed insulted. I am constantly bowled over by these people's generosity. I insisted I pay, the reason I gave 'Por tu esposa (for your wife)' I said. We said 'Chao' with him blessing us on the rest of our travels.

Laurent and I proceeded to a little cafe off the Plaza de Armas for food and, too tired to speak, we ate our food, both reflecting on what we had seen and learned from today. After our meal, we said goodbye with a hug and then went our separate ways to sleep off the 15km of walking today. At least it has prepared me for next week's trek.

Day 269 – Monday 13th July 2009

I am in a new class this week with a new teacher, Juan – on my own. It is really great as it is proving to be more intensive and he seemed really impressed with my Spanish. He said the things he was going to teach me, he didn't need to as I seemed to know them.

Tonight, I went out with Mike and Abby for a pizza and wine. I returned home, still aching from yesterday, collapsed on my bed and covered myself in the alpaca blankets and fell sound asleep.

Day 270 – Tuesday 14th July 2009

My Spanish has been so shit today. It basically started this morning when Belinda and Caesar bombarded me with questions and, considering I am not the best in the morning anyway, I could not understand a word. I even answered one question in English and this had Caesar rolling around in hysterics.

Then, I went to school and I learned reflexive verbs although nothing was sinking in. On top of that, I was forgetting even the simplest of things, which I know but could not remember them. Juan said he knows that I am good at Spanish but I just need to believe in myself, which is true. We just put it down to a bad day.

I returned to the house at about 16:00 this afternoon and I decided it would be a good idea to work on my Spanish as, by my standards today, it was poor. So, all I did tonight was to spend the time with the family and practice. I was given homework to do by Juan, which is the first time I have been given homework in 10 years. It turns out Adam has been offered a 2 year deal in Abu Dhabi, which seems like a good opportunity if he'll take it. It'll be gutting if he does as I'll not see him when I get home but he needs to do what's best for him. I say it seems like a good opportunity but, personally, I am not fooled by the whole notion of going out there to live in a world of luxury. On saying that, Adam and I are different guys. In essence, I hated the fucking place and those who see it as paradise have no imagination, no fucking sense of the world outside of the newest, flashiest commodity.

Day 271 – Wednesday 15th July 2009

"When the trumpet was sounded, everything on earth was prepared and Jehovah distributed the world to Coca-Cola, Anaconda, Microsoft and other entities"
Pablo Neruda; United Fruit Company (Microsoft added by Alistair Mirfin)

Just a quick update on the travel front – I have no flight sorted out from Cusco to get me to Lima so, instead of paying the hugely inflated prices on a flight, I am deciding to get a 20 hour bus journey and, after that, a 25 hour bus journey from Caracas, Venezuela to Santa Elena on the Brazilian boarder.

It is amazing in Cusco how the rich and poor are segregated. The lands of the Inca's have been rebaptized into Western republic – Banana republics. So much for liberty, so called by those so called restless heroes. Democracy and freedom mean nothing here. Nothing to the body that lies, nameless, a number rotting into the ground of an earth, which one so dearly held. The humble pauper on the street alongside which dogs are made, alongside which slaves are made. Neglected by the state. Neglected by a world, which is not fair. Ignored by the people outside who carry on their daily lives in pursuit of greed. Dignity is not a word you see around here, with the mother selling it for precious coins. Still the rich barter for a better price. Still he wants to get it for a better deal. The greedy bastard that only thinks about money. Not about the body that lies, in the morning mist, nowhere to go, just left to rot like used fruit. Another number to add to the pile.

<u>Day 272</u> – Thursday 16th July 2009

It was a bit of a philosophical day yesterday, but when I scratch the surface, that is the type of guy I am. But, that is what seeing hunger, greed, poverty, exploitation and hopelessness rolled into one, each day, will do to you. It is difficult to take when you see that you have so much and they have so little. It is not

fair. I'd give all I have in the world just for things to be equal. Not in some lame 'let's abolish one form of apartheid to replace it with a more, socially acceptable form of apartheid' way. But for real and true equality, where everyone has a fair chance to succeed. I am not saying I have much to give up in comparison to fellow citizens in the UK but I have more than the people here or in Africa – the forgotten world. Why? People talk about careers in the Western world but what are they? A kiss arse way to earn more money, while someone on the street in a far off land struggles to make ends meat. I think I have come to a crossroads in my life about which path to take. A crossroads I will have to seriously think about. I have to question if I am shallow enough to be motivated by money. Because no matter how much you defraud or not, no matter how much you have – it is never enough. But, I am motivated by a desire to make the world a better place, somehow. But, to those that hear this, I am a crazy fool. A crazy fool because I actually might want to achieve something better than mediocrity, talking about flashy possessions, new cars and bigger houses all the time. Let us see what the future brings.

<u>Day 273</u> – Friday 17th July 2009

Today, I left the school after spending 2 weeks there. It was funny standing there giving a speech to everyone in Spanish. Most people had prepared something to say, yet I just got up there unprepared as I was confident in my own Spanish. The speech went something like this (translated into English):

'I would like to say thank you to all here; Teachers, workers and my fellow students. I have learned much from my time here and each and every one of you has made this time special for me. I also wish to thank the people of this country for their kindness. Long live Glorious Peru'.

After the cordial speeches I headed to the market to buy Belinda some flowers and I bought some wine for Caesar. When I returned to the house, they gave me an abrazo (hug). After lunch, Caesar and I sat and enjoyed the Chilean Vino I purchased, talking endlessly about politics as former Peruvian President Alberto Fujimori has just been jailed for corruption. Caesar was surprised by my knowledge of political affairs in this country. We did disagree on the Chavez and Morales debate, with me being in favour of these 2 men, while Caesar affectionately referred to them as dictators. He did say, however, that it is nice to see a person from Europe of the USA caring so much about what happens to the people in South America.

Tonight, I headed out with a few people from the school, going to a bar and a club. I hooked up with a girl called Emily, from Melbourne, Australia, who has just arrived and is due to start the school on Monday. Again, we shared a kiss on the steps of the Cathedral. This did not go down too well with Theresa, who was out with us as she disappeared home. It was also the last night of a guy called Andy from the US. He is a great laugh and we got on really well so we hit the shots pretty hard. Tequila at first and then I introduced him to Mr. Sambuca.

Day 274 – Saturday 18th July 2009

I awoke at 10:00 this morning with a mighty headache and we shared our final breakfast. After that, I had to leave so I said a fond farewell to the family, thanking them for accepting me into their house like one of their own. Belinda, as is customary now, placed both palms of her hands on my cheeks and gave me a kiss goodbye – warning me to take care on the rest of my trip. I left them behind, like so many other people I have done on this voyage around the world.

I got the taxi to my hostel – The Flying Dog. It seems a cool place and, after making a cup of tea, I went back to bed with my head pounding to the beat of a Latin hangover una Resaca.

Around 16:00, I decided to get up and venture for food, still with a pounding head like a football against a wall. So, I headed to an Irish pub, Paddy's, on the Plaza de Armas and ate a beef sandwich with 2 panadol. After that was devoured, I took a beer and made a good impression with the barmaid.

Tonight, I shared a beer in the hostel with a guy called Luigi who works here and some gorgeous Peruvian girls. One girl, Greta, was up my street and she is the best looking girl I have met so far in Peru – probably this trip. However, I am unsure if the feeling is mutual. They were heading out to a club and asked me to go. However, I could not muster the effort for this and, beautiful as she was, I turned it down. After watching the 2 Steven Soderbergh films Che, I called it a night.

<u>Day 275</u> – Sunday 19th July 2009

Around here, you never know what is going to happen with your days. I got up early today so I could watch the open golf tournament at Paddy's, so I spent the afternoon there enjoying food and cervezas.

After that, I went to the hostel where I met Luigi. He, Greta and I (along with a few others) headed down to Luigi's Mothers house near the airport for Sunday lunch – jungle style. Luigi and his family originally come from the jungle in Peru, yet Luigi and his Mother a few years ago ventured to Cusco so Luigi could get a better education, leaving his father behind. Apparently, his father would not cope well in a city like Cusco. The food was really interesting and Luigi's other friends and family all seemed to enjoy having their stories heard by extranjeros (foreigners) such as myself. I was only too happy to hear about what I was eating and try everything they offered. Luigi gave me an energy drink, which is supposedly good for the libido. Others weren't as curious to try it as I was and the effects proved useful - later. Luigi showed me a scar on his leg, which is from when he was a boy playing and he was attacked by an Anaconda. We ate all sorts of food including pig dishes and fish from the river. It was a great experience to meet a family that are pretty much untouched by modern civilization. I gave Luigi's mother 20 soles to cover food costs. She looks about 108 but was still spritely enough to cook for us all. Luigi said she does it every Sunday and enjoys guests from all over the world.

Tonight, Luigi, a Dutch girl, Joanna, and I went back to the Irish bar where I met one of the barmaids who served me yesterday, although she was on the more social side of the bar this time. She is a Peruvian girl called Karina and we got chatting about local customs etc. I headed with her friends to watch a band in a bar and then we went onto the club Mythology. Things led from one thing to another and we ended up at my hostel. The guy who worked on reception had to let us in the front door – he was asleep upstairs and did not look too happy. Anyway Karina was not allowed upstairs into my dorm so we sat on the sofa in the reception area, while this other guy went upstairs to slumberland. As we couldn't go into my dorm, the two of us, clearly inspired by the Latin vibe, had to make do with a table in the kitchen. However, it was then decided we needed to find somewhere more private. So we left the Flying Dog hostel and went in a taxi to a motel near the airport. We were met at the door by a guy demanding 80 soles for a room. I went for my wallet to find it missing. I then had a flashback to the kitchen at the Flying Dog. 'Fuck' I thought. In the heat of everything I had just slung my wallet wide open on a table after searching for contraceptives and forgot completely about it. We rushed back in the taxi, again waking the slumbering man from his sleep, and I went into the kitchen to find my wallet lying there on the table in the kitchen, wide open with cards and money showing, with an empty durex wrapper lying next to it!!! We both had a chuckle to ourselves. At this, it was about 04:00am and we headed back to Mythology for a drink with Karina's friends who were still there. What an eventful day.

Day 276 – Monday 20th July 2009

I had a lazy day today considering the events of yesterday. I knocked about at the hostel for a bit and, at around 17:30, I nipped into the Plaza de Armas to say goodbye to Joanna, who I met this weekend. I had something to eat with her and then Luigi showed up after his shift at the Flying Dog. We decided to go to a British Pub in Cusco and there was a pub quiz on tonight. We participated but were utterly hopeless due to the language barrier but we had fun all the same, even though we finished bottom.

Afterwards, we headed to Paddy's to meet Karina. After a bit of salsa dancing at Mythology to which I still cannot get the hang of, much to the amusement of everyone in participation, Karina, me and her friends headed to a bar in San Blas to see another band. At around 03:00am, we called it a night.

E-Mail:

Hello everyone,

Just a quick update from Peru. Everything is going well over here. I left the Spanish school where I was studying, on Friday and left my host family's house on Saturday, checking into a hostel for 3 nights. Tomorrow, I go to a hotel in Cusco for one night and the day after I begin a 5 day hike on the Inca Trail, taking in the Sacred Valley. On the final day, we go to Aguas Calientes and ultimately, finish in Machu Picchu.

Last night, I went to watch a Peruvian band in Cusco with some local girls and it turned into a late one but it was fun. Yesterday afternoon, a few of us went to a guy called Luigi's house, where his Mum cooks food for everyone every Sunday. Luigi's family are indigenous people originally from the jungle in Peru - his Dad still lives in the jungle in Peru. So the food consisted of things they eat in the jungle, which was quite an experience.

Next week, I have decided to take a 21 hour bus journey through Peru to get back to Lima. Then I've got to get a flight to Caracas, Venezuela where I will spend one day before taking another 22 hour bus journey to the south of the country. It's all good fun anyway.

Day 277 – Tuesday 21st July 2009

I awoke this morning to check out of The Flying Dog hostel, which will serve me fond memories. I headed to the hotel from where we will be collected for our Inca Trail trip on Calle Matara called Hotel Prisma. However, they are fully booked tonight so we had to make our way to another hotel across town. Also, there is a taxi strike on today, which meant I had to walk more than halfway there and hope to look for one on the Avenida del sol. Luckily, I managed to blag a taxi driver to drive me the rest of the way as I was pretty shattered by now, with the weight of 2 rucksacks to carry. I got there and found out, as it is high season I'd have to share with another guy, although he is a cool guy, Adam from Australia. When I got to my room, I had a shower then a sleep after last night's activities.

Tonight, I went for food, which was paid for by the company used to book our Inca Trail, due to the mix up of the hotel. It was nice of them to offer and it gave me a great chance to get to know Adam a bit better, who is such a laid back guy from Western Australia.

I left Adam to return to the hotel as he was shattered and I then went to meet Karina who wanted to go to a hotel or come back to my hotel but I couldn't as I start my trip of a lifetime tomorrow and I can't wait. I want to be able to say I have done all these amazing things. I still firmly believe that the way I am living is right. This is why I came travelling. These people, who are rotting away like used fruit, with their career orientated lives do not seem to get the point. When we are old and grey when the grim reaper is knocking on the door we should be able to have a story to tell, about a world that we are meant to see and people we are meant to meet – people we are meant to help. Not to say 'I earned so much money sitting behind a desk'. What is the point in that? We need to do all these amazing things before it is too late because we never know when it may be over. We need to be making a difference, each and every day, while we can. As Albert Einstein said:

"Only a life lived for others is worth living".

Chapter 16 – Living The Dream

Day 278 – Wednesday 22nd July 2009

The Inn of Ollanta
"Oh, little bird! Abstain from eating
My princess's crop.
Don't steal him
The corn that is their food
Tullallay! Tullallay!
The fruit is white
And their tender leaves;
Up to now they are delicate,
I fear you to settle in them.
Tullallay! Tullallay!
They will cut you the wings,
They will pull up your fingernails,
And you will be captured
And tightly caged. Tullallay! Tullallay! "*(*I break into fragments of the Drama of Ollantay., 1938)

Through the windy mountains we travelled on a bus today on the first day of our Inca Trail. I just can't do anything but take a step back sometimes, breathing it all in.

The first town we came to (located shortly after Tambomachay) was a pretty little mountain village called Pisac, located on the Urubamba River. One of its more notable features is a large *pisonay* tree, which dominates the central plaza. The hillside is lined with agricultural terraces constructed by the Incas and is still in use today. These terraces were created by hauling richer topsoil from the lower lands by hand. This enabled them to produce surplus food more than would normally be possible at altitudes as high as 11,000 feet. It was destroyed by Pizarro and the Conquistadores in the early 1530s. The modern town of Pisac was built by Viceroy Toledo down in the valley during the 1570s. I found Pisac to be quite a beautiful part of Peru and surprised at how friendly the locals are as we get further into the mountains. The ruins remain perfect and you can't understand how, or why for that matter, the Spanish Conquistadores destroyed them in the manner they did. It beggars belief.

The drive to Ollantaytambo took us further and further away from Civilization and, upon arrival, I learned much more than I thought I knew about the Inca existence, which in my opinion, was all too brief at only 3 centuries. I am not saying that they were a perfect model of civilization, but they had a culture that was far better than any I have known so far. However, the Spanish had guns. The Inca's understood the Equinox and they devised Ollantaytambo in the shape of a llama as a fortress for Manco Inca Yupaqui. Just as Cusco is shaped like that of a puma, Ollantaytambo chose the other famous Inca animal, the llama.

On 21st June at Inti-Raymi, the llama's head is illuminated by the sun through the gap in the mountains opposite the terraces at Ollantaytambo. The Inti-Raymi ("Festival of the Sun") was a religious ceremony of the Inca Empire in honour of the god Inti. The ceremony was also said to indicate the mythical origin of the Incas, lasting nine days of colorful dances and processions, as well as animal sacrifices to ensure a good cropping season. The last Inti-Raymi with the Inca Emperor's presence was carried out in 1535, after which the Spanish Conquistadores took power, however Inti-Raymi still occurs today. The centrepiece of the festival is the all-day celebrations on June 24, the actual day of Inti-Raymi. On this day, the ceremonial events begin with an invocation by the Sapa Inca in the Coricancha square in front of the Santo Domingo church, built over the ancient Temple of the Sun. Here, the Sapa Inca calls on the blessings from the sun. Following the oration, Sapa Inca is carried on a golden throne, a replica of the original which weighed about 60 kilos, in a procession to the ancient fortress of Sacsayhuamán, in the hills above Cuzco. With the Sapa Inca come the high priests, garbed in ceremonial robes, then officials of the court, nobles and others, all elaborately costumed according to their rank, with silver and gold ornaments. A white llama is sacrificed (now in a very realistic stage act) and the high priest holds aloft the bloody heart in honour of Pachamama. This is done to ensure the fertility of the earth which in combination with light and warmth from the sun provides a bountiful crop. The priests read the blood stains to see the future for the Inca. As the sun begins to set, stacks of straw are set on fire and the celebrants dance around them to honour Tawantinsuty or the Empire of the Four Wind Directions. In ancient times, no fire was allowed that day until the evening fires. The ceremony of Inti Raymi ends with a procession back to Cuzco. Sapa Inca and Mama Occla are carried on their thrones, the high priests and representatives of the Supas pronounce blessings on the people. Once again, a new year has begun. June 24 is also celebrated throughout Peru as Indians Day or Peasants Day.

The buildings constructed at Ollantaytambo are supposed to be earthquake proof and walking around here you get a sense of something great. A race I wish to reach out and touch and understand.

Tonight, we spent the night in Ollantaytambo. Adam and I went out for food and a couple of beers to experience this quaint little town, with the terraces on the mountain looming over us making us feel humble to be eating here. This experience is really touching me

Day 279 – Thursday 23rd July 2009

Today, like my first few days in Namibia, I have seen things that will stay with me for the rest of my life – probably changing the way I will do things.

The Lares Trek began by procuring some bread, fruits and biscuits for local children we will meet as we pass through the mountains on this quest. Quest: for what? I do not know. But I bought a football to share with some children along the way. I also needed to buy some

Coca leaves from the market for the altitude. We stopped at a market, virtually in the middle of nowhere and the local children took great interest in this group of tourists yet the adults remained hugely sceptical by the look in their eyes. Upon purchasing the fruits and football, I tried talking to the stall owners about Peru etc. I was greeted with a frosty reception. At least I tried, whereas the others in my group bought what they needed to buy and went to stand by the coach. To be fair to them, I think there is only Adam and me with a reasonable knowledge of the Spanish language.

Once we reached Nevado Sirihuani, the trail began as the road was at its conclusion. I procured a poncho from a local, who appeared to be one of 10 just standing around in the rain with nowhere to go, nothing to do but to get saturated and have their dignity stolen by people from lands they will never know.

The trek began after a ritual ceremony with the locals to Pachamama (Mother Earth). This involved choosing 3 good sized coca leaves and saying a prayer, giving thanks for the land. It is meant to judge how lucky you will be. I think Marco mentioned that if the prayers are answered, Pachamama brings good weather. We did this in our Poncho's so we were optimistic to say the least and so it proved as it pissed it down all day. The trek started and I coped very well with the altitude although I am not too sure if it was because of my good health or due to the coca-leaves I was shoving in the corner of my mouth. You are supposed to add 3 at first where the molars are located and then keep topping them up. I stayed up front most of the way with Marco, our guide, to practice my Spanish although he also taught me how to say some phrases in Quechua for when we meet the people along the way. Most speak Quechua around these parts, which is the native language of the Inca's so it would go down well to learn a phrase or two. Marco was also impressed with my Spanish.

Along the trek, we met children; children on their own in the middle of nowhere in the freezing cold, with nothing on their feet but sandals and raggy clothes to keep them warm. We, the ones with money, gave dry bread and fruits to each one we met and the kids were just so happy to receive it – anything to stop the hunger. One little girl just stood there looking at me, blankly, while eating the dry bread. At one point, I asked a little boy 'te gusta pan (you like bread?)' and his eyes sparkled as he knew I had food to give him. Certainly more appreciative than any child I have met in the UK – or anywhere else for that matter. I just keep thinking to myself: it should not be this way. Something needs to be done.

We had to stop to do another ritual, which was to pay tribute to the mountains. This involved collecting a stone at the foot of a mountain and carrying it up to the top, to treat the mountains with respect. Mountains can be split up into male or female and if not treated with respect, mountains can cause damage, accidents or headaches.

Along the way, I did practice my Quechua saying 'Imatah sutiykiri? (what is your name)' and replying with 'n sutiy Alistair (my name is)'. It is a little touch that the locals seem to appreciate and that is all it takes to make a good impression to people of the world. A bit of consideration to accept their cultures and customs. Also, along the way, I gave my Coca leaves to a gentleman who I sat with and conversed with him in Spanish. I asked him if he liked living here and he replied simply 'Yes'. He told me this was his life and was how he and his children had grown up, farming the lands and raising crops. He knew very little of my country except it is 'where the rich people live.' I desperately want to understand these peoples. Through Peru and Latin America, you will find subtle differences amongst the peoples. However, I get the feeling that these differences can only be spotted by those from around here and not the ignorant Europeans or Americans. I am trying to develop an understanding of the fine Inca Culture. How is it possible to understand something I never even knew?

And so, we hiked and hiked in the freezing mountains and I couldn't imagine how people live in such conditions, although they seem happy enough. We made it to our lunch tent as the porters had gone on ahead of us. We ate soup, followed by a course of trout and vegetables. However, I still could not stop thinking about the kids who were getting nothing except bread given to them by us. Families living in freezing cold conditions, unable to do anything about the world in which they lived. Try telling these that democracy works.

After another 4 hours trekking, we made our way to the campsite for the night at around 17:00, just before it was getting dark. Tea consisted of chicken and vegetables followed by a chocolate dessert. The food, if I can say so, does taste good although I have a heavy stomach of guilt. We are camping in the middle of a field, which consists of a hut, in which a family of about 20 sleep and a toilet. Upon visiting the toilet, which is a hole in the ground and the dignity is covered by the vertical sheets of corrugated iron, I was met by an unimaginable stench and I was very fortunate where I put my foot as one wrong move would sent you 10ft below into an oblivion of stinking shit, piss and god only knows what other horrors lurk down there.

The cold night began in our tent in freezing conditions. Everyone complained, yet I thought how lucky I was to have a tent, a sleeping bag and plenty of warm clothing to get me through the night. Most of the natives I met today do not have that. And it is a disgrace.

<u>Day 280</u> – Friday 24th July 2009

"Rise like lions after slumber In unvanquishable number. Shake your chains to earth like dew. Which in sleep has fallen on you. Ye are many – they are few".
The Mask of Anarchy: Percy Bysshe Shelly

Today has probably been one of the coldest days of my life but one which has opened my eyes and brought me closer to this, for me anyway, strange human race.

The inequality that exists sickens me to the very soul. I cannot stand to see kids suffering like this yet the people in our group only seem to care so long as they can get a photo out of it to show their friends back home. One girl even used the word cute describe it. Some girl showed of her prized photo of poverty at lunch when I asked what she planned on doing about it when she returned home. All I got was the pitiful response people give back home 'What can I do?'

In a private discussion with Marco he agreed with me about the state of things. He used a good phrase for the governments who force people into living in such ways - 'bastards', which I agreed 100%. He agreed with me that these governments should do less propagandizing the illegal wars that their regimes start against a false 'axis of evil' and spend more time and money (much more money) in promoting social utility for the ever growing poor of this world. It is this belief that is becoming my raison d'être.

Marco and I discussed this topic as we continued the trek and the lack of education that the children receive is astounding. The trek continued until we reached our second and final campsite at 4500 meters. We had a game of football with the guides, porters and local children with the ball I procured at the market. It was fun – even if it was on a round pitch covered in llama shit. I gave the ball to a pair of local children, who seemed over the moon to get such a gift.

After dinner, it was time to get ready for bed on the snowy peaks where we are sleeping. It had been snowing so I put on 3 layers of clothes, shorts, football socks and I snuggled into my sleeping bag for the cold night that lay ahead. Today has brought me closer to this world – closer in respects I cannot yet understand but, in time, we will see.

<u>Day 281</u> – Saturday 25th July 2009

So, now, after many years of waiting for it, I am on the cusp of going to Machu Picchu. It was 21:37 and I was ready for bed in the hotel room in Aguas Calientes (Machu Picchu Village). It is located around 6km from Machu Picchu. Originally settled by a few farm families in 1901, the tiny settlement was transformed into a busy railway worker's camp, called Camp Maquinachayoq, during the construction of the railroad through there in the late 1920s. The town was the central hub for worker lodging and their equipment up until the railway was finished in 1931. It is such a surreal place surrounded by mountains and we are deep in the heart of the rainforest. However, it is very touristy.

So, Adam and I have to get up at 04:00am so we can get the 25 minute bus ride up the mountains to Machu Picchu, just so we can try to get a ticket to climb Huayna Picchu. It is going to be an experience I am never going to forget. No-one will ruin it for me.

The coldest day of my life got colder this morning when Adam opened the tent. At first we thought we heard rain hitting the side of our tent but, upon opening the door, Adam just said 'Mate. It ain't rain.' I looked out and it was a scene of mountains, snow and other tents. It was like a Christmas Card. We decided to brave the conditions outside and literally froze our bollocks off taking a piss. God knows how the people living around here cope. I was stood there with around 4 layers of clothes on and 3 pairs of socks on whereas one child was stood next to me wearing only sandals, some flimsy jogging pants and the customary Peruvian poncho. Marco and I discussed it and he said proper shoes are 'muy caro por ellos' – too expensive for them.

So, we finished the hike and then had lunch after visiting a 95 year old lady where we learned how they make a variety of potatoes. A stuck up girl in our group from Milton Keynes asked to look in her house, which was a rubbled shack with only one room and a thatched roof. She pissed me off at doing this. Not only are 12 strangers from, as far as this old lady is concerned, another planet, coming to take a look in her garden, they also want to poke around in her house. Faye only wanted to look in to see how the poor live whereas I didn't have to look in a house to see for myself. Instead, I got Marco to translate into Quechua a few questions to the lady on how they grow the crops and to where they are then sent once they are ready. I asked Marco to say, on behalf of us all, a thank you to this lady. She gave me a nod of her head and a smile, showing no teeth and a face that looked ravaged by time and hard work. Even though a connection is difficult to establish with these people, I always try my best. I wish I could say the same for my fellow group members.

We then took a train from Ollantaytambo, through the jungle and the mountains, to Aguas Calientes, which like I say is nice but touristy. Tonight, the whole group went to a pricey restaurant; where I had to put up with bullshit about wine – the people here already seem to have forgotten about what they have seen over the past 2 days. It will probably be burned into my memory – forever.

Machu Picchu

In 1874, German Gohring already registers the names of Machu Picchu and Huayna Picchu. Before US born Haram Bingham, who is widely acknowledged to have discovered Machu Picchu in 1911, farmer Agustin Lizarraga established in the zone during his exploration of agricultural lands in the year 1900.

In the early 20th Century, North American Professor, Bingham, who was researching the military campaigns of liberator Simon Bolivar, took an interest in the Inca culture and its different aspects. He started his journey in Cusco through the Sacred Valley as I did, following the direction of the Urubamba River. He and his translator arrived in a place called Madorpampa. It was there they met a farmer, called Melchor Arteaga who received a tip in return for information about the existence of some "ruins" at the top of the old mountain (Machu Picchu). On July 24th 1911 (just over 98 years ago) the explorers arrived at the "Royal Tomb", then to the "Principal Temple" and at last, to the "Temple of the 3 windows". Since then, this date is known as the Day of the Scientific Discovery of Machu Picchu or as Bingham referred to it as – The Lost City of The Inca's.

<u>Day 290</u> – Sunday 26th July 2009 – Machu Picchu

"Then, I climbed to reach you, Machu Picchu. Mother of stone; spume of the condors"
Pablo Neruda; The heights of Machu Picchu

After days of trekking through the poverty I finally reached my dream. You are everything I imagined and more. Sat atop the roof of the world on the famous young mountain, I contemplate what is going on in the world and what part I play in it. I look at the stone upon stone, mountain upon mountain. I think back to those days and imagine the colonial repression as it is now. Do things change? But Machu Picchu: what a sight. I never thought I would get here. Now a dream has flown with the condors, what do I do now? Find another?

I awoke this morning like a child on Christmas morning at 04:00am. I had a shower and we made our way to the queue of tourists, whom I do not really want to be a part of. Queue after queue after queue – nothing to do. Arrival at the gates of Machu Picchu and more queues. Queue to get a permit for Huayna Picchu. We had nearly given up hope of getting one as only 400 permits are issued in a day to climb the mountain and we had 7 in our group. However, a guy handing out the permits came up and I managed to get 394-400 for us all. I was selfish at grabbing 394 as, although the people in my group are OK, I had to climb Huayna Picchu. I want to take all of Machu Picchu in. The sun gate, the empty houses, which one so dearly held. I'll walk, crawl or drag myself up your peaks but never carried. I just wish I could have said something justifiable. Something that was worthy of such greatness but I couldn't. Capped with breathlessness and, for once, having nothing to say, I just stood there, silently trying to understand why I am so lucky. I still can't understand. I look out into the jungle and think of people living their lives with no understanding of the outside world. I think of people, back where I call home, and think the same. The only difference is where I come from at least there is the possibility, which is where ignorance stems from.

Adam and I climbed the steep, Huayna Picchu Mountain alone and, dare I say, it was tricky. I traversed the steep, rocky incline that has led numerous people to losing their lives and, at times, I thought the mountain would beat me. When I reached the summit, I collapsed on the stones at the top and looked up to the sky to say thank you. Thank you to the Inca's for building this place and I looked down on Machu Picchu, not knowing what to say or how to feel. Although there were about 10 others who made the summit, it was silent and I felt as if I was alone. It was tranquil and beautiful and I do not think I will see anything as beautiful again. Nothing has happened before that has led me to stand there, lost for words. I do not even know what I thought about. It was as if the world had stopped briefly and I was the only person in it. I stopped to make a few notes as I pondered what these travels are doing for me. They are changing my outlook on life, an outlook that wants to now be useful somehow – useful to people.

A dream came true for me today and I do not know how to tell you or how to make you understand what this means to me. It may sink in later. Days, weeks, months, years? I do not know how to answer. I think I am still lost for words at this place.

"Hold fast to dreams, For if dreams die, Life is a broken-winged bird, That cannot fly"
Langston Hughes

We left for Aguas Calientes around 13:00 and met Marco in a bar for food. Marco treated Adam and me to a beer each for being 'the best people he's guided on the Lares Trek.' He thanked us for speaking in Spanish and, at times, learning Quechua. Most people, he said, just want to come to Peru to take what they can before returning home to their lives of luxury. Although he had to retain an element of professionalism he said he was happy that at least 2 people actually wanted to learn. Adam then had to rush to get his train as he was booked on an earlier one to Ollantaytambo and Marco and I had the chance to share a beer together before getting our train. I asked him if he enjoyed his job and he said 'For Peru, it pays well.' This did not really answer my question and I sense he would be happier doing something else. I managed to get the point across in my broken Spanish that he is good at his job and he is bringing happiness and enjoyment to a lot of people. However, we both shared the same sentiments that somehow we want to be of use. Marco and I headed for the train back to Ollantaytambo and we were sat opposite a 21 year old girl from the States who was sat next to me on the return bus from Machu Picchu to Aguas Calientes. She is travelling with her 75 year old Grandmother who is of Puerto Rican descent and speaks no English. I had huge respect for these 2 people. Number one for the old dear who is still making the most of life, taking on a challenge that could flummox a person in their 20's. Secondly, for this young girl who wants to travel with her Grandmother. The 4 of us enjoyed a nice chat on the return to Ollantaytambo.

We arrived back from Ollantaytambo to Cusco at 18:00 and it felt good to have a shower in our hotel. After, Adam and I went for pizza and beers as we were both ravenous. We discussed the past few days and the striking differences between the lives of ourselves and the people we met on the Lares trek, as we stuffed our faces overlooking the Plaza de Armas, full of children trying to sell items to strangers. I still cannot get the images of the freezing, starving children out of my mind. Maybe I do not know what life is really worth but I am beginning to understand.

Day 291 – Monday 27th July 2009

Adam and I awoke for breakfast this morning in the hotel and I proceeded to pack away my things. I checked into my new place shortly after midday and it is not as cold outside as it is in my room, which is pretty cold but judging by how the folk are living in the mountains, I cannot complain.

So, this afternoon I watched Goodfellas, which is on cable TV here in the hostel. I thought to myself that it would never be shown at this time in Britain but I was happy as it is in my top 5 favourite films. After, I nipped out to get something to eat and it consisted of Pie and Chips – I just fancied it OK!! But as I sat and watched the faces of people from the same land as me, I couldn't believe what I saw. People sat playing monopoly, eating cadbury's chocolate. We should be out there learning about the Peruvian culture instead of doing something we can do at home. With that, I picked up my bag and headed for a wander around the museo Inka once again for 20 minutes before returning to my hotel.

It has been pretty much boring day apart from that to be honest. I watched The Godfather tonight and called it a night early.

Day 292 – Tuesday 28th July 2009

I had a good sleep last night making the most of a room to myself. I had a walk around Cusco today, with my thoughts. You know, it is funny, the locals here just see me as a walking pound sign, because I am from Europe, have blond hair, blue eyes: I must automatically have money. But I do not. I wish I could give to everyone but I can't. I hate seeing old ladies lying on the street, hands out stretched begging for money. It is hard for me to take in. An old woman who has probably worked hard all her life, reduced to begging on the street. In their eyes is a plea: a plea for forgiveness that doesn't come from many people.

Tonight, I headed to a pizzeria on the Plaza de Armas. On my way back I bumped into Greta who, funnily enough, was on her way to eat. She asked me out to a club tonight but I am not going. She is so beautiful and I do not know why I said no. I am pretty knackered. I know, come tomorrow, I'll regret it as she is a perfect girl for me in every sense. What a fool I am.

Day 293 – Wednesday 29th July 2009

There was me saying that I have not had any trouble since arriving in South America. I went out with Karina tonight after she finished work, just to a few bars and that. At about 03:00 or 04:00am, we were heading back to my hostel room but decided to have a sit down in the Plaza San Francisco. We were sharing a kiss when some guy ran from nowhere, stealing her bag and running off. I was after him without any thought of what might happen – on pure instinct. He couldn't have been armed as he was running away. So, I chased him down a side street shouting as I got closer like a cheetah catching it's pray. 'Fucking come on' I shouted at the top of my voice. 'You wanna fuck about' was the last thing I shouted before I rugby tackled him to the ground, giving him a few punches and, if things hadn't stopped I don't know what I would've done. I stood up ready to kick him, which I know you should not do to a guy when he is down but the way I saw it was fuck that – he's stolen a lady's bag. He lost all rights the moment he did that. On standing up and putting pressure on my leg, the pain of what happened kicked in and I realised I had ripped my jeans and cut my knee. Fuck, I thought. This gave him just the chance to leave the bag and run away before I did something that I might've regretted. My hand, covered in the blood of this lad who was about 18, was still clenched. I always said that if I caught anyone stealing from me or worse, a lady I was with, I would not be responsible for my actions. Now I had this lad at my mercy – in a way I am glad he got away. Anyway, we got back to my hostel and headed to my room. On taking off my jeans, we found that the cut was worse than I first thought. It is right down to the bone and in a right mess. We may need the hospital but I do not want to go. I used a couple of plasters to bodge it up and a bandage given to me by the receptionist who labelled me a 'hero.' It does not hurt so much now but I know that, in the morning when the beers wear off, it will be a killer. But the main thing was to get the bag back. The one thing you never do is steal a lady's handbag. But, once again, I showed that I am not scared to tackle anything out here. I'm going to live forever!

Day 294 – Thursday 30th July 2009

As I thought, this afternoon when I woke up, my leg was so painful it took me about 1.5 hours to get out of bed, not least because my knee was stuck to my sleeping bag. My plaster must've fell off during the night and now there is blood everywhere and it looks like a scene from a horror movie. I managed to get up and, by this time, Karina had left. Getting changed on my own was a bugger as I could not bend my leg as the cut went right across my knee joint. I had a shower to get things cleaned but the pain was excruciating. I then headed out into Cusco for food. Now, I always say that when travelling it is best not to draw any unnecessary attention to yourself. I stand out anyway with my blond hair, but now I am walking with a huge limp, I stand out even more. It is tricky walking up and down pavements, stairs etc. I just have to take them one by one and I have a technique that, when going up the stairs, I go left leg first and drag my right leg up then when going down stairs I go right leg first and follow with left leg – a step at a time. This is all to prevent flexing my right knee although, at times I have forgotten this and I have let out a range of expletives.

Tonight, I went out to meet my mate James from Santiago who has just arrived in Cusco from Dublin. I told him via the internet what had happened and we arranged to meet. He noticed me across the Plaza de Armas as the guy limping along and, upon showing him my war wound, he was pretty much sickened. We went to Paddy's to meet Karina who, on seeing it today, said I need to go to the hospital and pretty much everyone who saw it agreed. We went to a couple of bars with her friends and, by now, I couldn't focus on anything else apart from the agony I was in – even though I tried to put on a brave face. For once, I relented and let Karina take me to the hospital at 00:00, where we were seen pretty much straight away. I needed to have it cleaned, injected and then stitched. I was saying a few more expletives during this (even in Spanish) much to the amusement of Karina, the doctors and a nurse on duty. At least I had a girl there to hold my hand and mop my brow. The standard of healthcare was good yet Karina informed me that this was a 'hospital for Gringo's'. I would have been curious to see what the other hospital was like and I do not like the fact that I could get better healthcare due to me being from another country. Now, I have a huge bandage on my leg and I am told I am not to flex it. Karina wanted to 'put me to bed' so to speak but I said 'I am not in the mood.' We said our goodbyes on the steps of my hostel and I went to bed knowing that tomorrow is going to be a long day for me.

<u>Day 295</u> - Friday 31st July 2009

My last few hours in Cusco were fucking shit but I won't judge Cusco on this. It turns out I did have to pay for my hostel, which they told me at 13:00 when I was about to leave (I was obviously trying to get the room for free). We then had to rush around to the bank and then to Cruz del Sur for my bus. It was such a pain getting in and out of taxis with my bad leg but I made it to the bus OK and now I am away to Lima. It has just gone 16:00 and the bus journey will be about 21 hours. Luckily, I can stretch out my leg and there is a nice, middle-aged French couple sat next to me. The lady seems interesting and I get the feeling due to her hair and her frail nature, that she has been unwell and this is a trip of a lifetime for them. She mothered me slightly due to my knee and the fact I am travelling alone.

The journey was fun and we got the chance to partake in a game of bingo. The French man next to me was hugely disappointed when bingo was called with him requiring only one number. I, on the other hand, was well off calling bingo. His wife and I enjoyed a laugh at his competitive nature and it seemed like this gentleman would never get over this misfortune. We were served food like you'd imagine on an aeroplane and we watched the movies that were on the television.

<u>Day 296</u> - Saturday 01st August 2009

I arrived in Lima at about 11:00am today and got in a taxi to get to my hostel. Anyway, the taxi driver said he knew where it was when, in reality, he did not have a clue. So, he drove us around Lima for ages to no avail. I was getting frustrated but I enjoyed talking to this taxi driver who told me all about his life and his frustrations. He stopped off at a street vendor where he bought 2 bags of pastries - one for me and one for him. They were delicious and he said they are for you, my friend. We chatted long about Peru and Lima and his family as he drove me around the city, not having a clue where my hostel was but insisting I would pay no more than the money he quoted. Fair enough. Many people hear the scare stories about taxi drivers in South America and the general dangerousness of South America, which puts them off coming here. With respect, that is bollocks. These people who believe everything they read in their shit newspaper or what the BBC decides to tell them on a particular day are suckers - they've no balls. The people of this fine continent are the finest I have ever met. Yet one negative story printed in Europe about the drugs trade in South America is enough to put people off coming here. Not for me. I am lucky I have developed an intelligence where I do not believe everything I read in the paper or what I see on the news. I am not saying the countries on this continent are 100% safe – not by any means. The streets are raw and can be, at times, dangerous. But so can the streets of Glasgow , Manchester, London. New York; that city we are made to believe is the greatest city in the world – it is full of danger. New York, in my opinion, is for those that are easily manipulated and the "shop 'til you drop' mentality is pathetic. As for Las Vegas - Las Vegas, to me, is a city for uneducated, wannabe playboys who have been manipulated by modern day capitalism. Manipulated into believing its greatness when, in reality, it is built on extravagance – stereotypical of modern USA. Like the old saying goes "A lie told a thousand times becomes believable". Hence, if we are told enough times that something is great, then the masses will believe it. This technique was adopted by Joseph Goebbels, Minister of Propaganda, in Nazi Germany and look what happened there.

Then take those 5* 'luxurious' places like Dubai, Monte Carlo or St. Tropez, whose soul could be bought with enough money. People think these places are the best on earth because of the wealth but they are blinded by excess and, let me be quite frank when I speak of this, the only justification of their being is for money. I do not hold one desire to visit such places. I have been to Dubai in the past (briefly) and I do not hold one shred of desire to revisit a place polluted by greed. My time belongs here – with the people. With people who have struggled to form a life and whose daily life is a continuous struggle. My time belongs to trying to help people rather than waste it in a casino for 2 weeks, gambling money which could go to providing food to an African or South American family for a month. Maybe this point of view is too naïve.

After much driving around, we found the hostel where I checked in and I basically bummed about for the day because I can't go anywhere due to my leg. I must say that Peru has really taken to me and on this, my last day, I have had a wonderful time. The culture and the friendliness of these people are by far greater than anything else I have previously seen. It has also been difficult to try to identify with a race I can hardly begin to understand. I think having spent the past few weeks living in this fine country that a foreigner such as myself cannot understand the subtle ethno-geographic differences of people of this fine country and, also, the continent in general. Only a person who is really from these parts is able to do that. I just hope that the people I have met during my time here acknowledge that I am not just another backpacker and that I have actually listened to their circumstances. It is difficult to change the way things are for these people but surely something must be done to give the children a fair chance – access to education, clean water, clothes – things we take for granted so much in the Western World.

It will be sad to leave this amazing country but the bright lights of Caracas and the Latin atmosphere of Venezuela awaits – home of the legendary Simon Bolivar.

ow: Plaza de Armas, location of the execution
upac Amaru)

ow: With lady at Tambomachay market)

elow: Freezing cold in snow with sandals

(Below: Museo Inka, Cusco)

(Below: Luigi is centre with long hair)

(Below: Disparity of a cruel world)

Chapter 17 – The Tip of this Grand Continent

Caracas

Caracas lies on the Northern tip of the greatest continent on earth – for me anyway. It was founded more than 500 years ago when the famous Caracas Valleys were then populated by indigenous folk.

Francisco Fajardo, son of a Spanish Captain, made unsuccessful attempts to drive out the indigenous groups. In 1567, the governor of the province of Venezuela ordered a complete conquest of the valley, and Captain Diego de Losada finally defeated the tribe and re-established the settlement on July 25 of the same year under the name Santiago de León de Caracas.

Francisco de Miranda (b. 1750) is largely credited for paving the way to the independence movement, and Simón Bolívar (1783–1830) for actually achieving it. However, the independence struggle was not easy. In 1810, a group of *Caraqueños* formed a coup to take over the government, denouncing the Spanish governor's authority. The clash continued until July 5, 1811, when Venezuela finally declared its independence from Spain.

The city again lost 10,000 people to an earthquake that struck and destroyed the city in 1812. Spain finally recognized the independence of Venezuela in 1845. The modest growth of Caracas in the first part of the 20th century made the city very silent. The discovery of oil in 1914 at the Maracaibo basin had ignited the boom of the city's economy especially in 1970s. The economy and population of Caracas then suddenly boomed. The oil money was mainly credited for the booming of Caracas which is now a modernized and highly industrialized capital city. The earthquakes and modernization destroyed most of the remnants of the old town.

Yet for all this history, Caracas is still the power base of Venezuela. Hugo Rafael Chavez Frias was democratically elected in 1998 and began to undertake his Bolivarian Revolution, which aimed to rid Venezuela once and for all from the ruthless corruption that had bled it dry for decades from government officials and the 'friend to the north', the United States of America. From the Carlos Andres Perez regime to Marcos Perez Jiminez, Venezuela has been blighted. Chavez has aimed to rid Venezuela of such actions. However, it was due to his left-wing stance that in April 2002, he was victim of a CIA backed coup d'état to oust the democratically elected president. However, the following day the crowds took to the streets from the barrios, demanding their president be returned to power from the base on an island where his captors were holding him. The power of many voices won out and Chavez returned to presidency and was subsequently re-elected for another term.

Day 297 - Sunday 02nd August 2009

I awoke early today to get my flight to Caracas, Venezuela or affectionately called "the murder capital of the world". I arrived at the airport and, like in Chile; there was a problem with my ticket. It turned out I had to pay an extra $150 just because I changed the date on my ticket. I asked how much a ticket for the plane costs if I bought it now and was told a little over $160. So I am paying nearly as much for admin fees than the flight costs.

I got on the flight to Caracas and, luckily, I met a guy called Jorje from Valencia, Venezuela. He said he'd sort me out at the airport with money and taxi's so I'd be safe as it was my first time visiting Venezuela and it is dodgy. We arrived at immigration being met by a huge billboard of President Hugo Chavez, with a beaming grin; arms outstretched saying 'bienvenidos (welcome).' It was a nightmare getting through customs. 1000 people arrived at once with only 3 counters open, then I had to queue around 1.5 hours and, once through, I had to collect my luggage. Immediately I was surrounded by people trying to sell us money on the black market, which is very typical of this airport. Someone once said that I would be lucky to escape the airport alive, let alone Caracas but it is not all that bad – although you do have to watch yourself.

Jorje managed to negotiate us a good deal on the 'mercado negro', which is the only way to change money in Venezuela. Bolivars, the currency of this country after the great liberator Simon Bolivar, are virtually impossible to get outside of Venezuela and the banks here charge an extortionate rate so we do it on the black market. A 2009 United Nations Report stated that the cost of living here is 89% higher than its baseline, New York City. Considering the disparity between the earnings of the citizens, it does not seem fair but like I say it is not a fair world. Hugo Chavez has much work still to do if the Bolivarian Revolution is to take off.

Jorje introduced me to his family and they all packed me off in a taxi to Altamira neighbourhood. Jorje said he would have given me a lift but there was no room in his car, even though my hotel was in the other direction. What a generous guy. He gave me his number and took the taxi's details, urging me to call him when I got to my hotel as there have been reports of tourists being taken at gunpoint by taxi drivers and held for days until their bank accounts are empty and, once surplus to requirements, they are usually dumped in the middle of nowhere, or simply executed. I said I would be fine even though I was supposed to be met at the airport by a representative of the place I will be working at. However, the company I used for this project made a mistake and I am here a day early. A report I read last week said that, in December 2008, there were 510 people murdered in Caracas alone., ranking Venezuela as 4th on murders per capita behind Jamaica (3rd), South Africa (2) and Colombia (1). However, Venezuela has a reputation for being one of the most murderous yet happiest countries on earth.

The drive from the Maiquetia airport to Caracas is longer than I expected taking you through the main stretch of highway that splits the valleys in two and on the mountainside you see the famous barrios, which look in a desperate condition, looking down on the CBD in an imposing fashion. They are old, wooden shacks, built on top of one another and give a depressing image of poverty and degradation. On the way to where I was staying, I saw various groups staging a protest in support of Manuel Zalayeta, deposed in a coup in Honduras last month. My heart (still beating with injustice) wanted the taxi driver to stop for me to join in the protests in favour of Zalayeta. If it hadn't been for my knee, I may have joined in.

Anyway, I got to my hotel and proceeded to take a wander around Caracas for food etc. I am watchful not to have any flashy possessions on show as I do not want to appear an easy target. Tonight, I headed out to a bar on recommendation of a guy in the hotel, in Sabana Grande Neighbourhood. On first impressions of Caracas, I do not know what to make of it. I'll reserve judgement, por ahora.

Day 298 – Monday 03rd August 2009

Venezuela seems OK. I got up early this morning to get my breakfast and then I ventured out further into the heart of Caracas, meeting the locals, while standing out like a sore thumb with my knee in its horrific state. At one point, I got lost and ventured into an area, where I got the feeling I should not be there, which is not good. I turned and walked away in the Caracas sunshine. It does seem like a pretty city, especially where I am staying but this is the 'rich part of the city'. I stopped outside to talk to a woman called Luisa, a woman from Jamaica, who informed me that there are dodgy places in Caracas and to be careful. I told her I knew this and that I had walked about a bit struggling with my knee. She was worried by this and told me I had to be careful. Caracas has the highest murder rate per capita out of any city in the world and people will just shoot you for anything. Luckily, I take this with a pinch of salt and when it is my time to go, it is my time to go. However, I have a great belief that, at the moment, I am indestructible and I have much work yet to do.

Tonight, I went to a local bar for pizza and a few Solera beers. The service I find in Venezuela, so far, is very rude compared to what I have been used to in Chile and Peru. They have a sniggering look in their eyes when you ask them something but never mind.

Day 299 – Tuesday 04th August 2009

> ***"Life is what is happening while we are busy making other plans"***
> John Lennon

I undertook the 25 hour bus journey to Santa Elena to start the Community Project I am volunteering for, for 4 weeks. I was collected at my hostel by Oswaldo our driver. I met the other 2 girls I am travelling with (Jen and Hannah) and we headed to the bus station where

Oswaldo procured our one way tickets to the south. We waited around for 3 hours in the shittiest of bus stations until the bus arrived, which gave me a chance to chat to a couple of local women who are travelling to Miran to visit family. I told them what I was doing and where I am from and, clearly Chavistas, asked what I thought of their President. I said, after reading much on Chavez before travelling, I liked his policies yet, having been in power since 1998, he still has much to do. I said I was happy that he managed to survive the CIA backed coup in April 2002 and the Venezuelan people should be happy that they preserved democracy in this country – a democracy USA does not understand where, if a President is elected by the people, then that should stand.

We got on the bus at 15:45. Oswaldo said he'd give us the first row at the front of the bus so we could see the scenery of the country, which was beautiful. However, all we saw for the first 2 hours was a traffic jam, then it got dark and there were no lights as we made our way through the llanos to the Venezuelan lowlands. Hannah and I put the world to rights although she is a little naive in her judgments. We decided to get some sleep and, sat in the front corner enabled me to perch my head on the window as I slept with Hannah on my shoulder. I was rudely awoken with a prod during my time of slumber. As I angrily turned around to remonstrate with the culprit, I saw a member of the Guarda National, standing there armed with a huge machine gun saying 'passaporte'. So, I had to find my passport while he searched my bag. This happened a further 3 times on the trip making life difficult to grab any sleep. Military checkpoints are located all over Venezuela but, if you have nothing to hide, there is no need to worry.

This has not deterred me from looking forward to this project. I imagine it is going to be really rewarding and I am going to meet some great people. I am also laughing at those people judging me for wanting to volunteer my time to do something good. Those folk who are now sat in the pub, drowning slowly without ever having lived life. I also have this niggling feeling that I am being judged by the poor I am meeting, for having opportunities or what they see as opportunities. It is sometimes difficult to take because there is my own willingness to want to do well, yet my own guilt at what I see is clearly wrong with the world. I don't know what to think sometimes. I can only be me and try to be the best I can be everyday I am above ground, telling death to go to hell and helping people who need it. If I can do that then, for me anyway, I am a success. Success is not about having a flashy car, a nice house or attractive wife, as naïve people would have you believe. Is naïve the right word? Greedy people may be more appropriate. Success is about what you have done to help your fellow man and not about wealth. Let us face it; Adolf Hitler had all the wealth in the world. Was he successful? I think not.

Chapter 18 – Revolution and Revolt

Day 300 – Wednesday 05th August 2009

So, we arrived in the sleepy town of Santa Elena de Uairén a little earlier than expected at around 11:00. We had to phone the foundation and wait for a guy called Kelvis to collect us from the station. So, I lay back on the ground and lay in the intense sunshine of the deep Venezuelan south. So deep, in fact, we are only a 10 minute drive from the border with Brazil. Kelvis collected us, and then drove us to the foundation – our residence for the next 4 weeks in the jungle. On first reflection it seems nice and the view over the Savannah and the village is immense. This seems such a rewarding project that does well for the community and the children of the community. The director of the foundation, Manfrede, moved here with his pregnant wife in 2002 during the CIA sponsored coup d'état to oust democratically elected President Chavez from power. This turned Caracas into a dangerous city and Manfrede got on a bus to the furthest, safest place away from Caracas, which was Santa Elena. That's how this project was set up and Manfrede poured his time and money into it. So, the CIA in organising that illegal failed coup back in 2002, did a little good in the end in that this project would not have existed otherwise. Probably the only thing the corrupt CIA has ever done.

We had our introductory talk with a German volunteer, Jobst, who is very pedantic but seems OK. He explained everything about what we were supposed to do and I am looking forward to starting to teach the children. The only problem I have at the moment are some daft 19 year old girls – a similar problem to what I had in Namibia. They just seem to be unaware of anything. It is something I will have to cope with as there are only 7 volunteers. It is not a problem of major proportions. My mosquito net is up but I have had a load of bites already from little insects the locals call Puri-Puri. They are such a pain in the arse.

This afternoon, Manfrede took us on a drive into the local village and informed us of what is what. He did have a very apocalyptic view of drinking and said many local men just spend all their families' money on the booze. Jobst, the German, agreed wholeheartedly. However, I said to Manfrede and Jobst that I would reserve judgment until I saw it for myself and I would not judge anyone based on what other people have told me. That is all I try to do these days. Not judge anyone until I get to know them properly. I was told that on Friday I can go down to the local medical centre, run by Cubans, where I can get my knee looked at for free as it is proving really difficult for me at the moment. The Cubans can always be relied upon for free healthcare. Always free, always a good service. Not like the so called 'friend to the North' where they check your wallet before they'll check your pulse. No insurance? You have to go home to die. That is why I am in favour of the Cuban Revolution. I do not listen to the conspiracies of my government or the US government. History has been written by those who have hanged heroes. I am in favour of free healthcare for all. It is the only way for a better life

Santa Elena de Uairén & La Gran Sabana

The small town of Santa Elena de Uairén is the headquarters of the Aldeas de Paz in Venezuela and the heart of La Gran Sabana National Park. The town has about 25.000 inhabitants and is at an altitude of 900m-1000m (3000f - 3250f) with a nearly perfect climate (16°C / 45°F - 28°C / 79°F all year round). The town was founded in 1922 as a Capuchin mission, and grew in the 1930s with the establishment of gold and diamond mines in the region.

Santa Elena is surrounded by breathtaking scenery, and a wealth of nature. The region is one of the oldest geological sites on the planet where prehistoric flat topped mountains are like ecological islands with endemic species such as carnivorous plants and lots of other natural treasures. The Guyana shield, located in La Gran Sabana, is the earth's oldest surface. It is estimated to be 2 billion years old, and was formed when South America and Africa were still part of the super continent Gondwana.

The area known as La Gran Sabana, "the Great Savannah" is located in the south-eastern corner of Venezuela, at the border with Brazil and Guyana. It is a high plateau, a land of wide open spaces (75,000 square kilometres), tropical forest, spectacular tepuys (flat-topped mountains), rivers and gorgeous waterfalls. It is also home to the Pemón aboriginals. It is unknown when La Gran Sabana was first occupied, but there are artefacts that demonstrate that indigenous peoples were occupying the Orinoco Delta at least 2 to 3 thousand years ago. At the time of the arrival of the first Europeans, La Gran Sabana was inhabited primarily by Pemón aboriginals. Besides flat plains, La Gran Sabana also features tropical regions, jungle and cloud forests, rich in palm trees, fern trees, orchids, and bromelias. Also, animals including tapirs, jaguars, pumas, deer, anteaters, and snakes, are all native to the different ecosystems of La Gran Sabana.

Day 301 – Thursday 06th August 2009

I am settled in now. It is a really cool town in Santa Elena and I notice already that, although poor, there is a strong sense of community here. I visited the local hospital this afternoon to spend some time with the children playing games and, generally, trying to do my bit to put a smile on their faces. However, I got the feeling that the parents did not really want us to be there. It was a little uncomfortable. I understand this. Why do they want gringo's poking their noses in? I wouldn't want it for my kids. The hospital itself is not a big building and the paediatric ward around the back corridor consists of only 2 shared rooms, with a shared bathroom. Next door, is a room crammed with people with all sorts of afflictions alongside their families. The staff are nice enough and are trying their best with the limited resources available.

While at the hospital, sat outside the children's room on a chair to rest my knee, a pleasant local chap came over for a chat – in Spanish of course. He was there with his son who is in a bad way. I popped my head in the door to say hello but got no response except for some eyes that looked as though they were dead already. His Father insisted that he sustained bad injuries at work. He works a 4 hour walk away down a mine and, when I asked the chap “es pelegroso (it is dangerous)”, I got an affirmative nod. Although I didn’t understand much regarding the conditions these guys have to work in, I did get the sense it was extremely dangerous. This gentleman said that they want to airlift his son to another hospital in Estado Bolivar, which is a 1 hour flight away, yet he doesn’t want to let his son go as, firstly, he may not see him again, and secondly, he wants his son to be around his family when he dies. This gentleman was clearly in distress, signalled by the tears in his eyes, but still very concerned about my predicament. He had eyes that had given up trying – that seemed fed up with the way things were – the way things are. He was happy that he had a government that was trying to improve things, yet after 11 years, nothing much has progressed but, for him, it was even worse under Carlos Andres Perez – supported by USA. I felt for this man. He seemed to want his story heard not only for himself, but for all those others who work hard in unimaginable conditions. Those folk who say that they work hard, sat in an office back in the UK are wrong. They have no idea what a hard days graft is. I know that. Compared to these people, I have not worked a day in my life.

While I was at the hospital, I also popped in to see if they could look at my knee. The doctors kindly agreed but it seemed a free for all in the A&E part near the main entrance, which does not have a reception. You simply have to approach a Doctor or Nurse to tell them your problem. It is a long corridor where everyone who has an injury sits on beds, chairs or whatever else they can find to take the weight off. An elderly lady was put on a drip and had to lie on a bed. On this corridor was a doctor’s station consisting of a desk and I chatted to a nurse, explaining what happened to my knee. We proceeded to the very end of the corridor, to a room on the right where I was asked to take a seat on a bed. This nurse looked at it and cleaned it as it had got very dirty. She agreed that it looked a mess but they can’t yet remove the stitches. A big scar is already starting to form although this is not important considering the afflictions of many more people I have seen today.

The guys I am living with at the foundation seem OK. Nothing more. Nothing less. The German guy, Jobst (who shares my room) is such a control freak and likes to be seen to be doing everything – all the time. He also takes great enjoyment in telling people what to do – all the time too. But he is OK (just OK). Our room consists of 2 bunk beds and, as we open the wooden doors, we can see out over the Savannah and it is an amazing view.

<u>Day 302</u> – Friday 07th August 2009

Bloody mosquitoes and puri-puri are getting on my nerves now. They just seem to be biting the fuck out of me but never mind. Today, when we had the children up at the foundation, I was getting bitten to death. They are just so frustrating.

Anyway, I felt I made progress with some of the kids today. Two young girls, Jennifer and Maria were especially nice who are around 9 years old. They wanted me to help them with their English and seemed really happy to learn – although at times they could be cheeky. Some of the other kids seemed to be showing encouraging signs. I stayed doing my lifeguarding duties by the pool, keeping an eye on the 4 kids who were not allowed to go horse riding. My duties are a little stinted due to my bad knee. I said to Manfrede 'I will do anything where I can be of use'.

During the debrief afterwards, I found it really sad when I learned that some of the 14-16 year olds cannot read or write – even in Spanish. I raised this point 'what is the point in trying to teach them to read and write in English when they do not know Spanish?' Naturally, I volunteered to spend time with a kid called Jonathan who was sent to work age five, receiving no formal education. He cannot read or write in Spanish and the only reason he's being taught English is because it is easier for those volunteers teaching. Manfrede asked next time he comes up if I will spend time with him, teaching him Spanish. So, that is my role.

Tonight we spent time playing cards and, ruffling a few feathers, maybe being anti-social, I said I was going to bed as I'd had enough of cards. So I went to read Quixote and fell asleep under my mosquito net into a deep slumber.

<u>Day 303</u> – Saturday 08th August 2009

We have had the day to ourselves today. I was awoken at 09:00 by Hannah saying they were going into town so I went and called at the hospital on the way. I met a Venezuelan Doctor who spoke English. She was about my age and very pretty. She didn't have the curves of your average Venezuelan woman: she was slim but unbelievably pretty and there was me – a raggy bohemian traveller with a fucked up knee. I should've asked her out but, under the circumstances, it wasn't the best time. She still could not take out my stitches as I keep aggravating the injury by flexing my leg, but I cannot help it. Each time I venture the 30 minute walk into town, we walk a rocky path downhill and I constantly put pressure on it. She told me to return to see her personally on Monday when she'll be working. So, my knee is still stitched up. Bugger.

After the hospital, I decided it was a good opportunity to go for a haircut – bad idea! At first, the lady was doing it in the style like Zach's from Saved by the Bell, which was funny but it looked a mess all combed back. Then, she took off my beard with a dry razor, which was probably the most brutal thing that has happened to me, topping it off with some cologne, stinging me to the core. I couldn't wait to mess the hair up in my style, which is what I did on leaving the shop.

After meeting up with the others, we made the 30 minute walk back up to the foundation (so much for resting my leg) and then we sunbathed by the pool for the afternoon. Tonight, we went out for pizza and beers enjoying the 2 bars that are here in Santa Elena. Jobst was his usual, weird self. I have never met a 37 year old bloke like him. We all visited a bar;

sinking a few beers while playing pool with the locals. Kelvis and Junior, the guys who work at the foundation, are glad to have a proper guy around. Kelvis even said he had always wanted a friend from Manchester and now he has one. We drank to our football team, Manchester United, and both tried our best with the local ladies with me getting far more attention!

On arrival back at the foundation, I fell asleep in a hammock while overlooking the Savannah lit up by the moonlight. It really was beautiful. I'm happy to be away from the cities.

<u>Day 304</u> – Sunday 09th August 2009

Sitting here, looking into the jungle and over the town of Santa Elena de Uairen, I am wondering where do I go from here? I am still yet to discover where or what I want to do with this short space of time we call life. Make a difference? We all want that (in a way). But how? I do not want to be another 9-5 guy who goes about life, making as much money as possible to get by and not really caring about how others are living their lives. I am at a dilemma now I am nearing the end of my trip. But, let me tell you this, I will figure something out.

I woke up this morning, with my bandage torn off and you could clearly see the Wounded Knee. So, I took it off and now my open knee, still bleeding, is on show for the world to see. I have just stayed around the foundation today, frustratingly for me. There was an outing to a waterfall where people had the chance to swim etc but I could not go as I am not allowed to get my leg wet. It is a pain because I really wanted to go but I didn't want to go just to watch everyone else having fun. So Jen and I watched a film and had a sunbath for the rest of the day.

Once they arrived back they all went to play volleyball but, again, I couldn't because of the knee. Jobst wanted me to watch but I told him where to go with that idea. Watch? What for? If it was the Brazilian's women's team then yeah. But for a stuck up, lanky, skinny German. No thanks.

<u>Day 305</u> – Monday 10th August 2009

Today felt like my first real day working with Peace Villages Foundation. I pencilled myself in for the mobile school, which is where 4 volunteers (Jobst, Marina, Jen and I) go into town with a few educational activities for the children. About 22 kids showed up today and I was bowled over by their desire to learn and how enthusiastic they were. Plus, they did everything with a smile and they are so polite. Poor but polite. Many spoiled, rich kids could take note in the UK. But they won't because they have too much money to care. That is the problem with the world. I have come to a point of self-realisation now where a poxy job that may pay well back home does not matter to me. It is my deepest conviction that the world needs more projects like Peace Villages, more people like Manfrede and more people willing to give their time promoting social utility, than those who booze it away it away day after day, not giving a toss to how the poor of this world are living. I am certain of this.

This afternoon, we had the kids from the shanty town up at the foundation. I say shanty town as it is called the 'invasion.' This is where poor people can build homes upon useless land, in order to find a place to live. This law was passed by President Chavez, although naturally it found opposition from the rich landowners. So, this afternoon, I had the responsibility to teach some kids, like Jonathan, to read. I see Jonathan is embarrassed as he is 14 and learning alongside 6, 7 and 8 year olds. Especially when an 8 year old girl can read at an advanced stage to him. He sat on my shoulder and tried to take in what I was telling him and I used the phonetics method of teaching. We made a little progress and I gave him a pat on the back to make him feel he was achieving something. The kids find it hard to concentrate for a considerable period of time. But, I firmly believe now that there is good in the world. I am in a socialist country and, although I knew it before, I am proud to say I have socialist sympathies. Down with the upper classes who want to keep the revenues to themselves. We need a world for the millions and not the millionaires.

<u>E-Mail:</u>

Hey everyone,

I am in Venezuela and I'm staying in a town called Santa Elena de Uairen close to the Brazilian boarder. It is virtually in the rainforest and the foundation I am staying at has about 6 volunteers, plus 3 staff. It basically involves working with the children from the local shanty towns helping them to read and write etc and also aiding community development. Some of the older children can't even read or write, which is a shame so the other day I sat down with 2 of them to help them out. This morning, we went to the local park with the mobile school where we can help the kids learn maths and Spanish, from ages 3-11. They are so happy and eager to learn - it amazes me. I ready feel like I'm making more of a difference here than doing a crappy job back home where no-one is appreciative. I think the world needs more projects (and people for that matter) like this, which actively sets out to make things better rather than asking the useless question 'What can I do?'

My knee is still a right mess from the accident I had in Cusco on my penultimate day there (for those of you who don't know, I was out with a girl and at about 3:00am we were sat on a bench in one of the plaza's. Then, out of nowhere, some guy ran past and stole her bag off the bench. So I ran after him down the back alleyways of Cusco, rugby tackled the git and bust my leg off the pavement when we fell. But I got the bag back). Now I have a few stitches in my leg, which still can't be taken out as it is still bleeding. I need to go everyday to the hospital (again in about 15 minutes) to get it cleaned. Luckily, I am seeing Cuban doctors and not American doctors a.k.a healthcare is all free - one of the advantages of Socialism.

The living standards are very basic and I have to endure being bitten alive by mosquito's and the puri-puri bugs which seem immune to repellent. So, my whole right arm, right side of my back and right leg are covered in bites but it could be worse. A snake was spotted last week and other bugs like wasps (giant wasps) have infested the camp but nits all fun.

OK. I need to go to the hospital now to get my leg checked out. I also managed to give myself an electrical shock yesterday from one of the light systems in camp.

Day 306 – Tuesday 11th August 2009

I needed to visit the hospital this afternoon (again) to have my wound cleaned as it was black with dirt and some yellow puss was coming out of it, along with blood etc. So, I got there and saw a nurse who informed me that it is 'muy infectado (very infected).' However, she took out the 2 centre stitches and the wound popped open. Basically, it means I have a big hole right where my knee cap should be so it is all bandaged up again. Also, I walked there and back, which was a pain in the arse – walking down and up the rocky road for 30 minutes each way did not help it. The doctors at the hospital warned me to take care of this bandage as their resources are running low and even the basic of items such as bandages are scarce. They have plenty of iodine but, when I return I will need to have my knee cleaned and dressed with today's bandage.

This morning, I was helping Kelvis and Junior doing odd jobs around the foundation. They are two 20 year old guys who work permanently on the foundation and are smashing guys. We had a laugh about things – women, football etc. At one point, I asked Junior if there were any dangerous animals knocking about, to which he replied 'no.' Then, while I was moving sacks of horse shit, we found a little rattlesnake. It was only a baby but deadly. 'Muy pelegroso(very dangerous).' So, it is now being kept in the workshop we have here on the foundation along with its little friend we found 10 minutes later. I asked a relevant question that if we have found 2 baby rattlesnakes, is there the possibility that maybe a Mummy and Daddy rattlesnake are lurking close by to bite any unsuspecting workers? Undeterred, we moved the horse shit, which proved really bad for my knee. Plus, there were thousands of ants biting me and I was warned against a particular species, found close to the base of trees – the bullet ant, which can hospitalize you. Kelvis was pretty watchful of these as the pain is meant to be like being shot by a bullet, hence the name. This insect has the reputation of having the world's most painful sting. Some Amazonian tribes actually use the bullet ant as part of an initiation ceremony but, judging by the fear on Kelvis' face, I would not like to find out.

Day 307 – Wednesday 12th August 2009

What a dull day it has been today but I cannot complain as I have been lacking in motivation if truth be told. There was a painting activity this morning, which I took part in for about 30 minutes but decided it was not for me. There is no point in doing something that is not for you if you can clearly see that from the get go. So I planned some lessons for the children on Friday. This took me a while to do, so I volunteered to stay as guard of the foundation this afternoon.

I thought as I looked out into La Gran Sabana what will await me when (if) I get home. I want to keep travelling, not staying in one place too long – weeks at most. Then keep on moving and meeting the world because I have learned more in the past 10 months than the rest of my life. I feel I understand people and, more importantly, the world.

Tonight was pizza night. I had to cook lunch for everyone today and, let it be said, the rice was a bit of a disaster. As with Mark in Australia, it is proving to be my nemesis.

Day 308 – Thursday 13th August 2009

Thursday's are great here at Peace Villages Foundation as we seem to get a lot achieved (after our lie in, in the mornings). The mornings consist of a weekly meeting to establish the next week's workplan and we have to do our cleaning duties. It may sound routine and pretty dull but it all goes to sustaining this project.

Anyway, once all the tasks were assigned, we headed to Mana-Krü. I enjoy the mobile school more than any other tasks as we enter the neighbourhood, meeting the local parents and children. The parents seem really keen to know where I am from – especially the young Mothers who take a keen interest. I sat with one kid, Jonathan, while he did Maths sums and he was such a clever lad. He sat and concentrated for about 30 minutes and you can clearly tell that these kids have a more stable upbringing than those kids from the invasion who attend the foundation classes. Jonathan was 8 years old and he said that he enjoyed going to school but, at the moment, they are on holidays.

The nights here prove to be very boring yet they do give me a chance to catch up on my reading. At all times I have Pablo Neruda for inspiration and I have immersed myself in the classic 'Don Quixote' tonight. It is more preferable to hearing the pretentious bullshit Jobst comes out with. He is an intellectual guy but he thinks he is always right. At one point I realised I was getting nowhere during a discussion with him so, during his ramblings, I picked up my Neruda book and went to sit in the hammock overlooking La Gran Sabana, cutting him off mid-sentence. Maybe he was a bit pissed off but I'd rather take that than listen to his pretentious ramblings.

Day 309 – Friday 14th August 2009

I tried gardening today in the vegetable garden with Junior, getting totally bitten alive by the Puri-Puri who are feasting on my open wound on my knee. It is still a complete wreck and I only managed about 1.5 hours work, stopping in absolute agony. Junior managed to find a tropical looking spider he was not too keen on so he crushed it with his boot, which I had to laugh at as it was amongst a big pile of weeds we had just collected with our bare hands. I proceeded to get a pair of work gloves I took with me on my travels, but had not used until that point. Once I had finished, I gave them to Junior as a gift (Yunior, un regalo para ti). He was made up with the gift, thanking me on numerous occasions.

I had to cook lunch for everyone again today alongside the new guy Eduardo. Earlier this week, I had a nightmare with the rice but today we did Ok even though we did not have much to go on. Eduardo is a dick. He is a 21 year old from the USA who goes on about how spiritual he is but, in reality, he is not. He does not practice what he preaches. He goes on how eating meat is bad but says he loves a burger. He says he doesn't drink yet 30 minutes later he went on how much he like getting wrecked and could drink me under the table. To be a good liar, one needs to have a good memory.

This afternoon, we had the kids from the invasion up at the foundation and it was OK. Jonathan, the 14 year old lad, has really picked up something I taught him and he now approaches me when he sees me and shakes my hand saying 'hola professor' (hello teacher). Even though I was just meant to watch the kids play football, I joined in, which I shouldn't as bending my knee leaves me in fucking agony. However, I soon stopped after I had a kick and hit one kid, Nato, flush in the face with the ball, reducing him to tears. He was inconsolable. I had to use all my reconciliation skills to rectify the problem and I soon had him on his feet smiling again. It all turned out fine.

Kelvis nipped out after much persuasion by me to buy some beers. Manfrede does not like much alcohol being consumed at the foundation but he was OK with it so long as no children are about, which is understandable. Eduardo, who doesn't drink remember, drank about 6. I said yesterday he does not practice what he preaches. What a daft arsehole.

<u>Day 310</u> – Saturday 15th August 2009

Jobst and Eduardo are officially pricks. Going on constantly about how bad it is to eat meat and drink alcohol (even though Eduardo tucked 6 beers away last night). All this afternoon they both gave it to me big style that drinking is bad and eating meat is, in Jobsts' opinion, is bad for the environment and eating meat, in Eduardo's opinion, is bad spiritually as it is taking another life. I said during this debate that I do not give up meat because I could not. They said you are weak. I retorted that 'Yes. I am a weak person. But does it not take a strong person to admit that?' That left them thinking.

This morning we went to La Linea in Brazil for money as the rate is supposed to be better to get Reals to change to Bolivars, but the cash machine did not work so we had another walk around. Another German volunteer, Marina, did my head in. She likes to dictate people with what to do. I am beginning to realise I do not like the people I work with here. They are too self-righteous and it pisses me off.

We met up tonight at a fiesta in Mana-Krü after Jen and I had went for a pizza in central Santa Elena. I arrived to find Eduardo and Jobst sharing a beer so I reserved comment. But, how I did I will never know. When they talk about how strong willed they are, having principles, and then they do the opposite, I feel that reflects badly on them. At least my principles are principles I can keep to: doing good by people and treating people how you'd expect to be treated yourself. Nothing more. Nothing less. I respect my family. I stand by my friends. I'd do anything for my women. Plus I try to be as friendly and open with people as possible. These principles are not too bad and at least I can stick to them.

So, tonight, the whole village got together for the fiesta in Mana-Krü. I made a friend called Orlando, who was a great guy. He was in his 40's and clearly having a good night. Jobst and Marina did not want to talk to him as they thought he was a pissed up fool, obviously believing what Manfrede had told them about men going spending all their families' money on drink. They even laughed at him behind his back. Fair enough, this guy was pissed and, at times, was a fool. However, I stuck with him to hear his stories and we chatted for ages. Jobst and Marina were angry with me for this as they thought that a Peace Villages Foundation volunteer should not be mixing with these types of folk who are bad to their families. They left, with the last torch, away to mix amongst themselves and ignore the plight of the people. Basically, they had judged Orlando before speaking to him. Upon speaking to him, I found the only reason he was pissed was because his older sister worked on a stall selling beer and she gave it to him for free. As I was a new found friend of Orlando's, I was told I would not have to pay for a beer all night, ultimately joining Orlando in his state of inebriation. The generosity of these people is amazing if only you would give them a chance. It turns out that this gentleman was part of the local indigenous Pemon population and he works hard in the tourism business. He informed me that he is one of the few indigenous populations who are opposed to President Chavez and his Anti-American stance. Taking his anti-imperialist view, Chavez is affecting tourism in Venezuela for guys such as Orlando. However, I counteracted this debate and pointed out that Orlando, as an indigenous Pemon fellow, is lucky to have a job in tourism at all. There are many who do not have that opportunity and it is for these that Chavez is defending. We disagreed on certain points but Orlando was happy that I was able to talk compassionately about an issue that clearly meant a lot to him.

I then met a family from Guyana who seemed so welcoming. They told me their stories from Guyana and it sounded amazing how they ended up here, with the Mother working in the local hospital. I showed her my knee and said she'd probably see me in the next week or so. The language barrier was easier with this family as in Guyana it is a split between English and Spanish. However, I wanted to practice my Spanish and they English so I'd ask a question in Spanish to be answered in English and vice-versa. While Jen and I chatted away to this family, the father informed us that his son had cracked open his heel on a metal canister. At the time, due to lack of medical facilities, the family left the wound unattended. But, once it got serious they had to travel to Venezuela to get it looked at. They also informed us how they had another son and daughter who came to the hospital in Santa Elena, who suffered from malaria, but, tragically, they died. When I wrote in Namibia that death (for me) is just matter of fact – it is hard to think that now. I tried hard to fight back the tears on listening to this man, who was worried that his other son was suffering with this terrible affliction. He was so thankful for Aldeas de Paz for the work done with his youngest son, playing with the children and giving the adults someone to talk to. We took photo's with this family as a keepsake – for them and us.

Jen and I made the walk back, alone without a torch. We stopped off in Santa Elena in a bar in the centre. We made the 30 minute walk back up the mountain without a torch and only had the moonlight and the stars to guide us. We stopped near the Ruta-Salvaje for a 'romantic moment', which wouldn't have happened if I'd not been full on alcohol. Luckily for me, we were interrupted by a rabid dog, seemingly intent on devouring me. All I could see in the darkness were the piercing eyes and the sharp teeth ready to pounce. While the dog barked furiously I urged Jen to back away while I stood eyeball to eyeball with this beast. Just as I was about to let out a telling kick to its face with my left foot (as my right leg is buggered), the owner appeared calling it indoors. I needed to explain our presence at such a late time, stating that we worked with Manfrede at Peace Villages. We were let on our way. Upon arrival back at the hostel, we climbed into the same hammock, and fell asleep overlooking the view I have come to love –the Gran Sabana.

Day 311 – Sunday 16th August 200

The day today has been spent knocking about at the foundation and I have not even been bothered to get out into town to achieve anything. We eventually woke at 06:00am in the hammock and went to bed so that meant I awoke at mid-day and had some ribbing from Kelvis about the antics last night when we arrived back at the foundation!

The scrambled egg I made for lunch set me up for an unproductive day and, to be quite honest, that is what it has been.

The other volunteers are doing my head in slightly with their blinkered ignorance, which is getting me down about being here. The two German's were an embarrassment to the foundation last night with their attitude and their disdainful look to Orlando and his family. On reflection, I am furious with them for it – not just for treating Orlando like a piece of shit but for judging me for wanting to hear his stories. When I volunteered in Namibia there were 40 volunteers so I could ignore the ones I did not take to. Here, there are 8 of us – we got a new girl today called Alina from USA who, luckily for me, is really nice. But, apart from Jen, the rest seem all negative people.

Tonight, I met a gypsy lady, with a shaven head, who gave me some sort of fabric bracelet, which will keep me safe during my travels apparently. I sat with her, listening to her stories on travelling this continent and she had me wanting more from it. She had obviously travelled a bit and spun me some yarns about this and that but she seemed really interesting.

Day 312 – Monday 17th August 2009

Football season started today and Jen and I had regular updates from her boyfriend in Leeds. We beat Birmingham 1-0 and the Scousers lost 2-1 to Spurs. I informed Kelvis who gave me a big high 5!!

Jen did not cook lunch as she was supposed to today, instead walking with me to the local hospital. This caused a few problems as I told her it would when she walked down with me. We all had a meeting and, mainly the Germans, were complaining. But they were complaining about things that are not even important so, even though it didn't affect me, I had to say something. I was still annoyed with their lack of respect to Orlando the other night, laughing behind his back. I said 'You all need to get a perspective and realise that people in this world are starving like who I saw in Namibia and the mountains of Peru.' All I ask for is perspective.

Anyway, I went to the Cuban Medical Centre and a local lady who was there with her child assisted me with the Doctor's – even though I didn't ask her to. Initially she was sat outside with me and then, when I went in to see the doctor, she followed me in and sat next to me, chatting away to the nurse and myself about my injury. I enquired about Medical Care in Cuba and said I heard great news of Medical Treatment over there. The Doctor gave me some antibiotics to prevent infection as, at the moment, it is very infected. It was all free as healthcare should be.

Today, at the foundation, we only had 3 children so it was a little quiet. I stayed out of the lessons contemplating things for a while. Contemplating what (in the next few months) I will do or how my life will progress from here. I do not want to turn back into one of those people with no balls. I have realised that people are, in my home country, freer than they think. They do not have to subscribe to the idea of job, mortgage, marriage and death. There is more to life. It is all about realising it and realising your full potential. It is there if only you search for it but many just find safety in mediocrity to achieve anything special in life.

Day 313 – Tuesday 18th August 2009

My knee, even though it is getting better, is still buggered. Maybe it is my own fault because today, when we had the kids up at the foundation, I started to have a kick about with one of the young kids, twisted my knee slightly and thus let out a huge cry of pain. This caused the knee to start bleeding gaining the attention of all the curious children but, now, it is OK and I am at peace again.

The kids really are a pleasure to teach even though they may not be learning much. At least they want to learn and, despite the kids who want to disrupt things, the others are a pleasure to teach. I enjoy it here as I have said before. Some days are better than others but, when you actually sit down to contemplate things, that is life.

The weather here can be a bit unpredictable but, at the same time, predictable. It is sunny for most of the day but, at about 17:00-18:00, a huge downpour will occur that brings so much rain and, with it, the possibility of snakes.

The food today has proven to be a rarity – it was nice. But, on saying that, it is my turn to cook tomorrow so the nice food thing will not last long.

Day 314 – Wednesday 19th August 2009

We had the mobile school this morning but we could not find a decent spot as the fiesta is still ongoing so we had to make do with an open football field. The weather was so hot, which just sapped all my energy but, on the other hand, the children just seemed to get stronger and stronger. They are amazing. I was on lunch today with Jen and we managed to cook something that resembled a shepherd's pie, albeit with soya meat so figure that one out. There was just enough, which left me feeling hungry afterwards although I do not know the meaning of that word in comparison to much of the developing world.

This afternoon, we had the children up at the foundation and, if I am honest, I do not prefer it as much as the mobile school. It is funny because, at first, I thought I would not like the mobile school but I love it. The reason is because you get to mix with the community and learn more about their lives and how they live.

Tonight was a little dull. All we tend to do is sit around debating, which I like as it can prove to be a good way to pass time in company – but it needs to be the right company.

Day 315 - Thursday 20th August 2009

Eduardo, Jobst and I sat around talking about world events tonight, pre and post September 11. But, on reflection, Eduardo is a still a self-righteous know it all who likes the sound of his own voice. My views on him have mellowed since he first moved in last week and at least now we can share a laugh together. Anyway, their blinkered ignorance to USA's foreign policy is totally shocking. I do not know why people won't see it. Maybe you are the same. But their complicit denial of USA's activities in Central and Latin America, staging coups to oust democratically elected presidents most notably in El Salvador during the 1980's where the US government were responsible for the death squads leading to the deaths of up to 75,000 people – all so there would be no left-wing government in the country. Do not forget the coup in Chile either. All in order to dominate these lands as USA sees Latin America as "its back yard." Not anymore.

This morning was consistent of Thursday's around here. We did our usual cleaning duties with mine being to clean the pool. This gave me the opportunity to catch up on some reading and, as always, Neruda was with me along the way. I also read a lot upon the failed coup attempt against Chavez in 2002. What went on at that time can only be described as illegal, undemocratic and unconstitutional. But, as it served US interests, it was approved.

The US government has stated that this Chavez regime is undemocratic. However, he won by majority in 1998 elections and then won the second election a few years later – although by a lesser percentage of votes than in 1998. However, in 1999 a law was passed by Chavez called the Venezuelan recall law, which means an elected official can be subjected to a recall referendum if a petition gathers signatures from 20% of the corresponding electorate. Chavez was subject to this in 2004, which he won by a 58-42% majority. Naturally, opponents claimed 'fraud' but after winning successive elections and the recall, Chavez has proved that democracy does work in Venezuela. I could argue these points all day long.

We had the mobile school today and Santa Elena is preparing for an annual fiesta so the whole village is being set up for this. Venezuelan's love an excuse to party and I am really beginning to see this free-spirit that defines the Latin race.

Day 316 – Friday 21st August 2009

I awoke this morning at 06:00am to go to the market with Kelvis. We walked around the market for ages, buying the provisions for the week. I managed to speak with a few local market traders who welcomed me as one of their own and even gave free samples of juice to try.

Kelvis then dropped me off at the local hospital where I waited for 2 hours with people with numerous afflictions. Along this narrow corridor that constitutes an A&E department, I was sat, with my knee pouring with blood, next to an elderly lady who was lying in a bed and I was squeezed in on a chair next to her. In this, her dignity was taken away completely but we got chatting, although I did not ask her what was wrong. She said that, in the UK, I must be really lucky. I said 'I am' having realised that matter on this trip. She also asked me why I came to Venezuela if the UK is such a nice place. This flummoxed me slightly but all I could answer was 'to make a difference – somehow.' The world is unfair and I want to do my little it to make it fairer. I said that many people and many friends of mine, where I live, do not really care about what is happening in the world. They simply choose to ignore it and I didn't want to selfishly waste my time on a holiday or a pointless job when there are so many worthwhile causes I could be helping. As I said this, she managed to muster enough energy to reach out and touch my hand and let out a smile – a smile on a face that signifies years of hardship. This, in my opinion, was worth more than any pay-check you could ever give me.

I was eventually seen and a beautiful nurse ensured that, alongside her, one of the main doctors in the hospital would sort out my infection. I had seen her last week where she just clean my knee with Iodine yet she had a go at me for not returning to see her as I went to the Cubans. She was affronted and asked 'why?' I said I didn't know why as she is so beautiful and, out of that, I managed to ask her out tonight to a local pizzeria to which she said 'yes.' But, the doctor undertook some medieval shit on my leg today, which I was only too happy to watch. Firstly, he injected my knee a few times, causing an unimaginable amount of blood to squirt everywhere. Then, to get rid of the infection, he took a razor blade and cut it out, right down to the bone and I could feel the vibration if not the pain. Blood was everywhere and I have never seen so much from my body. Then he stitched it up and, in a funny way, it felt nice. Maybe it was because of Marianna being at my side during it just as Karina was in Peru. Even more nurses came in fussing over me and it was a laugh. I arranged to meet this young lady at 20:00 tonight.

After that was done, I headed to get money in La Linea, Brazil, which is the border town. On arrival at the border, the Guarda National wanted to see my swine flu vaccination certificate. However, I explained that I did not have it on me (even though I haven't had it) and they wanted to inject me with the vaccination there and then. I said I didn't want it and, at one point, there was a standoff between me and these 3 Guards, each armed with heavy machine guns. In the end they relented and let me through although after searching my bag and seeing my passport. It turned out that the bank did not accept international bank cards and we would have to make the 2 hour trip to Boavista. However, I headed to a supermarket where I met the owner and I had to pay 20% interest to get Brazilian Reals from here to change into Bolivars in Santa Elena. This still worked out cheaper than going to a bank in Venezuela. I said to the man in the supermarket – 'because I am paying 20% interest, can I get a free beer out of your fridge.' He looked at me, smiled and said I can take two! This made my day and I sat in La Linea enjoying a beer with my knee all bandaged up. As the anaesthesia wore off, the pain, at times, has been unbearable. I can only grin and bear it as others have it much worse.

Tonight, I went for pizza and it was amazing. We had a good talk about Venezuela and, it turns out, that a doctor in Venezuela does not earn that much money. In fact, they earn only 500 Bolivars more than someone who works in a Burger King but Chavez is trying to change this. I am not too sure how accurate this figure is but, if it is true, it isn't too great. I asked if she enjoyed her job and she said 'yes. She is helping people.' Her dream is to visit Europe but she doesn't think it is possible for financial reasons. It is such a shame.

Afterwards, we headed to the local fiesta in Santa Elena, holding hands, where we had a couple of beers. I was not allowed back to hers as she still lives with her parents and they are 'muy catolico' (very Catholic). Her Mother is apparently very strict and from what I gather this is symptomatic of many Venezuelan ladies. They live with their Mothers until a late age and the Mothers do have a huge say on things involving relationships. I told her that it was not possible to come back to mine due to it being a foundation. However, I said as I leave next week and, if she wanted to make the 30 minute walk up the mountains, she could come back and 'share a hammock.' She thought for a second and then declined my kind offer. We said goodbye and went our separate ways, never to see each other again.

Day 317 – Saturday 22nd August 2009

Jobst, Marina and Eduardo headed for an excursion this weekend to stay with a local indigenous family in the jungle. However, there was much trekking involved through the jungle so it was decided that I was not going to go. So, Kelvis, Jen, Junior, Alina and I headed to a few bars in Santa Elena this afternoon, playing pool. I decided it would be a good idea to show the two Venezuelan guys what drinking with Scottish people is like and, let it be said, Junior was pretty far gone. I also managed to find out that Manchester United beat Wigan 5-0 away, which cheered me up.

I also looked into getting a flight from Miami at the end of September. I have seen one via Dusseldorf for $500 but I may pay an extra $100 for a direct flight to Manchester. Also, I urgently need to sort out my tax refund as the tax back company has my money but I need the International Bank Account Number.

Tonight, Jen and I braved the torrential storms to head down to the fiesta in Santa Elena for the continuation of the fiesta and all the community turned out. I like the sense of community that exists here in Santa Elena de Uairén. We do not have that in the UK – not since Thatcher ruined it during the 1980's, turning man against man, instilling this competitive drive that has polluted our society. This town is different to many I have seen before and, in my opinion, it reflects better. Coincidentally, it is probably because this town has yet to feel the full effects of westernization.

Day 318 – Sunday 23rd August 2009

I cannot believe the amount I have eaten today. I woke up absolutely starving and I needed something to satisfy it. So, Kelvis, Jen and I headed to a Brazilian restaurant in Santa Elena, which does the best meat I have ever tasted. You just sit down and they bring salad, rice, sauce and spaghetti to your table. Then, every so often, a guy would come with a joint of meat on a stick and cut it at your table. It was amazing – particularly considering we have lived off Rice and vegetables for the last few weeks. I just at and ate and ate. Kelvis could not believe it and, to be fair to the waitress, neither could she. May I am a bit greedy but today I do not care. All we paid was 30 Bolivars.

Kelvis, Jen and I then went to Mana-Krü to a family's house where we keep the supplies for the mobile school. This husband and wife have 3 children, one of whom, Jonathan (a common name in these parts) is disabled. They welcomed me into their home, offering me a malta soft drink, which tastes something similar to flat cola but very sweet. It is brewed from barley and hops, similar to beer. It is non-alcoholic but very refreshing all the same, looking similar to a stout. I told them that is my last week and that their daughter (who attends the mobile school) is very clever and very polite. They thanked me and blessed me on the rest of my travels.

Kelvis, Jen and I then went for ice-cream where I chatted to a local gypsy lady who has turned into a friend of mine here. She is skin and bones with a shaven head but her outlook on life is amazing. I am pretty sure as I look into her eyes that she has encountered hardships along the way to living in this peaceful community but she always has a way of looking on the brighter side of things. She understands, as I do, that she is lucky to be alive and that each day is a blessing. Her life as a happy wanderer does strike a chord with me and she even said that she can see that I have this desire to just live without the shackles of modern capitalism and wander the earth meeting the people. We discussed politics sat in the dusty, dirty streets of Santa Elena and shared our outlook on life. I then said I leave for Caracas on Friday, with her leaving me with 3 words "FOLLOW YOUR HEART".

Junior was on guard at the foundation today so he and Kelvis went into town for pizza tonight and brought a big one back, which we devoured. So, we sat there eating pizza.

I am now into my last week here. I cannot believe nearly a month has passed and, if truth be told, I cannot believe nearly a whole year has passed since I started travelling. I want to stay doing this but, on saying that, I also miss my family and friends. I think now is the right time to go back to what I knew before. I have had fun.

Day 319 – Monday 24th August 2009

I awoke today to find we had a new guest in town – a young boa constrictor snake the others found on the road up here. The bad weather probably flushed him out. Naturally Eduardo says he knows everything about snakes but, later he forgot he said that and said he knows nothing about them – after being bombarded with questions. To be a good liar you need to remember what you have said to people. But he does not.

It was my turn to cook today so I did a Spaghetti Bolognese, with tuna meat but Jobst and Eduardo do not like Tuna. It never ceases to amaze me how so many people just take a dislike to a lot of foods when others in the world would kill for it. I hate fussy eaters. People who make others stand on eggshells to satisfy their appetite. Just eat it and shut your mouth I say. I would try anything given to me. I am open minded in that way. The only reason people are fussy eaters in the Western World is because they have the opportunity to be. It is the same reason Obesity is a crime that occurs primarily in the Western World.

Anyway, the day has been a bit dull and all I could do was to sit around and think about things, which for me, is a bad thing. You start to have regrets and I always said I would never have any as when you are travelling it does not do any good to have them.

Day 320 – Tuesday 25th August 2009

We had the usual Tuesday morning of the mobile school today and, for once, I was in charge. It is nice to see regular faces there now – regular faces who bring in new people with them. The local family, where we leave the materials once we finish, have really taken us in. As I said on Sunday, they have 3 beautiful children but they youngest, Jonathan, is disabled. He can walk but I think he is just a little 'slow' and it is really sad to see. I spent a little time with him today and he is constantly smiling at the world, which is amazing to see. All the children are full of joy and, Grisel who attends the mobile school, is such a clever, funny girl.

This afternoon we had the children up at the foundation and I took responsibility for teaching English. So, I focused on verbs and pronouns as I feel pronouns and verbs are the most important facet to learning English. It is so frustrating when they learn it for 30 seconds and then it is forgotten. But, it is also frustrating when a kid, like Harry, who wants to learn but is being disturbed by others, letting himself be distracted. Maybe I was like this at school. But, he did learn and even came up to me later and said in English 'I want to play football'. 'Harry,' I said, 'that was excellent.' I gave him a pat on the back and we enjoyed a kick about. He seemed proud that he had learned something.

Day 321 – Wednesday 26th August 2009

It has put down an incredible amount of rain today. It started at about 17:00 and continued non-stop until about 20:00, acting as you'd imagine it in a monsoon. I lay in my hammock reading, occasionally looking down at the village below, contemplating how those in the 'invasion' are living in their corrugated iron shacks. The houses (if you can call them that) are built on the flat lands, right at the foot of the mountain where we live and are, in my opinion, susceptible to flooding, and dangerous with all the dodgy electrics knocking about.

I challenged Jobst to a game of chess tonight and I lost miserably, 3-0. He is a thinker and outthought me.

The children never showed up at the foundation today. On a reflective moment sat overlooking the Gran Sabana and the table top mountains, I decided to buy a flight home from Miami. Why would I want to travel the USA for longer than I have to? Another city is not going to top what I have seen, especially one in the so-called friend to the north – or so said in the Monroe Doctrine.

I may do it one day, but for now while I still have a vision and imagination, pathetic cities like New York are bottom of the list. Maybe, just maybe, if you think about it: South America has completed my trip. Why do the poorer countries have so much more to offer? Europe? US? No thanks. In the future I feel I am destined to return to Africa and, definitely, South America. Not only does it have more to offer for those who appreciate it but, day after day, the people continue to bowl me over with their affection and it is really touching.

Day 322 – Thursday 27th August 2009

I cannot actually believe today has been my last day here at Peace Villages Foundation. The time here has gone so quickly and I made a conscientious effort to write a memorable piece in the guestbook today, which went as follows:

First and foremost I would like to apologise for any inconvenience I may have caused due to my damaged knee. Believe me, it is not how I wanted to spend my time here. At times I have felt frustrated by it and I feel it has hindered me from doing a lot of tasks. However, it has been a privilege to have worked here and I only wish the people I know back home would feel the same.

Manfrede: What you have created here at Peace Villages Foundation is to be admired. I only hope my small contribution can help sustain the project for years to come. I am sure you would agree, however, that there is much work to be done but with more dedicated volunteers as I have witnessed here at PVF, I am sure it is possible. If only there were more of us in the world.

Kelvis y Junior: Mi amigos! Eres la vida de la fundación. Cuando vienes a Manchester, llámame y vamos a Old Trafford ver Manchester United – el mejor equipo en todo el mundo. Nunca olvidas este! Siempre hay una habitación para ustedes en Manchester. Mi tiempo aquí fue bueno porque ustedes. Muchas gracias por todos. Patria socialismo o muerte!

Spending time here at Peace Villages Foundation has allowed me to view a better side of human nature. I see voluntary work as an essential part of promoting social utility. It means people are working for the sake of working, instead of seeing the monetary reward at the end of it. I think it is about time more people gave up their time to undertake projects such as this instead of ignoring the plight of the poor of this world.

As you are all aware, I have been travelling the world now for almost 1 year and, after working at PVF, I intend to return to what I call home in 'Manchester'. This is probably a good time to sum up what I feel about my travels. During the time I have travelled, I have encountered many different people in various continents from Africa to Asia to South America. Amongst the volunteers and local communities in Santa Elena de Uairén, I have met many more. It is my deepest belief that the petty nationalism's that seem to divide us are purely an illusion – a myth. We, in my opinion, are all one people irrespective of race, religion, ethnicity or nationality. From the deserts of Namibia and the Middle East, to the Outback of Australia, to the Mountains of Peru and the Gran Sabana of Venezuela, we as people share the same characteristics. The only thing that separates us is the extreme gulf between the rich and poor of this world (the haves and have not's). I said this when I departed Africa and visiting South America has only served to reconfirm my opinion– people assume in this world that Apartheid has died. It hasn't. It has merely been replaced by the socially acceptable version of apartheid. People now are not divided between black and white (skin colour) but divided between rich and poor.

After spending one month at Peace Villages Foundation, I have developed the belief that people around the world, instead of blaming each other for problems that exist, should instead look at themselves. Many people talk about 'with the help of god' we can achieve

this or that. In my opinion, we can only look to ourselves to make a difference to the world. We can also look to blame corrupt governments in the world for problems that persist. But again, if we look at ourselves, we can make a difference. As I look at my fellow volunteer's commitment over the past 4 weeks, I have been blown away. I am happy to see that other people are happy to give up their time to make a difference to the world. So to Eduardo, Jen, Jobst, Marina and to all past and future volunteers – you are to be commended for your vocation here. I will forever remember your selfless acts of generosity. We, as volunteers, (when we leave) need to continue this effort every day. If we all try to make a difference and make the world better every day, then maybe, just maybe, it can be.

I will miss visiting the mobile school and interacting with the local children – always a smile on their faces. In my opinion, a smile is the greatest gift anyone can receive and it costs nothing. Thanks to everyone for the memories. Todo Bello (all is beautiful). Forever, Alistair.

I hope many people could take note of this entry but, whether it be to a sincere ignorance or a conscientious stupidity, I fear that they won't. I sincerely hope that this foundation flourishes in the years to come.

It was my last day at the mobile school today and I was sad to leave the children behind – particularly those who have become regular attendee's over the past few weeks. 2 little sisters in particular. One girl, Katarine (pictured left behind me), really took to my heart with her never-ending, infectious smile and her willingness to constantly learn. When she saw us setting up today she came running over from her house with that smile she always has and a hug for me as it is my last day. All the other kids down there are just as great and it was pretty sad to say goodbye to them all and one can't help wonder where life will take them.

Tonight, we had a barbecue in the woods while drinking a few beers and a bottle of rum. The guys all had a cigar each and we did a ritual of smoking 'herbs' out of a pipe procured by Eduardo. I am not too sure what the herbs were but we procured them off a Gypsy lady in town last week. Eduardo, who said he is never sick off drink, was inevitably sick off the rum. I told him he had meet his match in me and everyone else laughed as he passed out on the floor but we had to move him as he was getting covered in ants. Kelvis and I were still going on strong at 03:00am and we had a good chat about things and, finally, I came to a conclusion. Kelvis has said for the past few weeks that it is his dream to visit London and, maybe go to a Manchester United game. However, he informed me that it would cost him a year's salary to do this. But it was during this conversation that he said he is very happy with his life. He said I should not feel bad because I have more opportunities to travel than he does. He said:

'You can't help where you are born in life. All you can do is to make the most out of what has been provided for you' Kelvis Reynaldo Padron; 27-08-2009

Kelvis had a point on saying this. All I can do is to now do all that is in my power to help people and be of use, somehow. I can't be feeling guilty for having more opportunities than someone else but all I can to is to aim to reduce the inequalities that exist so other people can enjoy the freedoms and privileges I have. Kelvis actually opened my eyes to this and made me see my own sense of usefulness to the underprivileged.

Anyway, at around 04:00am Kelvis called it a night. The Germans, Jobst and Marina went to bed about 23:00 although that did not surprise me. I decided it would be a good idea to mess around with the boa constrictor and I did give it a kiss goodbye on the head. What was I thinking? Instead of going to bed, I lay in a hammock overlooking the town which I will be leaving behind and I left behind what was me and is now us.

Day 322 – Friday 28th August 2009

I cannot believe I didn't go to sleep last night. I just stayed up contemplating things but I can catch up on sleep on this 25 hours bus journey to Caracas. A hangover occurred but no-one has seen Eduardo today as I think he will be delicate from last night.

I said my goodbyes to all at the foundation and Kelvis took me to town to the market to do the weekly shop and we stopped off for Empanada's. After an abrazo at the bus station, Kelvis and I said goodbye and it was sad to say goodbye to a friend I may not see again. As he walked away he gave me a fist of defiance to which I imitated this. Goodbye Santa Elena. It was nice knowing you and maybe, just maybe, I will return if I can get the opportunity. I will always remember you, your children and the fiesta's.

As I waited for my bus, the National Guard came and dragged me to a back room to check my luggage. Obviously they were checking for any narcotics and, hungover, I was obviously pissed off. They only did it because I look like a gringo and, generally, gringo's are in this part of the world to smuggle drugs. It is annoying and impersonal but that is life. I thanked them saying it was a chance to 'limpiar mi bolsa' (to clean my bag), to which they did not see the funny side. On the bus, the National Guard again caused me problems as I tried to catch up on my sleep. Constantly, there are checkpoints and, being the only white guy, I was subject to searches and this happened twice in 1.5 hours. To make matters worse, on flexing my knee on the bus, 2 centre stitches pulled out of my knee while sleeping, causing it to bleed profusely and, on drying, the wound stuck to my jeans. So, National Guard willing, I slept all the way to Caracas.

Day 323 – Saturday 29th August 2009

So, I rolled into Caracas at 09:00am on the dot after the bus journey and I was a little groggy to say the least. As soon as I stepped off the coach, I had a taxi sorted out, which was just as well as I was close by to the barrios of Caracas, which with a busted knee and 2 heavy bags, is not the place to be. I could literally smell the crime emanating from the area.

I had been warned to watch out for the cabbies over here but if I spent my life listening to other peoples fucking fears I would not have undertaken this amazing trip so, in essence, they can just carry on living in fear. I was a little skeptical at first on seeing his Cadillac for a car but he was a cool guy who had a wicked sense of humour and did warn me of certain areas as we drove through the city – he even acted as a tour guide. He has even arranged to collect me tomorrow to go to the airport at 05:30am, which is decent of him.

So, I got to my hotel just wanting food and to sleep but the guy on reception said I could not check in until 14:00. So, that gave me a chance to wander around Caracas still on my busted knee. When I look at the barrios (from afar) a sick part of me wants to go in to see how people are living their lives, even though I have been told by all Venezuelan's that I am risking my life if I do. But, on saying that, no part of Caracas looks safe. As you look around at security measures on buildings, especially around the more affluent neighborhoods of Altamira, you sense that locals are doing everything possible to protect themselves from crime.

I saw the last 10 minutes of United v Arsenal on the internet – we won 2-1. The rest of the day has been spent knocking about, contemplating my time in South America, the greatest continent on earth. I have achieved so much here, met so many different people and I can safely say my Spanish has improved tenfold. So, it is with regret that I have to leave. I want to now just skip the US and return to see my family and friends to maybe persuade them that not all that glitters is gold. The greatest challenge lies ahead.

E-Mail:

Hey everyone,

As it's my last night in South America, I thought I'd send you a quick update to let you know what's going on. I rolled into Caracas this morning after a 22 hour bus journey from Santa Elena. My last day in Santa Elena was eventful on Thursday and the farewell party went on all night. It did give me a chance to sleep virtually all the way on the bus. I've just been to a local fiesta in Caracas, which is not as scary as you're made to believe. I know some people who are avoiding it because they listen to other people's advice on how to live their lives. It is dodgy in parts and, if I'm honest, you do risk your life going to them places but its no reason to avoid the city. I love it here.

I'd echo the same sentiments for South America in general - the greatest continent on earth. This is why I'm sad to leave. Everyone needs to visit this place at least once in their lives. Obviously, for me Machu Picchu and the Lares Trek in Peru were the stand out points but my time in Santiago and Valparaiso in Chile were awesome. However, the last 4 weeks working with young kids in Santa Elena were amazing. Kids always with a smile and eager to make the most of education. It is sad to see 14-16 year olds just learning to read basically because they have never had the chance as they have had to work instead of being at school. So, now, I have to go to USA - something I'm reluctant to do as I ask myself the question - what is the point? I am into the final chapter of this trip and it has been pretty special and I class myself as extremely lucky to be able to do it. My friend Kelvis in Santa Elena says that he would need to work a whole year just to fund his flight to London, which he says is his dream. OK. I'm going to bed now. I have to get up at 05:00 to catch a flight to Trinidad and Tobago (Port of Spain).

Day 324 – Sunday 30th August 2009 – Venezuela to Trinidad & Tobago

My taxi driver picked me up earlier than expected at 05:20 in Caracas and after seeing the barrios for one last time, we made the way to the airport. As I am different with blond hair and blue eyes, I was asked for my passport and searched again. It is just as well I am not a drug dealer as I would be totally fucked and, let it be said, the prisons in Venezuela are by far some of the harshest you will see anywhere in the world. I got on the plane with no fuss (after the police and sniffer dogs checked me over one last time)and made my way to Trinidad & Tobago. On the way, I was sat next to 2 nice ladies from Trinidad, who were outgoing to say the least and they had that Caribbean mentality you'd expect. We had to relocate seats to sit near the emergency exists as we spoke both English and Spanish.

Trinidad & Tobago

Upon arrival in Trinidad & Tobago, the nice Air Stewardess asked if I had a change of clothes. I asked the natural question 'why?' Apparently, it is illegal to wear combat clothes of any kind in Trinidad & Tobago – I was wearing a pair of combat shorts. I said 'I do have other shorts but they are in my main bag.' She looked worried for me and said 'they will stop you. For sure. This is not good.' Anyway, luckily I had a jacket, which I used to form some sort of sarong as I made my way through passport control to collect my luggage. However, on arrival in the terminal a guard approached me, asking me to remove my jacket. His face was of utter disgust like I had walked in there with 20 kilos of heroin. I said I was unaware of this law and that I would change immediately once I collected my bags. He escorted me to get my bag and then took me to a wash room where I had to change my shorts. I was then free to leave. I had a walk around the airport until it came time for me to leave for Miami. I found Tunnocks Caramel Wafers in a little shop, which reminded me of back home in Scotland. All I needed was a bottle of Irn-Bru or pint of Tennent's and life would be perfect.

(Below: The height of my dreams at Machu Picchu)

(Below: Looking down from Huayna Picchu)

(Below: Teaching at the mobile school)

(Below: In Brazil)

(Below: With children at the mobile school)

(Below: Sharing an ice-cream with Kelvis)

Chapter 19 –The 'Friend to the North'

Trinidad – Miami

The flight was fairly uneventful if I may say so. American Airlines try charging $10 for a sandwich to which I said 'no.' But, on the plane, I did manage to drink my first cup of 'proper' tea for about 4 months. It was OK. The Air Stewardesses were nothing to write home about.

Miami

Upon arrival in Miami, I had to go through the worst ever immigration checks. Two hours in a queue and then I had to endure some kid asking me loads of questions. What is your purpose here in the US? How much money do you have? Where have you been? When I told them I had been to Venezuela, I was interrogated further. Obviously it was because of the tense relations between the Yanks and the Venezuelans. Diplomatically, I said I went to volunteer in the south of the country near the Brazilian boarder. What I really wanted to say was that Venezuela is a socialist country where I felt I could learn a lot more than coming here to learn how to be greedy and live the myth that is the 'American Dream'. He asked how much money I had. I retorted by asking 'Why do you need to know that?' I relented and said 'About 500 bucks.' Clearly lying, as all I had in my back pocket was about 20 Bolivars I smuggled out of Venezuela and aware that I had scraps of money left in the bank. I explained to this guy my plan was to go LA and interrupting me he said 'how long are you going to be here for?' I asked him to let me finish, explaining I **was** going to go to LA but I am now going to just buy a flight home next week as I am tired of travelling. In the end, I just said anything to appease him so I would not have to look at his smug face again.

I got into a Pakistani cab to head to my hostel on South Beach. He was a nice guy and his optimism of how great it is in the US 'the land of opportunity' was heartbreaking and I am sceptical at this. 'Anyone can achieve anything here' he said. 'You arrive with nothing and can become a millionaire.' 'How long have you been here' I asked. 'Nearly 30 years' came the response. Nearly 30 years and still driving cabs. But that is what the illusion of the American Dream does. It convinces you that anything is possible, when in reality, it is not for most people. It forces people into living beyond their means, in a lifetime of greed and beyond their reach.

We got to my hostel and the Yank on the reception is a total dick. Very tired and hungry, I was not amused with his smug attitude. I headed to my room to be met by a guy called Christophe, from France. During the night at 04:00am another 40 year old guy, Phil, showed up with a bird he'd picked up who was from Croydon and who looks like E.T. Anyway, I was pissed off at first with the noise and the fact he put the light on etc, which in a hostel, you do not do. Anyway, I got chatting to Phil and it turns out he went to the same college as me (although a few years before me) and he is from Rawtenstall, but now lives in Venezuela. It is such a small world. It is all good. I'll reserve judgement on Miami for now.

Day 325 – Monday 31st August 2009

So, my first morning was spent drinking an 8.1% lager with my room-mate Phil and we went out for a well needed breakfast. After we finished, we headed to a bar called D'vine on Lincoln Road, where we enjoyed happy hour (or 3 of them) while watching the ladies walk by. We talked of back home, which made me feel nostalgic. Phil's friend Luis, from Venezuela, then arrived and he is also staying in our room. They are both neighbours in Miran and when they talk Spanish I can understand every word so I feel I have learned a lot.

But, tonight after a few beers in the hostel, we headed out to play pool and then went on to an Irish bar. Loads of Aussies are in the hostel, which is not necessarily a bad thing. My first impressions of Miami are that it is what I thought it would be. Extravagant and it breathes excess at every turn. Miami is a buzzing town though, which always has something going on. Tonight though, a load of us left the Irish bar to return to the hostel. However, it was found that one of us has a wheelchair and none of us knew where it came from. One of the Aussie guys somehow punctured the wheel on a kerb. I had visions of a disabled fellow without his equipment so I suggested to Phil that we return it. However, I also had visions of being caught by a group of thugs, angry at us taking it. So, as we got near to the door of the Irish bar, I wheeled it through the door and we proceeded to run away in self preservation.

Day 326 – Tuesday 01st September 2009

As yesterday, a lot of drinking has been done today, which is not bad per se but I feel I am not learning a thing. However, it is still fun and the people seem to be OK in my hostel. But most are just out for a good time, make money and not a difference. Take Phil for example - a typical capitalist who scoffs and laughs at my notions of helping those less privileged. My argument is that if there were more people with my attitude in the world then maybe it could be a better place. But he, and another girl from Manchester, Lorna, could not comprehend this idea. But, more fool them I say.

This afternoon, Phil, Luis and I wanted to go to the beach and, on our way we stopped off at a pub and stayed 5 hours drinking beer. I think the barmaid took a shine to me although Phil and Luis said the same about themselves. Tonight, we visited a Mexican place for Burrito's and then we headed to another Irish Place where we seemed to play fusbol for ages, drinking beer. Good times.

Day 327 – Wednesday 02nd September 2009

What is it with this place and drinking? Everyday so far has been hit hard and I am achieving nothing. Phil just has me on it all the time but we'll see what occurs.

Today, a new guy arrived in our room called James, 30, from New Zealand. He is a really cool guy and typical of all the people I meet from New Zealand – calm and laid back. As soon as he unpacked, we started on the beer and it continued into tonight. We were having a goodbye party for Lorna who leaves tomorrow for New York. After many beers, we headed to the bar we went to yesterday afternoon, which turned out to be dead. Undeterred, we livened it up and I ended up playing pool with a girl, Anna, from Hawaii. She could talk and talk and would not let you get a word in edgeways – typical woman! But she was friendly enough although it was a pity about the looks. Again we stayed up putting the world to rights until 07:30am. I am infuriated by Phil's unwillingness to accept my views on how to make the world better. The world needs less selfish people.

Day 328 – Thursday 02nd September 2009

The excess to which Luis and Phil are spending is getting to me now but I am refusing to say a word – each to their own. I have developed certain nonchalance to my lack of money and to everyone's preoccupation with it. It seems to fit in with the bohemian life I have adopted for myself. Why do they think my attitude to it is so absurd? One person once remarked to me (I don't know who so they obviously are not that important or maybe made little impression) that I only do not care about money because I have it. Well, now I do not have it and I still do not care. Go figure that one out.

Tonight, after a few drinks in my hostel, we went to a bar in the city. I left after 2 beers as I just was not in the mood for making the effort. Phil and Luis astound me with their lack of morals. I like them and they are great guys but they chase women at every opportunity even though one is married with children and the other is in a long term relationship with children. It rests uneasy with me to see how people these days lack so many morals yet I seem to be judged as 'funny.' I do not understand it. But, I met 2 of Luis' mates tonight. One guy from Buenos Aires who now lives in Fort Lauderdale was a great guy who gave me an abrazo when I left. All good people.

Day 329 – Friday 03rd September 2009

It looked, at one point today, that I would be sleeping rough tomorrow night as I had not made a reservation here and, when I asked on hostelworld.com they had no spaces as it is labour weekend. So, I was planning to spend the night on the beach or something to that effect. But, it worked itself out tonight and it turns out I can keep my bed in my room. But, on reflection, for a city that is built on affluence and prosperity, why do I see so many people destitute, starving and homeless. You see people at the side of the road, with nothing except a shopping trolley to keep their belongings. 2 old chaps sit at a bus shelter, day-in, day-out with nowhere to go and they can be found sleeping there at night. On another part of South Beach a gentleman sits, afflicted by the same circumstances. These are the people failed by the notion of Americanism.

My personal financial situation got better tonight as my tax rebate came through so I can now buy a flight home next week. It will be nice to see my family. So, as it was James' last night tonight before he heads to Costa Rica, a few of us went out but it was spoiled by a miserable German cleaner who, normally, is friendly. But, a guy called Flo who stays at the hostel, from Austria, was so funny, pole dancing in a bar full of meatheads. The evening ended with James and me eating a Pizza in Pizza Rustica on Lincoln Road, and drinking a Peroni.

Day 330 –Saturday 05th September 2009

Phil and Luis left today as no beds were available for them and, in a way, I am glad as I can relax a little from partying. Saying this, I was in an Irish bar this afternoon watching football. One Irish bar wanted a $20 cover charge to see the Republic of Ireland game. So, I watched the Denmark v Portugal game for free on the other side of the pub. It turns out, if I'd showed up at 10:00am I could've seen Scotland beat Macedonia 2-0.

Tonight, I headed out with some Argentinean's to watch Argentina v Brazil but, again, the Irish bar wanted $20 to watch it. So, we went to a place called The Food Factory, which had it on a plasma TV and we watched it there over a few beers. Brazil won 3-1 and the Argentinean's were fuming. So, we trudged back to the hostel and had an early night. I need to achieve some things tomorrow in Miami. I have not done so since my arrival.

Day 331 – Sunday 06th September 2009

Today, I have had my head in a book called 'Into The Wild' by Jon Krakauer. It was passed onto me by James and is one of those books that is being passed over the world. Anyway, I have heard this subject before, about a guy called Chris McCandless who abandons his life of luxury with his parents in search of the ultimate experience – travelling a Tolstoyan existence to Alaska, Into The Wild, where he ultimately perished due to starvation. He had set fire to all his money and only took a bag of rice and a gun and that was it. A lot of people I spoke to about this simply have tunnel vision regarding Chris. How could he do that to his parents? How could he ignore them and treat them that way? He is too idealistic. But, this story struck a chord with me. I would never do what he did as I get on with my parents but on viewing this story, you need to look at both sides. Chris left as he felt he was being held to ransom by his parents. He wanted to shrug off the bourgeois existence that had encapsulated his life. Money is money. Life is life. Life is not money and Money is not life. At times, when we are young, we can feel like we are being held to ransom by our parents. One time, for me personally, was when I had bad grades at school in 1998. On seeing the report my Dad threw it on the floor and saying something to the effect of 'that's crap that is,' before storming out. A few days later I was called into the dining room on a Sunday morning for a 'chat.' Well, I was informed about what had been purchased and the things my parents had done for me. Examples include taking me to the football, buying me a Playstation for Christmas etc. Material things, you know like those with no imagination judge things. Anyway, you get the point. It was supposed to say that I had let them down and that if I did not work harder, there would be no more rewards – basically holding me to ransom. I thought (and still do for that matter) that success cannot be judged in terms of a material reward. At the time regarding these grades, other extenuating circumstances were not taken into account. I had let them down as they bought me something and I had achieved less than they expected. Back in those days, times were more turbulent for me but these issues were not taken into account. Therefore, nowadays, I try to take external matters into account and I have an intuitive mind that if something is wrong, we need to work out ALL the factors as to why it is wrong. The 'Carrot and Stick' method adopted by many parents is, in essence, nonsense. It is the same now with my feelings towards poverty in the world. Chris held similar sentiments. We are idealists, which I am proud of. It sickens me to be criticised for idealism. If only more people thought this way and acted on it, then the world could be better. That is not to say I do not respect my parents and I am so grateful as, without them, I would not be here now. I understand, unlike Chris did, that they grew up at a different time, with different experiences so, at times, it is hard for them to understand. But, the point I am trying to make in all this is that I would not want to criticise this guy as many people do without knowing the facts. So, I have been unable to put this book down. So much so, I went to the beach for hours and took too much sun – all on my back, which now looks like a mahogany table and my front looks like a pint of milk.

Day 332 – Monday 07th September 2009

I got up early today and went on a tour to the everglades – I hated it. It was one of the typical tour things I can't stand. 'On your left you find... on you right here is...' Along with crumby patter it made for a dull day. Plus the tour in the everglades was shit and the alligator show was crap. I felt sorry for this poor alligator who was taped up with a belt around his mouth while a guy sat on his back. The staff all wanted tips for doing nothing. Amazingly disappointing.

It is so sad to see in Miami folks in wheelchairs, asleep with nowhere to go. A guy on Collins Avenue sits at the same bus stop with an eye patch all day and night. The 2 homeless guys sit at the other bus stop on Washington Avenue – all day and night. This morning, I saw a guy at 08:05 on Lincoln Road, flat out asleep in his wheelchair. Land of the free doesn't exactly match here I guess.

Day 333 – Tuesday 08th September 2009

So, tonight, I bought a flight on the internet, which will take me back to England via Dusseldorf. On Friday, I will arrive in Stansted Airport.

So, at the moment, it is so hard to describe my emotions. I am excited about the prospect of going home. To see the people I left behind. To see if anything has changed, when all I can do is to believe that it has not. It is an excitement I believe will not last long, but, for now, it is not diminishing. I can't wait to see my Mum's face on Friday when I turn up at the house. I want to give them a hug and share a beer in the pub with my Dad on Saturday. All I want now is to make things better in the world but I haven't a clue how to go about it. It is difficult. Maybe I already have but I don't think I have done enough. Mum said online yesterday that Wes and my Uncle Ronnie are on a mission to find me work in UAE. Fuck that, I thought. That is the last thing I want. To be out there with folk thinking it is great to earn loads of money (tax-free), blinded by the excesses life has to offer at the expense of others. I am an idealist – I do not mind admitting it but, I ask you, is there anything wrong with that? When I first came away, I had certain beliefs: certain beliefs that left me for a time in Australia. But, now, they are back with a vengeance. The injustice of South America still exists. It is a cliché to think I am trying to be like Che Guevara. Great men inspire others much in the same way Mandela, Ghandi or Martin Luther King did. We are now richer than ever before. But why do people still go hungry? Why do many people not care for their fellow man? Why do people want to live in a country just because it is 'tax free?' Selfishness stems from Capitalism. I can't get out of my head the images of kids in Namibia and South America, no food, no home and just alone with nothing to do. An anger fills my heart and rushes through my body. All these are questions I need answers to but no-one wants to know. That is the tragedy.

<u>Day 334</u> – **Wednesday 09th September 2009**

It is hard to describe how I am feeling at the moment, on this, my last day of travelling –for now. What an expedition it has been and, to say the least, I have learned a lot about people, the world and, more importantly, about myself. I am a much stronger person now than before I left. I now have lost the sense of fear. Before going into the unknown, I had a certain sense of foreboding that I could not understand. But, now, that has gone and my attitude to the world has completely changed.

Today, after all these days on the road, meeting new people and experiencing life as it is meant to be lived, I have come to the end. My last day and night of a trip that has taken me to the greatest places on earth yet, in a way, I am excited to be going back. Not because I miss it as such but, when I return, I need to tell people how great my life has been over the past year. Every other day I seem to be telling strangers about what I have done but I have yet to discuss it with the people I care about most in this world. One person I discussed it with called it 'epic' but I do not know if I would go that far. It was close but epic is too strong a word to use.

I have enjoyed my last day in Miami on the beach and went on a walk around the shops. This afternoon, I headed to try to catch the Scotland v Holland game but the Irish Pub, Waxy O'Connor's wasn't showing it so I spent the time with 2 guys from Glasgow watching Northern Ireland lose 2-0 to Slovakia at home. It was just as well really as we lost 1-0. I was glad those 2 turned up when they did as I was nearly involved in an argument with a drunken American man at the bar. He seemed Ok at first but when he said to me 'welcome to the greatest country in the world,' I had to respond with 'Where's that? I thought I was in USA.' He was adamant that USA was special and, frankly, his views on the Iraq conflict were sickening – 'someone had to go in there and show 'em how great America is.' I said 'tell that to the innocent kids who were studying in school when a misplaced Yankee bomb fell through the roof.' He knew he obviously pissed me off. Talking about Barack Obama I said I was happy that the American nation finally showed some sense and elected the right guy. However, this chap, a clear racist, did not take to Obama purely and simply for the colour of his skin. He was also against Obama's reformation on America's healthcare. I asked 'why exactly?' He was off the opinion that you should only be entitled to healthcare if you can pay for it. I said tell that to the millions of people in your country who can't. At this, I cut him off and turned to the Glaswegians to talk football who agreed with me what a tosser this other fella was – a greedy, repugnant American.

After the game, we went across to the other Irish bar where we met 2 other guys from Birmingham and we enjoyed a beer or 2 with them playing pool.

Tonight, Flo, Phil and Kathy and me had some beers in the hostel and I smoked a celebratory cigar on completion of my trip. We headed around the corner to the bar we have come to frequent. The nicest looking Colombian barmaid was working who was ideal for me but she could not understand any of my Spanish. Walking with Lions is now at an end. I have achieved much yet my thirst for the road has not yet nearly been quenched.

Day 335 – Thursday 10th September 2009

What was I saying yesterday about the completion of my trip? Well, I'll explain.

I got up at mid-day and headed to get some lunch as it was going to be a long day and night. So, after that I packed my few remaining belongings into my rucksack and headed early to the airport with my friend, Marcel from Slovakia. He called me his hero on account of all the places I have been and all the stories I could tell him. I was at the airport around 5 hours early, but we split the taxi so it worked out OK. After the initial hanging around, I went with my bags on a trolley to the Air Berlin check in desk. I got to the front and handed my passport to the attendant. The next thing, I am waking up in hospital – again.

I had another seizure, right there at the check in desk, which subsequently led to me missing my flight. As soon as I came around in the hospital, a woman who was a terrible representative for US dental care was stood there wanting my insurance details. I said 'what for?' She said, 'well you have to pay for your medical care.' At this I was fuming as it is what I have said for the past few years where (in the US) they will check your wallet before your pulse. I said to her 'can you at least let me have some first before you start emptying my pockets.' I gave her a number a little later on but it turned out it was not the correct one she needed. I was then called into a room off the A&E department reception, which looked like you'd find in a bank. 3 attendants sat behind a Perspex screen and she said I would need to pay $5200. I nearly fell off my chair. Bullshit. I refused point blank to pay and she said 'you have to.' 'Not if I can't afford it' I retorted and 'try getting blood from a stone.' She gave me the bullshit that if I do not pay it will affect me if I want to return to the USA. I just said 'maybe I do not want to return.' Then I declared I do not have the money and she asked if anyone back home could help me out. By this time, in the UK, it would've been 03:00am and I said my Mum and Dad would not have that money to hand. This girl was a proper snotty bitch, who was totally unsympathetic to my cause. All she wanted was to get money from the patients. Let's hope Barack Obama's plan works out. Earlier, I asked a nurse who was a nice guy, if he could clean my busted knee while I was here. 'No problem' he said and he did it 20 minutes later. Then I saw him walk over to a computer and punch it into a touch screen monitor like he was ordering burgers at Burger King. The seizure thing should've cost $4800 and they wanted $400 to clean my knee. $400! In Venezuela it is free. More benefits if it is needed for Socialism. The good thing about Capitalism is that is constantly provides us on the left with ammunition to win our argument. The shitty system it represents is for millionaires and not the millions. As in the words of Engels:

"It is totally indifferent to the Bourgeoisie if the working class starve or not so long as he makes more money and what makes no money to him is unpractical, idealistic bosh"
Friedrich Engels; The Conditions of the Working Class in England

The nurse asked me if I had anywhere to go tonight to which I said 'no.' They asked if I wanted to stay so, in the state I was in I said 'OK. Thank you.' He was a nice guy and he understood my predicament. All they had, however, was a tiny store room at the back of A&E, which was just big enough to fit in one of the A&E beds, although my bag had to wait outside. I was grateful for anything and, as soon as the nurse and I shook hands, I got to sleep, which was badly needed. The way the capitalist system works keeps people as slaves everyday and makes us succumb to its myth that making money is more important than making a difference. But it is not and so long as there is a breath in my body or fire in my heart, I will never succumb and be made a fool of. I will never sacrifice my morals for money. Some things are more important.

Day 336 – Friday September 11th 2009

Well, eventfully, I made it on the plane back to Europe but it was a long time getting here and not without its trials and tribulations.

I was awoken shortly after 06:00am by the nurse who was looking after me last night. He informed me that I would need to leave as their shift was over and, if the new shift found me sleeping in that room, they could get into trouble for authorising it. I did not mind and I thanked him, sincerely, for all he had done the previous night. So, I gathered my belongings and walked out the front exit, completely unaware of where I was. I headed for the nearest main road, made a left and walked for 2 minutes until I came to a Burger King where I had breakfast but I could not use Wi-Fi. So, I then headed to McDonalds down the road and, as it turns out, you have to pay for the Wi-Fi there. But, luckily for me, the young girl behind the counter took pity on me and lent me her mobile phone so I could call a taxi to take me to the airport. So, at about 07:30am, I showed up at the airport at the same place as yesterday. I asked anyone who would listen for advice on what to do and they said I should wait until Air Berlin opened, which was at the same time as yesterday, which meant waiting 9 hours. Fortunately, I met a guy called Alex from Germany who is getting the same flight. He showed up at 11:00 so at least we passed time in each other's company.

When the check in opened, one of the baggage handlers, who was working yesterday, approached me and put his arm around me – he was really concerned for my well-being. He said I was really agitated and he tried helping me but all I wanted to do was fight him, telling him to fuckoff and shouting. He explained how he helped and I did not have the heart to tell him he was wrong in what he was doing. He said he wished he had something he could've put in my mouth to prevent me biting my tongue off during my seizure. At this point I said this was the wrong thing to do as I could've choked. But, he was a really nice guy and sorted everything out for me, leaving notes for the right people yesterday so they expected me. I also apologised for my behaviour yesterday, saying that I am not normally an aggressive person. Under the circumstances, he understood.

I had to wait for a nice lady to turn up to change me on to today's flight but she had to go through Germany to arrange it. The guy she spoke to in Germany said I would have to pay the difference at $162 to which I tried arguing that it was not my fault I missed the flight yesterday and I was using Air Berlin in good faith. However, she retorted that it was not Air Berlin's fault either. Touché. I feel I am doing them a favour today as the flight is by no means full. But, maybe, I can claim on insurance. Once, just once, I'd like businesses to show a little compassion – especially in extenuating circumstances. But, all they care about is making more money, much more money. They pretend to care about their customers but, in reality, they do not. All they want is to screw you over, the same as the whole Capitalist system does from morning to night.

Flying on September 11 was not too bad given what the United States is like these days but I am sure there was more security than there usually is. I actually forgot I was flying on September 11 until I took a look on my ticket

This trip has enlightened me in more ways than I can possibly understand. I am not me anymore or I am not the me I was. A fire has been ignited in my belly against all forms of injustice and prejudice. All I can try to do is to set an example each and every day. To try to make the world a better place. But, I hope people will take heed. I hope other people can become enlightened to the injustices carried out in the name of money. I hope one day, I can see the Promised Land where all forms of apartheid are abolished. I hope for a better world for everyone. I hope. I hope. I hope.

Day 337 – Saturday 12th September 2009

Home

It turned out I had to pay the excessive $162 to get back to Europe but I managed to get a few hours sleep on the plane. Air Berlin would not change my other flight from Dusseldorf to Stansted so I had to buy a new flight for 221 Euros to Birmingham. I coughed this up, begrudgingly, and headed to Birmingham.

After nearly 12 months travelling I finally landed back in UK, under a smokescreen, no-one knowing if I am here or in another land. On first reflection as I listen to the daft Chav's on the train, laughing amongst themselves, mocking old ladies, it makes me wonder why I came back but, now I know. It is to see the people I care about, not the people I don't. The police invaded the train to apprehend someone. It has only taken 30 minutes from me setting foot back in the UK. All I wanted was to get back to Manchester to watch Spurs v United at White Hart Lane. I arrived at Piccadilly Station in the heart of my city to find it awash with blue as the bitters had just played Arsenal and won 4-2. I needed to find a boozer to watch our match but everywhere was packed. I headed towards a little backstreet Irish boozer, Mulligan's, where I got the bouncer to look after my bags, while I nipped in and enjoyed the best pint of beer I have ever had. Some girls mocked my Peruvian jumper calling it a dressing gown but I chose to ignore these comments and carried on watching the match. We won 3-1. Home.

"Modesty and civility are very becoming in the fair sex; whereas laughter without ground is the highest piece of indiscretion" Don Quixote

I hopped on the X43 bus home to a few curious looks from people as I had my huge rucksack with me. Upon arrival in Crawshawbooth, I called into a local Chinese for a curry and made my walk back home. My Mum and Dad were sat in the dining room as I walked around the corner and they thought I was someone selling something. After a few seconds, they twigged who it was and it sparked scenes of hysteria. They cannot believe I am back. It is strange to be home. I have spent nearly a year away from this place and, it is pretty much safe to say that things are still the same. The boy that left, however, has changed though. Seeing the world – all the injustice – has changed me. My eyes are now open and for once in all my life I can actually see. All I have left to say is that the person you knew (or thought you knew) before is no longer here. I am now we.

"Nothing in the world is worse than a sincere ignorance and a conscientious stupidity" Martin Luther King Jr.

(Below: With Roger in Namibia)

(Below: With Laurent at Sacsayhuaman)

(Below: With Adam on Lares Trek)

(Below: With family from Guyana in Venezuela)

(Below: With Yunior and Kelvis in Venezuela)

(Below: Sharing a beer with Phil & Luis in Mi

Chapter 20 – Let Us Understand One Another

So, you've read how I interpreted the world over a year visiting some of the most remote places on earth. No doubt you will have many judgements and critiques but, before you do, let me say this. All I want is to make things more equal for those who are starving day in, day out due to a rapacious economic system forcing people to live beyond their means, to bring an end to war, warmongerers and, in my opinion, those institutions that make war possible – weapons manufacturers, who go largely ignored in the modern world yet are responsible for all injustices that occur, as well as corrupt governments. Is this wrong? If so, lock me up and throw away the key now because I am guilty as charged. But, I do not think I am and, deep down, I think you would agree with me.

Upon arriving home and telling stories of where I have been, what I have experienced and what I have seen, I am fully aware of the ignorance of many people I know and the challenges that lie ahead. Although I cannot remember who I had this conversation with, I do know it was about the Thatcher issue and Chile. The person I was talking with was a clear Thatcherite but when I explained how Thatcher had supported General Pinochet during the 1980's, leading to the torture of around 31,000, the killings of many, disappearance of around 3,000 and the fact that, for this, Thatcher is detested in Chile, I was greeted by the response 'I do not care about the people in Chile.' These are the selfish attitudes we are dealing with. People who only care about what their government can do for them and not focusing on the atrocities their government commits overseas. Out of sight, out of mind springs to mind. This person who said 'I do not care about the people in Chile' may as well just have said 'I do not care about anyone else apart from myself. So long as it doesn't affect me, I am happy.' Ignorant.

But like I say, the one thing that gets to me most is war and poverty – none of which should exist, yet my nation of UK takes great pride in war labelling those who misplace bombs as 'heroes' for illegally invading another country. It doesn't matter if they are under order or do not agree with it. The fact is they are doing it.

"Of all the enemies to public liberty war is, perhaps, the most to be dreaded because it comprises and develops the germ of every other. War is the parent of armies; from these proceed debts and taxes ... known instruments for bringing the many under the domination of the few.... No nation could preserve its freedom in the midst of continual warfare."James Madison, Political Observations, 1795

As we are all aware the United States has the most formidable military spending. In 2008, the total military spending of the world was US $1.473 trillion of which the United States spent 48% of this. This, I am sure you'll agree, is a shocking statistic. In 2003, the US spent US $393 billion on its military, which is 33 times more than those seven nations it conveniently classes as 'rogue states'. Armed Forces from the United States and its allies (notably the United Kingdom) freely bomb innocent civilians in Iraq and Afghanistan, taking lives as they see fit and not caring about the consequences. When these soldiers are then taken down, they are given a pathetic heroes welcome for defending so called liberty and freedom for the west. This liberty is the right to freely invade another country as they see fit, causing an unimaginable amount of carnage, destruction and bloodshed. It is always the most vulnerable and marginalized groups who are affected by political policies.

By contrast, the wealthier you are, the more likely you are to benefit from economic or political policies. The amount the world spends on military, financial bailouts and other areas that benefit the wealthy, compared to the amount spent to address the daily crisis of poverty and related problems are often staggering.

"The people there are dead because we wanted them dead"
Pentagon Spokesman to CNN on the bombing of an Afghan village that killed 93 civilians

When you compare the military facts to the facts about poverty, it is alarming. For example:

- Almost half the world — over 3 billion people — live on less than $2.50 a day.
- The GDP (Gross Domestic Product) of the 41 Heavily Indebted Poor Countries (567 million people) is less than the wealth of the world's 7 richest people combined.
-Nearly a billion people entered the 21st century unable to read a book or sign their name
-**Less than one per cent of what the world spent every year on weapons was needed to put every child into school by the year 2000 and yet it didn't happen.**
-1 billion children live in poverty (1 in 2 children in the world). 640 million live without adequate shelter, 400 million have no access to safe water, and 270 million have no access to health services. 10.6 million died in 2003 before they reached the age of 5 (or roughly 29,000 children per day)

The poorest people in the world will also have less access to health, education and other services. Problems of hunger, malnutrition and disease afflict the poorest in society. The poorest are also typically marginalized from society and have little representation or voice in public and political debates, making it even harder to escape poverty as all decisions, in one way or another, are designed to help the rich.

The questions I ask may seem critical and uncomfortable. If these little comments prick at your conscious that is good – it shows you have one and it shows that you are acknowledging the fact that there are huge problems in the world to be sorted.

I now know that there is a world out there for those with imagination. It is an amazing place, full of amazing people. These travels have taught me so much about the world and the many injustices that exist and all I can do is to try to be a better person each and every day. The greatest reward for me is to be of use and not to earn money, much more money.

As Plato said:

"The greatest wealth is to live content with little."

The greatest reward I received was when a child in Venezuela, who could not before read anything, learned to read basic Spanish due to my efforts. You can keep your excessive salaries In the Western World. We all seem to want more yet, when we have it, we are never happy. More breeds excess and excess breed's greed. No matter how much you have or how much you save, it never seems to be enough. Then there are those people who earn extortionate salaries manufacturing weapons, tanks, warplanes, bombs, bullets and rockets, which are designed to cause suffering they will never know. All I ask them is: Do they think about the consequences of the weapons they manufacture? Can they sleep at night knowing people on the other side of the world are living in fear of one of their bombs falling through the roof? Having personally spoken to such people, I find their attitudes somewhat startling especially when they think of themselves as successful because they earn extortionate salaries and own flashy possessions.

Then we have the Royal Family, which for me, Britain does not need, leaching our resources. Prince Andrew has a £435,000 travel bill alone, which is met by the government – or the taxpayer. The Duke of York spent an astonishing £21,700 on himself and staff in 3 days at the World Economic Forum at the Swiss resort of Davos in January, 2009. He spent £30,300 on a 15 day trip to China while a further £27,000 was spent on visits to Vietnam and Singapore. Also, an overnight trip in Russia for talks with Dmitry Medvedev cost £4300. All these figures just shout out that Britain should be a Republic and not a Monarchy. Especially when many people are needlessly going hungry or many people are turned down for vital drugs by local Primary Care Trusts due to lack of funding. The Royal Family never go hungry at their 8 course banquet dinners and never seem to have to wait for treatment for healthcare when it is needed.

This trip had opened my eyes more than I thought. I hope that if you, too, have a thirst for knowledge and with the capacity to care you can actually change your concept on your way of thinking. I hope that you have enjoyed reading these notes and that they have been in part fun, educational and descriptive of what I saw, what I did and what I achieved.

They were written for you to read and, maybe if you are willing to open your mind, you will see these places for real one day too. If you ever let that happen, no doubt you will develop a desire to make the world more just. I shall leave you now with the boy you knew and the man I am.

Ever onward.

Forever,

Alistair.

Author's Afterword

As the moon lit the night's blackness and the stars twinkled overhead lighting the tops of the trees in *la selva* it made it difficult not to reflect on what had been seen.

Lying in a hammock, atop a mountain, overlooking a village in the remote jungle on the tip of this great continent, a figure remains still, calm, pondering. No movement occurs apart from the hammock as it gently shifts from side to side in the calm breeze of the jungle night. His eyes are focused, looking down on the village below; contemplating what has been said by every person he met. He had seen all the world had to offer, met the people and heard from their many arguments that continue to convince him.

As I approached to speak with him, he shook his head as if there was nothing at all to say for our time together on this earth. His eyes never moved off the village below and as our souls were nearly parted, he told me:

"Stay on the side of the poor for they need your help more than the rich. Dedicate your life to helping those who deserve it – to those who are suffering. Educate those who need enlightenment and help them to realise the atrocities committed in the name of freedom and money. The more you ignore the plight of the deprived, the more you sin against the people. You form no part of the current society, which is a myth designed to subjugate the proletariat to a lifetime of hunger. You are lucky that you are educated and have zeal in your heart to change the course of people's lives."

I saw his clenched fist - a fist clenched for the people below and those who need their stories heard. As our souls drifted into one, I now knew which path of history I would choose – and that is to help the people and be of use to them. As my left fist clenched tighter I was aware of my own sense of usefulness. I now see myself changing lives. Through my steely glare I see my own style of doing good to the world and resisting injustice. I prepare myself to be on the side of the underprivileged to give them a better world. To give them a better hope. To give them a better future...

Get Involved, Open Your Eyes & Be The Difference!

Making a difference to the world does not mean going out with a gun to another defenceless country in the name of 'freedom.' Often, it is simply opening your mind to learn about the facts through the many organisations that remain hidden who do great work to open our eyes to injustice. Changing your way of thinking is easier than you thought. All you need to do is seek the truth instead of the lies that are perpetually given to us by modern media. Here's a list of the organisations that may help:

Think Tanks

http://www.jubileedebtcampaign.org.uk/ - Debt cancellation campaign.

www.globalpolicy.org – Monitors policy making at the UN

Aid Organisations

www.actionaid.org – works to secure food, water, healthcare and education for people living in poverty, enabling them to stand up for their rights.

www.care.org – A humanitarian and relief organisation which also provides emergency food and shelter to survivors of wars, conflicts and natural disasters.

www.oxfam.org – UK based development, relief and campaigning organisation which seeks to end poverty and suffering around the world.

www.maketradefair.com – Information on Fair Trade.

www.globalissues.org - Provides information and facts on issues prevalent to the world

Gun Control

www.controlarms.org – World's largest anti-gun campaign, launched in 70 countries on 2003

Child Poverty

www.savethechildrren.org – Has an international perspective on child poverty.

www.cpag.org.uk – Child Poverty Action group lobbies and advocates for children and families in poverty.

www.ecpc.org.uk – End Child Poverty Campaign is an excellent source of facts and figures about the extent of child poverty in Britain

Acknowledgements

There are many people I have to say a big thank you to during this trip, who have helped to shape my view of the world, develop me into more of a selfless person and without whose help this book could not be written. Their stories provided me the inspiration to write this book and their attitudes towards life have proved pivotal in shaping my way of thinking.

First and foremost, I would like to say a huge thank you to all staff and volunteers at Harnas Wildlife Sanctuary, Namibia for their continuous and dedicated efforts to help and rescue animals. Frikkie von Solms told me they would die for their animals and this selfless dedication to a cause some may not understand proved to be very inspirational for me. I would definitely recommend this project to anyone wishing to volunteer their time to work with animals. For anyone interested, please visit www.harnas.org.

Secondly, I would like to mention a few close friends I made along the way. Roger and Siri from Norway, who acted as the kindest and sincerest people one could wish to meet. Their attitudes towards travelling were similar to mine and I really appreciated my time working in Namibia with them both. Ryan and Anna who I met in Australia. From meeting in Cape Tribulation to living in Melbourne, we kept in touch and they provided me with some great entertainment. Ryan and I both appreciated how lucky we were to be doing a trip like this and we often remarked upon this over a few beers. Then we have Diana, from Germany. She was only in Melbourne for 2 weeks but we really hit it off and we seemed to drink copious amount of alcohol, partying until the early hours. Although brief, our time together proved to be quite eventful. Through Diana I met one of the funniest guys one could possibly meet – Constantine. This guy, like me, would do anything for his friends. From Greece, he had a fiery temperament yet we both shared our passion for food, cheeses and wine. Naturally, I left my mark on this fellow by getting him into having a few pints. Then we have the group from Chile. The Chileans were the most welcoming set of people I have met and the stories I heard on the streets talking to the locals about politics, education and social equality will stay with me for a lifetime. Their tales of living in United States' shadow were harrowing and can change your perception on how unjust the world is.

Next, I would like to thank the family I lived with in Peru; Belinda, Caesar and their family made me feel welcome as if I was one of their own. The staff and students at Academia Latino Americana, who made my time learning Spanish fun. For anyone wishing to learn Spanish, while assisting the local area please visit http://www.latinoschool.com. It is worthwhile and, when travelling South America, you need to speak Spanish.

I would like to thank Marco, my tour guide on the Lares Trek to Machu Picchu. His friendly, relaxed guide helped us learn so much about the Inca existence and we held similar sentiments to the injustices of the world. For anyone interested in doing the Lares Trek please visit www.gapadventures.com/trips/lares-trek.

The staff at Aldeas de Paz (Peace Villages) and local community in Santa Elena de Uairen, Venezuela need a special thanks. Living and working in this remote community allowed me to grow into the person I fully intend to be. One person, who I neglected to mention in my writings, was Ruben – a worker at the foundation. Ruben was one of the most peaceful, genuine and thoroughly decent men I have ever met. Years of practicing Buddhism and regular meditation have allowed him to be at one with people and be happy and content with life. On talking with Ruben, I learned so much that I will take forward with me. This place also showed a greater sense of community than anywhere I have previously visited and the families and children I met will stay with me forever. For anyone interested in this project, please visit www.peacevillages.org.

I also need to thank all the healthcare staff, both Cuban and Venezuelan, when assisting me with my injured knee. All healthcare was free and their dedication to helping me as an *extranjero* was really touching. I must also extend this gratitude to the Air Berlin staff at Miami International Airport for assisting me during my seizure and the healthcare staff at Miami North Shore Hospital for their help. Even though the healthcare system in USA is flawed, the Medical Personnel were faultless. This gratitude must also extend to the healthcare staff in Australia for assisting me during my seizures.

Finally, I want to say thank you to you all for taking the time to read this book. My opinions are not always right but they come from a desire to make the world more just. So, I will leave you with a quote from Maya Angelou:

"Perhaps travel cannot prevent bigotry, but by demonstrating that all peoples cry, laugh, eat, worry, and die, it can introduce the idea that if we try and understand each other, we may even become friends".

For more information on **Walking with Lions: Notes on a Round the World Journey** please e-mail Alistair Mirfin at:

walkingwithlions@gmail.com

Add the author as a friend or join the **Walking with Lions: Notes on a Round the World Journey** group on:

www.facebook.com